D0376167

72-3144

iii

# Characters of Note
## The Fort and Cabin Creek
## Kaintucke

**John Flynn,** b. 1748. Veteran of War of Independence, horse-breeder, settler. Surname is sometimes notated as "Flinn" in historical documents

**Elizabeth Halstead Flynn**, b. 1757. Wife and mother.

Their Children:

> **Mary Polly (Polly) Flynn**, b. 1773
>
> **Nancy Flynn,** b. 1778
>
> **John Flynn,** b. 1781
>
> **Chloe (Cory) Flynn** b. 1783

**James Halstead**, b. 1747. Brother of Elizabeth Halstead Flynn. Veteran of War of Independence and Battle of Point Pleasant (Battle of the Kanawha). Officer in Kentucky Militia.

**Anne (Trotter) Bailey,** b. 1742. Liverpool, England. Frontier scout. Widow of Richard Trotter, wife of John Bailey, frontiersman and ranger.

**Marie DeForest,** b. 1769. Daughter of French/Scottish trapper/trader father and Delaware mother (deceased).

**Leonard Morris**, b. 1748. Scout in War of Independence, fought at Battle of Point Pleasant (Battle of the Kanawha), settler.

**Margaret (Peggy) Price Morris**, b. 1750, his wife.

# The Raiders

**Simon Girty (Katepacomen)**, b. 1741. Scots-Irish. Captured and adopted by Seneca as a child. First sided with Americans in the War of Independence, then defected to Loyalists and Indian allies (which included Seneca).

**Meneshewa**, Shawnee warrior.

**Meouseka**, Shawnee warrior.

# Kettle Town
# Also Known as Girty's Town

**James (Seamus) Girty**, b. 1743, brother of Simon, captured at same time but adopted by Shawnee, trader.

**Bets (Betsey) Girty**, b. 1748, captured and adopted by Kispoko Shawnee, wife of Simon.

**Kate Malott Girty/Katemeneco**, b. 1764, captured and adopted by Shawnee in 1779. Wife of Simon Girty.

**Nancy Ann Girty**, b. 1786. Infant daughter of Simon Girty and Kate Malott Girty.

**Jean Baptiste**, b. 1763. Voyageur from Montreal.

# The Natives and Adoptees

**Pelaawi Tepeke** (Spring Moon) /Tepeke/ Becky, b. ca. 1746, Shawnee Mekoche Healer, female peace chief.

**Chief Moluntha,** b. ca. 1692, Shawnee Chief of the Mekoche clan.

**Nonhelema/** Grenadier Squaw, b.ca. 1720, Sister of Cornstalk, wife to Richard Butler and Moluntha, mother to Tamanatha/Captain Butler, wife to Chief Moluntha, female peace chief.

**Tecumapease,** b. ca. 1758, Older sister of Tecumseh.

**Spemica Lawba/** High Horn/ Johnny Logan.

**Tecumseh,** b. ca. 1768-1771, Shawnee leader.

**Cheeseekau,** b. before 1760, older brother of Tecumseh.

**Seeawasekau,** b. ca. 1775, brother of Tecumseh, one of three triplets with Lalwethika.

**Lalawethika/**The Rattler/The Noisemaker, b. ca. 1775, brother of Tecumseh, one of three triplets with Seewasekau.

**Kisathoi/**Margaret McKenzie/Margaret Kinzie, b. ca. 1770, Shawnee captive adoptee, later wife to John Kinzie.

**Tebethto/**Elizabeth McKenzie, b. ca. 1772, Shawnee captive adoptee.

**TalithaCuny/**Priscilla Estes/Priscilla Miller, b. ca. 1770, Shawnee captive adoptee, later wife of Jacob Miller, cousin to Adam Mann.

**Sinnmatha/**Big Fish/ Stephen Ruddell, b. ca. 1771, Shawnee captive adoptee, close companion of Tecumseh.

**Prairie Deer,** b. ca. 1757, Shawnee Mekoche clan mother of White Buffalo, wife of Standing Elk.

**White Buffalo,** b. ca. 1774, Shawnee warrior, Kispoko clan.

**Standing Elk,** b. ca. 1755, Shawnee Kispoko father of White Buffalo.

**Dove Trees,** b. ca. 1776, Shawnee Mekoche girl, friend to Nancy/ Talitha.

**Blue Jacket,** b. ca. 1743, Shawnee war chief. Fought on side of the British in War of Independence, one of leaders of resistance to white settlement in the Ohio Territory. With Little Turtle, led the Indian confederacy to victory at the Battle of the Wabash (St. Clair's Defeat), the greatest defeat of US army by Native American forces. Signed the Treaty of Greenville on August 3, 1795.

**Little Turtle/** Michikinikwa, b. ca. 1747, a chief of the Miami people. During 1790's, led followers to many victories in the Northwest Indian Wars. Father of Sweet Breeze/ Waganapeth. Father-in-law of William Wells/Apekonit, captive adoptee of the Wea.

# The Villages of Kekionga

**John Kinzie/** Shawneeaukee/ Silverman, b. 1763, father Scottish surgeon in British army, but known as a French Canadian silversmith, fur trader, married to Margaret MacKenzie, Shawnee adoptee known as Kisathoi.

**Bright Wing,** b. ca. 1748, Shawnee cousin of Pelawii Tepeke, married to Henri, French trapper /trader.

**Henri** b. ca. 1736, French Canadian trapper/trader.

**Little Henri,** b. 1784, their child.

**Belle,** b. 1785, their child.

# Indian Creek

**Johann Jacob Mann,** b. 1724, Kraichgau Baden-Wurtemburg.

Barbary (Mueller) Miller Mann, b. 1734, Berk County, Pennsylvania.

> **Adam Mann,** b. 1758, Berk County, Pennsylvania.
>
> **John Jacob Mann,** b. 1751, Pennsylvania
>> Mary Kessinger Mann b. 1762
>>
>> Seven Children
>
> **Elizabeth (Elisabetta) Mann Maddy,** b. 1760, Peaked Mountain,wife of William Maddy.
>
> **William Maddy,** b. 1760, Somerset, Orange County, Virginia, Husband of Adam Mann's sister, Elizabeth/Elisabetta Mann, and brother of Mary Polly Maddy, the first wife of Adam Mann.

**Jacob (Mueller) Miller,** b. 1729, brother of Barbary Miller Mann, uncle to Adam Mann

> **Jacob (Mueller) Miller,** b. 1765, son of Jacob Mueller nephew of Barbary, cousin of Adam and Jacob Mann, husband of Priscilla Estes Miller (TalithCuny).

**John/Johann (Mueller) Miller,** b. 1733, husband of Barbara Mauzey, b. 1734, France, brother of Barbary Mann, uncle to Adam Mann.

> Michael Miller, b. 1770, cousin of Adam Mann
> George Miller, b. ca. 1780, cousin of Adam Mann

**Joshua Michel (Mitchell),** b. 1757, Paris, Ile de France, widower of Nancy Ross with two children by her, later married Elizabeth (Lizzy) Stigard, b. 1770, Austria. Veteran of Revolutionary War, fought by the side of Rochambeau at The Battle of Yorktown. Fathered ten children with Elizabeth/Lizzy Stigard.

**Daniel Jarrell,** b. ca. 1746

**Mary Davis Jarrell,** b. ca. 1750

Children: Gibson Jarrell, Elijah Jarrell, Simeon Jarrell, John Jarrell, Tomsey Jarrell, Betsy Jarrell, Lemuel Jarrell, Benjamin Jarrell, Polly Jarrell.

**Estill** Among first Families who settled along Indian Creek.

**Cook** Among first Families who settled along Indian Creek, owned Cook's Mill.

**Frogg** Among first Families who settled along Indian Creek.

# The Military

The Fighting Butlers

**Richard,** b. 1743, in Dublin, Ireland. Sharpshooter in Morgan's Rifles in War of Independence, second in Command to Washington at Yorktown when Cornwallis surrendered. Indian agent and trader in Pennsylvania and Ohio, most senior U. S. officer ever killed in combat. Married to Marie Smith and had four children. Married to Nonhelema with one Child, Tamanatha, who fought against Richard Butler at St. Clair's Defeat.

**Edward,** b. 1762, youngest "Fighting Butler" born in Pennsylvania, veteran of the Revolution, survivor of St. Clair's Defeat, artificer and adjutant general of General Wayne in Fallen Timbers campaign. At Richard's urging, carries brother Colonel Thomas, shot through both knees at St. Clair's Defeat, from the battlefield. Married to Isabelle Fowler, father of four children.

**William Clark,** b. 1770, in Virginia, grew up in Kentucky. Brother to George Rogers Clark. Adjutant and quartermaster in Kentucky militia. Commissioned by General Arthur St. Clair, served at different times under Major John Hardin, generals Charles Scott, James Wilkinson, and Josiah Harmar, and Anthony Wayne. Resigned his commission due to ill health in 1796, but later went on to lead the Lewis and Clark Expedition with Meriwether Lewis.

**General Wilkinson,** b. 1757, controversial character involved in many scandals and grudges. Served in Continental Army, became aide to Benedict Arnold just before retreat at the Battle of Quebec, led Kentucky Volunteers, and was brigadier general in Battle of Fallen Timbers. Constant critic and antagonist of General Wayne during the campaign, despite campaign's success, filed complaints against Wayne to George Washington afterwards. Throughout campaign, spied for Spanish government, alerting it to British and French movements in North America.

**General Harmar,** b. 1753, senior officer of the US Army 1784-1791.

**General St Clair,** b. 1737, born in Scotland, came to America to fight for the British in the French and Indian War, participated in The Battle of the Plains of Abraham. In 1776, accepted a commission from the Continental Army. Was aide-de-camp to George Washington, and was at Yorktown when Cornwallis surrendered. Became governor of the Northwest Territory, and in 1791 succeeded Harmar as commander of the US Army. Was commander at The Battle of the Wabash, also known as "Battle of a Thousand Slain," "Columbia Massacre," and "St. Clair's Defeat" (Americanized to Sinclair's Defeat).

**General/Captain Benjamin Logan**, b. 1743, Kentucky general who, in 1786, led a force including Daniel Boone and Simon Kenton, against Native Americans living on the Great Miami River in the Mad River Valley. Chief Molutha was killed during the campaign, and his relative, Spemica Lawba, taken captive. Spemica Lawba (High Horn) was adopted by Logan and later became known as Captain Logan. He fought for the Americans in the War of 1812.

**Captain John J Hardin,** b. 1753, known on the frontier as "Indian Killer." Fought in Morgan's Rifles in the War of Independence. In April 1792, sent by George Washington to negotiate peace with the Shawnee.

**William Wells, Apekonit,** b. ca. 1770, youngest son of Samuel Wells, captain in Virginia Militia in the War of Independence. Taken captive by Miami Indians when 12 years old, adopted by Chief Gaviahate, Porcupine. Found by his brothers around 1788 or 1789. Remained with Wea. Wea first wife was presumed killed in a raid by Wilkinson in 1791, after which Apekonit and his men destroyed artillery squadron at St. Clair's Defeat, 1791. Attracted attention of Chief Little Turtle, and eventually married his daughter, Waganapeth/Sweet Breeze, with whom he had four children. After continued contact with his brothers, he joined the American side in the Northwest Indian Wars, becoming a captain in the Legion of the United States, and a scout and translator for General Mad Anthony Wayne.

**The Miller Brothers, Chris and Nicholas,** Indian captives who along with eighteen others, became part of Wells' elite scouts in Battle of Fallen Timbers.

**General Scott,** b. 1739, scout in French and Indian War, served in War of Independence as Commander of Washington's light infantry and chief of intelligence. Later moved to Kentucky, participated in Harmar's Defeat. Was major general in command of 2nd division of the Kentucky Milita, who with Anthony Wayne's Legion of the United States, fought in The Battle of Fallen Timbers.

**General Jean-Francois Hamtramck,** b. 1757, born in Montreal, became captain in the Continental Army. Made commander of Post Vincennes in 1787. In 1790, moved against Indian villages in a campaign to distract native-led Wabash Confederacy (Indian

Confederacy) from Harmar's Campaign. Made lieutenant colonel of Legion of United States in 1793, cited for bravery at The Battle of Fallen Timbers in 1794. Was appointed first commander at Fort Wayne, where he owned a large farm with his friend William Wells, Apekonit.

*I saw her in my dreams.*
*More than once I saw her,*
*under green, over green,*
*floating down a ribbon of river.*
*There she is in a bark canoe,*
*Gliding beneath a lattice of leaves.*
*She is scared. She is silent.*
*But though she is small, she is strong.*
*If she had not been,*
*I would not be here to tell her story.*

*All America lies at the end of the wilderness road, and our past is not a dead past, but still lives in us. Our forefathers had civilization inside themselves, the wild outside. We live in the civilization they created, but within us the wilderness still lingers.*

*What they dreamed, we live, and what they lived, we dream.*

*TK Whipple, Study Out the Land, popularized in the frontispiece of Larry McMurtry's incomparable Lonesome Dove.*

## 1786 Ohio River Valley

*Five thousand whites, slaves, and freedmen are killed or carried into captivity between 1754 and 1794 in the continuous warfare between settlers and Indians that results from the encroachment of white settlers into Native lands. In spite of the danger, in 1784 more settlers pour into the area when Thomas Jefferson successfully lays the groundwork for The Northwest Ordinance, encouraging settlement north of the Ohio River and east of the Mississipi through land grants to those who make improvements on their plots, building structures and fencing in crops.*

# BEFORE
# FALLEN
# TIMBERS

©2015 NM Jarrell. All rights reserved. This book or any portion thereof may not be reproduced or used in any manner whatsoever without the express written permission of the publisher except for the use of brief quotations in a book review.

Bloodcrow cover font created by Dan Zadorozny of Iconian Fonts,
used by permission.
Background photo of Cabin Creek by the author.
Author photo by Irisa Taylor Lange.

ISBN: 978-1-68222-158-7

*For Valerie,*
*Fan of Cyclone Woman*
*I feel the brush of wings...*

# PROLOGUE

"I dreamt the red men came."

Elizabeth floated towards the murky light, willed herself awake. Daughter Nancy spoke in her sleep again. Her child's silhouette move towards her, spectral. Then she felt the clammy hands on her neck.

She sighed sleepily, pulled in Nancy the wakeful one, and tucked her closest to her. Her small children nested around her, surrounded by the scents and sounds of the slumbering fort—youngest Chloe was to her right, and five year old John to the left. Only missing was Polly, her eldest, who slept near the other young females. Of course the menfolks slept elsewhere, weapons ready.

"No red men will come to here to the fort, Nancy. Everyone is safe here."

"T'wasn't the fort they went to. T'was the improvement."

Elizabeth's scalp tingled. She reached for Nancy's hand, clasped it tighter. She felt the rough patch blistering there, a soap-making burn, now scabbed over. Her thoughts flew back to her daughter's dream.

Her eight-year-old daughter was lately tormented with nightmares and visions. The child was a puzzle to her. Her imagination was too strong. She was not like her other children. Sometimes she seemed nearly of an age with Polly, her elder by nearly seven years, while at other times she was as playful as young Chloe.

But these portents of hers, those were troublesome. Sometimes held truth. Shawnee raids *were* on the rise up and down this valley. Families had survived the recent war only to be ripped apart. Murdered or taken captive. Dreadful.

Bad luck for the Flynns that the land and horses willed to them by Patrick, her husband John's father, were situated right in the middle of the warpath that not so long ago flowed with the blood of those ancient foes the Shawnee and Iroquois—but now streamed with the blood of the westward tide of settlers.

And John Flynn was dead set to add to his acreage through making the improvements the new government required.

She shuddered. The dark cloud floating overhead settled right on in, made itself comfortable. If she was honest, she had to admit that she, too, feared going to the home place. And now Nancy with a vision. . . .

Not to mention problems with Polly, her eldest, usually such a good girl yet contrary of late.

Polly felt a draught beside her, a hollow where her sister Nancy had lain. She pulled her quilt around her tightly. Nancy shouldn't have been here in the first place, should have been sleeping with Mother, John, and Chloe. But she had snuck her way in with Polly and the older girls once they were asleep.

She often got up in the night after her terrors and visions and made her way over to Polly where she flopped and moaned and mumbled out her dreams. Tonight she must have gone back to Mam.

Mam blamed the visions and terrors on Pa's da, Old Patrick, their grandda from Ulster. He had loved to tell them gruesome stories of haints and spectres. But Grandda had passed on, been gone awhile now, and Polly had stayed at the fort often enough to know that Nancy wasn't the only one with nightmares. It was not unusual to be awakened with dreadful groans and cries as folks relived some horror they or a loved one had suffered, most likely at the hands of the Shawnee Indians. The tribe was on the warpath now, and that was why so many folks were staying at the fort for protection.

And now Polly was wide awake.

She glanced wistfully at her friend, Marie, face illuminated in a shaft of moonlight that beamed through chinks in the roof. She slept soundly, lips curved in a secret smile, her dark hair spread across her pillow like a raven's wing.

On the morrow, Marie would have worked with Polly on a new quilt pattern, one from France. And then she would have taught more dance steps: Jenny Pluck Pears and Rufty Tufty. Maybe even the waltz.

But no, Polly would not be enjoying herself with Marie and other friends staying here. Instead, she'd be bound for the rough work of the fields and woods surrounding their improvement.

She started. Marie murmured and chuckled in her sleep.

At least someone had something good to dream about. What *did* she dream? Of the big city she had left? The soldiers she had danced with at the balls in Philadelphia?

Sometimes it was hard to remember that Marie was half Indian, she knew so much of the world. After her Delaware ma's death, her pa, a trader, had sent her to an aunt in Philadelphia to be educated. Then Marie claimed she was too old for the school, and wanted to join her father in his work. He had left her here at the fort for safe keeping while he was away trading in the villages. Polly hoped he'd be gone a good long time. And if he was, why Polly would have a lot more chances to learn to make a fancy quilt and practice new dance steps.

She felt a tiny twinge of guilt. At nearly fifteen years of age, she *was* needed at her parent's property. There were plenty of rails waiting there to stack for fencing.

Mother would help Pa lay the fence.

No soldiers would accompany them this time. They couldn't be spared. Polly didn't mind. Marie had pointed out to her that one or two were sweet on her, but Polly cringed at the thought. She did not care for them with their awkward ways and rough manners, their lanky limbs and clumsy movements that reminded her of young calves.

Though some girls her age were already married and had a child or two, Polly was not in a hurry. Marie was seventeen already, and thought she herself still had plenty of time. It would be nice, though, not to have to rush to do the chores Mam and Pa always had lined up for her. She shifted, tried to get comfortable. Wished she could get her mind to quieten down.

Nancy pressed Elizabeth's hand. She whispered, and Elizabeth hugged her close.

"They tapped us…"

"Who tapped us?"

"The red men touched us all on the shoulder. But Pa they tapped on the head. Polly wasn't there. Where was she?" Nancy's voice trailed off.

The chill came back, coldly caressed Elizabeth's neck and spine. Did the vision have something to do with Polly's scheme to remain at the fort tomorrow?

Earlier today the girl had begged to stay behind.

"Please, Mam? We'll be working on a quilt. And then I can spin for us, and string more leather stockings."

Well. At least quilting and stringing beans was more useful than singing and dancing. Still, Polly would miss out this time. The Flynn family was staying together, and if one of them was going to be "tapped" by the Indians—whatever that meant—they would all be.

Together.

She tried to put away her thoughts and catch some sleep before the taxing morning arrived. She patted Nancy's back. The child's breaths were more regular, but she wasn't yet asleep.

"Nancy, hush. No more stories about red men. The British aren't here to help them now. We'll soon be left in peace. If we don't look after our land, the crows, bears, and foxes will eat all our corn. Then they may start in on the horses. Can't have that now, can we?"

She laid a hand on the moist forehead and gently covered Nancy's eyes. "Sleep now."

Half asleep, Nancy whispered, "Sing the gypsy song."

Surely a hymn would be more appropriate, but perhaps this favorite would get her daughter to drop off. So she sang, softly, " '*The gypsy laddie went over the hill, down to the valley so sha-a-a-dy, he whistled and he sang till the greenwoods rang, and he won the heart of a la-a-a-dy…*"

They fell into restless slumber.

*She dreamed again. Red men, yes. But* everyone *was turning red…*

# CHAPTER 1

## The Wilderness Road

**Polly**

The trail was slow going, meant for walking or single file riders. Stumps of walnut, maple, sassafras and other trees often blocked their way. Sometimes the forest was like to never end. Thick woods everywhere: cedar, hickory, small oaks and persimmon. Many trees bore girdling marks of the Shawnee. And once in awhile there was a break in the woods as they passed remnants of old Indian cornfields not yet taken back by the forest or by settlers like them.

More cornfields. Polly fingered the cornhusks she had stuffed in her apron pocket before they left. If she had time, she'd make dolls for Nancy and Chloe. She had scrap material for clothes—some pieces that would have been used in today's quilting. She'd make them special by putting curly wood shavings on for hair. Nancy, especially, would like that.

Pa's singing interrupted her daydreams. He sang "Pretty Polly." So she was still in for some teasing after all.

> *"Then she got up on the noble brown*
> *And led the dapple gray*
> *And she rode till she came to her father's hall*
> *Two long hours before it was day…"*

Polly *was* on the brown—the dun—horse, Dolly, and Mother and Chloe rode the gray. Pa, oh so clever making that song fit. When he reached the final verse, he turned and said, "Aye, Polly, ye made it away again." Winked.

She ignored him, looked off into the woods. Now young Johnny, who sat nestled in before her, twisted, jostling them, trying to wink, too.

"Why don't you sing, 'The Girl I Left Behind Me?' " asked Mam.

"Gypsy song, gypsy song!" Nancy shouted from behind.

"Dipsy one!" shouted Chloe. Copycat. Happy wherever.

"Oh! There're wee lassies among us who have the refined taste to appreciate my music!" Pa shouted to the air, and tried once more to catch Polly's eye. He started off again in his strong high voice, a tenor, some called it.

Nancy, who rode behind him, hugged his back and laid her head against him, gloating. She always wanted to be the one to ride with Pa.

This song had so many verses it might go on forever, like the forest.

"Mother sang the gypsy one last night," Johnny said. "It waked me up. Nancy wanted it."

Polly glanced ahead at Nancy, now singing with Pa on the verses she knew. You'd never know *she* hadn't slept much last night from the look of her. Her face was flushed and she was laughing. At least someone looked forward to going to the acreage, the improvement.

Here the trail ran parallel to the river, and though winter would be here before long, a spicy scent—wild ginger? —wafted up on the breeze. It was the scent of the river; they were getting closer. She glanced above to see clouds unfurled like floss against a wild blue sky, almost making up for this miserable, twelve-mile trail all to a cabin where stacking rails awaited.

The trail widened, and they rode two abreast. The young'uns began to sport and play, and Mother's horse, Pilgrim, disapproving, pranced. Nancy and John grabbed at Chloe until Mother had enough.

"Stop!" she demanded.

She pointed at the red spot, the burn on Nancy's hand. "That isn't healed. You're only making it worse. Leave Chloe alone."

She twisted around towards John. "And young man, you leave your sister be."

At this, Nancy reached behind herself to tickle him. Dolly, Polly's horse, stumbled over a large root in their path.

"Ouch!" yelped John.

The puckered skin on Nancy's wound tore against John's rough shirt, and she finally quietened down, wrapping the wound in the folds of her pinner while fixing him with a baleful stare. She'd burnt herself two weeks ago, playing by the soap kettle and Polly reckoned she was going to have a nasty scar. But Nancy proud of it because Pa made a silly joke about it being in the shape of Ireland.

Who cared what shape it was? Polly imagined she herself would sport fine gloves though she'dnever even had a pair—if she ever had a scar like that on her hands.

Messing with that sore made it ooze and itch again, because Nancy wouldn't stop scratching at it.

"Leave that be," their mother reminded.

Polly distracted her sister. "If you be still the rest of the way, when we get to the cabin I'll make you some poppets."

Nancy eyed Polly with both hope and suspicion. "Promise?"

"Yes."

They now passed the girdled trees that marked their property. The areas once filled with white oak and chestnut tree stands made good cornfields, fields that could yield twenty bushels per acre. And from just one of those chestnuts they could get two hundred fence rails. Plenty for Polly to stack while her parents laid fence with rails already split, stacked, and piled in the field.

She heard neighing of their many horses—fifteen in all called out a greeting—as they approached the cabin. Pa had more horses than anyone in the valley. Maybe when work was done Polly would ride a fresh one over to Margaret and Leonard Morris's place and tell news from the fort. She knew Mam hoped to visit Margaret Price Morris— Peggy—too. Leonard checked on the Flynn's stock when they were away.

They stayed out here in spite of the danger, and in spite of Margaret's urgings. Leonard claimed he didn't fear Indian attacks. He'd fought at Point Pleasant as well as in the late war. But Margaret said he'd never gotten over seeing a body scalped. He had her shave his head so that his thick red locks would never decorate a Shawnee lodge.

Nancy hummed a tune a waved her arms through branches over the path, excited to be here. Yonder was the stone chimney. Soon there would be smoke coming out and supper cooking. They had supplies stored here, of course, and plenty of corn, but Mam had brought salt pork and corncakes for supper. Late potatoes, cabbages, and turnips waited in the weedy garden patch.

The sky above beamed its autumn blue down upon them. Maybe today would not be so bad after all. Marie might show her what she'd missed at the fort some other time. While Mam set the food to cooking, she would craft the poppets. They wouldn't take long to make. And then when she worked in the woods later, she'd have some precious time to herself.

Yesterday when she had asked to stay behind with Marie, Mam had almost looked sorry for her.

"Not this time, Polly. But look at you." Mother had brushed a lock of Polly's hair back. "Don't worry, before you know it you'll have a family of your own to take care of." Though she didn't have a hankering for any of the fellows at the fort, Polly would think on all that, and on having her own way one of these days.

# CHAPTER 2

## One for Sorrow

*One crow for sorrow...*

**Elizabeth**

**October 1786**

The sky was bright, but the dark cloud reappeared, hovered over Elizabeth as she helped her husband John lay fence. He was cheerful, hummed "The Girl I Left Behind Me," not tired of it yet.

"Help me get this in place, Bess."

She picked up one end of the split log. Chestnut, she thought, idly. She and John guided the rail in at an angle. He stood back and admired the growing border that protected their field.

"This makes me think on a saying from back in the war. If'n a lad had a bit too much drink and was weaving back to camp, they'd say he was makin' Virginia fences."

John was still in his joking mood. Knowing she was supposed to join in, Elizabeth smiled.

"And here I thought we were in Kaintuckee." She tried to sound lighthearted.

"Ah, but you know Kaintuckee is still a part of Virginia."

Well, that was true, officially. But those from Kentucky, the name that graced this wilderness that aimed to be something more, were a rougher bunch. Genteel Virginians did not necessarily want to claim kinship.

His dark blue eyes questioned her before he spoke. "You wouldn't still be thinkin' on Nan's dream, would you?"

She looked down. "I can't help it." She leaned back against the fence, tested it with her weight. If it didn't hold her, it wouldn't hold back a bear. "You know sometimes those visions of hers come to pass."

"Well, she has the gift. 'Twas the same with me Aunt Maeve back in Ulster, me da said. Bit of a poetical nature, too, she had, like our Nancy. Like a changeling, she is. But look above."

She glanced up. Hawks wheeled lazily in the sweet October sky, and a whisper of smoke rose from the stone chimney of their small cabin. Laughter and shouts drifted from the windows.

"All's well with the world." He'd moved over beside her, draped an arm over her tired shoulders and gave her a squeeze. "You know we had no choice in coming here today." It was a statement but also held a question.

"Yes, I know." The Kentucky Cornfield Laws demanded they improve their acreage: Clear timber, put in crops, put up cabins, put up fences. No improvements, no new land. Their claim was further along than some because Old Patrick, John's father, was one of the first settlers out here and had left them the cabin and original plot. But with improvements, the government would add four hundred acres to their existing property.

Besides the cabin and land, John had also inherited his father's Irish love of horses. They had the largest herd around, even supplied some to the late war. Their neighbor Leonard Morris could not be expected to provide sole care of them. The autumn air suddenly felt colder. Winter was on its way.

John hugged her to him again, briefly, then released her and waved at the ridge behind them where Polly worked in the woods. "And I'm just as happy to get Pouty Polly away from the fort and that Marie for a spell."

Oh, the jokes again. He started up with one of the final verses of the song:

*"As he turned around and looked around*
*To view the leaves on the tree,*
*With all the strength this fair maid had,*
*She threw him into the sea."*

"You didn't need to tease her so."

"Sure and it's her favorite song of all."

"Not since she's grown. We may not have her with us that much longer. I told her the same thing the other day. Before long she'll have her own family to look after, some of her own choices to make."

"Oh, she'll not take up with any of those louts at the fort if I can help it. And Polly and I will make friends again later on. We always do."

The gobble of a wild turkey stilled their conversation, and they turned to stare.

Polly stacked and hummed and daydreamed. Marie had a book called *Soldier's Joy: Vocal Music or the Songster's Companion*. Back in Pennsylvania, she even had a harpsichord to play them on, and Marie taught Polly the words. These were not like the songs Pa sang, but sad songs that touched your heart, like *My Lodging it is on the Cold Cold Ground*.

It was too bad her parents did not care much for Marie, mostly because of a prank on Uncle James. But Polly loved having friends, loved forting. Sometimes a fiddler stopped in. Some knew tunes from Marie's book. When the one-eyed river-boatman Jean Luc Cruzatte visited, he'd play lively ones and always end with *Pop Goes the Weasel*, where he'd put his fiddle behind his back, snap a string on the "pop," and set the fort children—including Nancy, John, and Chloe—bounding up into the air like corks.

Marie, who had even been to Paris, found these tricks exceeding dull. And Polly was nearly too old for them now. No, now she wanted the soft, sad songs.

Along with lively dances like Rufty Tufty, Jenny Pluck Pears, and Hunt the Squirrel, Marie had taught her to waltz. Though some found the waltz scandalous, Marie said it was fine because even if it was a dance that came from the Palatines, George Washington liked it, and cut the finest figure when he waltzed.

There was no need to tell her mother about the waltz lessons.

She hummed her sad song now while she stacked the rails, and imagined the few birds that sang in the trees made harmony with her.

But suddenly she hummed alone. The woods went quiet. Songbirds were silent, and all that remained was a strange stillness. Just one crow bounced on a branch, fixed his bright eye on her like a spell.

Then there was another sound—the gobbling of a wild turkey—and a shot. Maybe Pa had shot the bird for roasting? As Polly pondered this, a scream rang out.

*Mother?*

Supper bubbled and baked in the stewpot and on the hearth. While the others worked outside, Nancy minded Johnny and Chloe. Wild, they were, but so was she. Already they'd done their chore, run down to the spring to bring back water, and now, finally, Chloe was wearing out.

One good thing: Polly kept her promise. She'd made them poppets with clothes out of some quilting scraps from Marie.

"You're a nice gal, ain't you?" Nancy asked her cornhusk doll as she drew a face on her with a piece of charcoal plucked from the fire. She admired her work, especially the pieces of flossy hair she'd glued on with candle wax. In her pocket was a scrap Polly had given her that would make a gown later on. For now, Nancy just wound the fabric around the doll.

John's doll already lay discarded near the fire. He didn't care much for it since he wanted it to be more like a soldier. Chloe's had the hair pulled off and the body crushed. But Nancy liked the look of her own.

"I'll keep you safe from the likes o' them two," Nancy told her corn lady as she tucked her safely into her own pinner pocket.

They tried out some games, but Chloe and Johnny didn't care about learning how to do a Cat's Cradle or Crow's Foot out of Mam's wool scraps. And the floss made the burn on Nancy's hand itch, the burn Pa said would leave a scar in the shape of Ireland.

She scratched at it.

"Mam said don't," John warned.

"I know. I'm trying not to. But it itches like the dickens." She let out a long breath and tried to just rub instead of scratch.

She wished she and John hadn't of chased that old fort dog, Lafayette, around the pot while she was supposed to be minding Chloe. Lafy, as they called him, bumped a pole holding the kettle, and when Nancy tried to right it, boiling lye and hot fat spilt right onto her hand and arm.

Uncle James had been out in the yard with some soldiers who were cleaning weapons when it happened. He ran to her, scooped her up, and dipped her down into the horse trough to cool down. John, not so fast since he'd been lamed in one foot, rushed to get Mother.

Mam came quickly, and Nancy held back her tears. John got a whupping for running around where he ought not. Chloe, of course, never got in trouble.

Uncle James had tried to make her laugh about the nasty wound. "There's the map of England!"

That's when Pa had disagreed and said it was Ireland.

"Let's just hope there'll be no scar," Mother said and dabbed some of her precious salve on it.

And Polly had said, "Too bad. Now you will always have to wear gloves if you ever want to be a lady." Nancy picked at it again. Being a lady did not sound like too much fun.

Chloe shrieked as John teased her with a skein of yarn.

"Johnny, she's not a cat. But I will tell you a story about one." Maybe a tale would help Chloe rest and fall asleep. Nancy reached down to tug her plump sister up onto her lap. A Goldylocks, she was, with her yellow hair. Mam's and Polly's yeller hair wasn't near so bright, and Nancy and John had hair the color of Pa's—brown with red in it.

But Chloe didn't act much like Goldylocks. Probably more like the bear cub in the story.

Nancy's stomach grumbled at the smells from the smoky hearth—corncakes along with the stew. The hot meal would be ready soon. That was something they didn't usually have of an evening. Maybe Pa'd shoot a wild turkey later on, a real treat.

Did she hear a gobbling now? She set Chloe down and went to look out the window.

A shot rang out.

Surely Pa hadn't hunted yet?

But before she could see anything, the door flung open.

Red men filled the room.

Last night's dream came real, and she was sick, dizzy. Time stopped. The room spun and swirled. Slow. Then it came right—though very, very wrong.

Chloe screamed and slapped as Indians grabbed her. Then they took Johnny, who had gone white and silent. And finally their rough hands pulled at her. She went quietly, invisible. The real Nancy was somewheres else.

The red men dragged them outside and then she saw her mam on her knees. One Indian held her arms back while another tied her hands together. They tied a long strip of leather around her neck. She hollered and cried.

Where was Pa?

Polly must still be in the woods, working.

The Indians spoke their own words, loud wild talk. Marie DeForest and some others at the fort would have understood that language, but not any of the Flynns. There were nine Indians in all. One of them looked strange, a white man dressed like an Indian. Some people came to the fort like that. They'd turned into Indians. These here had scarves tied round their heads and one—the white Indian—had a scarf pulled almost over his eyebrows.

She left off staring at him to see two Indians run back into the house and carry out their things. They even had the stewpot, bread, and blankets.

Why didn't Pa stop them?

Mam looked strange. She didn't scream anymore. She cried, but no sound came out. She looked at Nancy and the rest, eyes red, as the Indians held onto them.

One jerked Mam to her feet.

Chloe cried and reached out to her, but the Indians wouldn't let her loose.

Nancy seemed to fly right out of herself, looked down at Chloe from above. She needed to hush her sister. "Chloe, Chloe, it's fine. You can be with Mother later. Listen to your sissy." She reached over and patted Chloe's foot.

Chloe stopped crying, startled. She settled right down like riled horses did when Pa calmed them.

The Indian who held Chloe gave Nancy a strange look, then nodded at her, and said something to his friend.

Then they both looked at her, smiling.

How could they smile in all this?

Johnny sucked his thumb. His eyes were wide open, staring.

Where was Pa?

And still no Polly…Should they call for her? Better not. The woods, the whole world, was deadly silent.

In the sudden quiet, Nancy now saw these were Shawnee Indians. Most of them had shaved heads in the front with one or two feathers hanging from hair in the back. The white Indian was different; she couldn't see his head for his scarf, and its ends fluttered in the breeze as he helped others round up Pa's many horses. In the last of the day's sunlight, the Shawnee shimmered with the silvery circles hanging from ears, necks, and arms.

Nancy smelled smoke and heard crackles and popping behind her. The cabin burned. Angry flames licked at it like a hungry wolf. Then they smudged off into the sky, leaving black and gray wolf tails.

Where *was* Pa?

Then she saw him, in the spot Mam's eyes had been fixed on. Indians had stepped away, and Nancy saw where Pa lay still.

While she watched, an Indian reached down and cut off Pa's dark hair. Red leaked out of Pa's head, and thin fog—smoke? —came out from where his hair used to be. The ground beneath him went from red to black, and that Indian held Pa's hair up high, whooped and hollered.

Smoke from the flaming house brought water to Nancy's eyes, but she didn't cry. If she did, Chloe might start up again. Nancy remembered some stories, those she wasn't meant to hear, about crying babies having their brains bashed out by Indians. She would not let that happen to Chloe.

Through watery eyes, she saw the silver sparkling Indians in the field. They caught Pa's horses and tied leads to them. Light danced off their jewels.

Mother did not fight against the Indians or scream at them anymore. Nancy and her siblings, too, were quiet, as they were loaded onto the horses and moved into the forest under a darkening sky.

As if in a dream, Polly shakily climbed into the crotch of a tree and looked over the woods towards the cabin. Nancy's nightmare had come true.

There *were* red men scrambling all over their property. One was pulling their mother up from the ground.

*What was that on the ground by her?*

Others rushed for the cabin, coming back out with Nancy, John, and Chloe. Some came out carrying the food they had been cooking for dinner.

Try as she might, she couldn't spot Pa.

One Indian had a flaming stick of wood from the fire. He set this against the cabin and flames began to spread, going higher, higher into the October sky.

Paralyzing fear gripped her. Pa would never allow this to happen.

Then she spied him, saw his form lying near the fence, broken. Bitterness spewed up into her throat. Her body was no longer hers as she slid out of the tree and ran. The oak, hickory, and tulip trees, were no longer sheltering, but cruel obstacles. Hot tears blinded her. She stumbled on, deeper and deeper into the woods to the huge hollow sycamore log, the hiding place. It was big enough to hide all the Flynn children, who sometimes crowded into it, giggling, pushing, and squeezing each other. Inside, it was soft, wet, and splintery. She burrowed in.

There would be plenty of room for just her, now. She wriggled deep as she could into the log, her mouth dry, numbness settling over the rest of her. Tears flowed from her eyes, but she cried silently, shuddered, but made not a sound.

In the silence she heard Pa voice, singing, yet knew he was gone. One look over yonder had made that clear. But it was the song, "Pretty Polly" she heard in her head:

*Then she got up on the noble brown*
*And led the dapple gray*
*And rode till she came to her father's hall*
*Two long hours before it was day.*

Well, she couldn't ride, wasn't going to go down where Pa lay and try to catch a horse. But she would rise up. She'd go to the fort, raise the hue and cry. Just for now, though, she'd be still.

She made no sound till hours after her heart was pulled out, after she heard what was left of her family pass over her, felt the horses step across the log that sheltered her. She listened as their hooves and the muffled voices of the Indians faded into the distance.

She made no sound till she moved from her hiding place as the hoot owl called out on his nightly hunt.

Then she crawled from the stump and ran.

# CHAPTER 3

## The Dark and Bloody Ground

*"This ground is bloody
and you will find its settlement dark and difficult."*
Chief Tsi-yu Gunsini (Dragging Canoe),
Treaty of Sycamore Shoals, 1775
(concerning the land of Kaintucke).


**Nancy**

**Somewhere North of Cabin Creek**


In dusky twilight they rode in a line through woods that were now strange. Two Indians led the way, each leading one of the Flynn's horses. First in line was the white Indian with the scarf. She thought she heard the others call him "Simon."

Chloe was in the middle, riding in front of an Indian feller who had taken quite a shine to her. He'd touch her yeller hair, and say things to her in his strange Indian talk, and Chloe would pull on his silver decorations and laugh.

Mam and John rode together behind them, with an Indian in between who led their horse on a rope. Mam's back would go all stiff, like someone hit her, whenever she heard Chloe and her Indian laughing and carrying on. Though she didn't say anything, Nancy could see Mam was upset with Chloe, cutting up with an Indian who had killed Pa! But Chloe knew no better. She was still a baby.

Here was Nancy at the end of her family sitting right in front of a feller who led Mam's horse, Pilgrim. Behind him were more Indians, maybe nine in all, leading stolen Flynn horses.

Sometimes they changed from Indian talk to English, and from what Nancy made out, they were delighted to be running off with so many animals.

At least all the Flynns got to ride. That was one good thing.

Nancy had heard about kidnapped folks—and that's what they were now, wasn't it?—forced to walk till their feet bled and they scarce could stand. That was the end for them. John with his bad leg wouldn't have lasted long. She already saw one Indian point to it and call him, "*Que tas ke.*"

Then that Indian hopped on one foot, making fun, that mockingbird.

Now the Indians were close up, Nancy could see why they glittered so. They not only wore silver circles around their necks, but also had shiny armbands that glinted as they passed through the patches of light, brightness that was starting to fade. But still those medallions winked, and the earrings gently jangled, making faint tinkling sounds in the still forest.

Pa had told them once the Shawnee had silver mines. So like she'd reckoned before, these surely must be the Shawnee. She felt a lump in her throat.

*Pa.*

Mam's hands were tied. All tuckered out, Chloe now slept in the arms of her new friend. Johnny sucked at his thumb behind Mam, but he, too, looked as if he might be asleep.

Nancy had figured out where Polly was.

The log.

Pollywog in the log. Was she still there? Anne Bailey at the fort had told them about the time she escaped from the Shawnee by hiding in a log. Somehow Nancy could just feel Polly in there as the horses stepped over it when they left the burning cabin behind. Nancy had wanted to shout out to her. For some reason, Old Patrick's words for home and goodbye came back to her. The cabin had been his, after all.

*Slan*, Polly. *Slan abhaile!* That meant, "Safe home!" in Irish. But there was no home now. Where would Polly go? Back to the fort? The Indians had most of Pa's horses. Polly surely could not catch any of the wilder ones left behind. She wasn't good at that.

And would someone come to find *them*? Herself, Mam, Chloe and John?

As they'd gone over that log where she knew her sister was, Nancy pulled out a tiny piece of cloth. Her doll, wrapped in the bigger scrap of blue was still in her pocket. She clasped the piece in her fist, reached behind her, and when no one was looking, let go. From the corner of her eye she saw it flutter to the ground like a hurt bird. Polly might find it. Goodbye, Polly.

Pa was gone, Polly, too; she missed them already. The lump in her throat grew and she about choked. Tried not to cry. How come no one listened about the dream? Pa was gone, and Polly all alone. And where were they headed now?

They rode up onto a ridge. When they reached a spot high above a river, five of the Indians left with the extra horses. Two of them took colors from pouches they carried and painted marks on the trees. Before they left, one of them took something bloody from his bag and held it high.

Nancy tried to see what sort of animal this was. Perhaps they were about to fix a meal from some critter they skinned?

But as she and John stared, Mam hollered, "Look away." Her eyes locked onto theirs as the Indians made four loud whoops and then one long high holler. A shriek really, like the cry from one of those banshees Old Patrick used to talk about.

"Don't *look*, I said." Mam gritted her teeth. Her face was wet with tears.

The lump in Nancy's throat got big again, and her eyes stung. She kept her teary eyes down like Mam said.

Then those Indians rode off.

Now there were four with them: the white one called Simon, or sometimes called a name that rhymed with "Dirty," then there was the one with Chloe, called something that sounded like "Mouse-ka." There was another one named "Menshowy," and one more whose name she couldn't make out.

The harvest moon rose low and bright, and the light spilled out onto a clearing. The men slowed up there, held the horses. They got down, and while some Indians hobbled horses, others built a fire using a knife they scraped on a piece of flint. Meouseka unrolled a pouch and did something with tobacco, making motions and murmuring.

The one who rode at the end had some of Mam's supper rolled up in a blanket. There were corncakes, and cold stew inside pumpkin shells. Mam's pot hung empty from one of the packs they'd tied onto the horses.

That Indian tore off hunks of corncakes, dunked them into the stew, and gave them some to eat. Then he untied Mam's arms and offered her some, but she only stared away, angry.

Nancy was not hungry, but when John saw her watch him and Chloe eat their vittles, he held out a piece of corncake to her.

"It's still good," he said.

Her stomach growled and begged for a bite, so she gave in and had a bit.

When the Indians finished eating, Meouseka took Chloe—he still wouldn't let Mam have her—and held her till she slept. Then he wrapped her in a blanket, one of their own, taken from the cabin. He set Chloe down on a bed of dry leaves that he'd piled up into a nest and then joined the other Indians by the fire. They smoked tobacco.

The white Indian, Simon, came over. He sat down beside Mam and said, "You'll do no one any good by your not eating." Something in his voice sounded like old Patrick, Grandda from Ireland.

Some of the blankness left Mam's face. She seemed as if someone had just woken her up.

"How do you live with yourself?" she asked. "You didn't need to kill my husband. You could have brought him, as well. You would have gotten a good ransom."

Simon stared at Mam. His light eyes glowed in his dark face. His eyebrows were bushy, like the caterpillars Nancy and John played with this time of year. He sighed. "Sure you know a man like your husband doesn't make a good captive. Merciful it was that his death came quickly." He gave her a long look, made that mournful sound again, and dropped his head like a hound dog. " 'Tis not *always* quick, Elizabeth."

Even in the darkness, Mam's face paled, like a sad white moonlit flower. She was quiet. The woods were still now, too, though one could hear the shushing roll of the river winding like a snake down below the bluffs.

Simon raised his head and gave Nancy his attention. "She's Nancy, aye?"

Mam nodded.

"Nancy *Og*, I've a wee lass at home named Nancy just like yourself. Nancy Ann she is," he said.

Nancy was worn out, but she felt a spark of interest. The white Indian had a baby?

"Did you steal her like us?"

He started, stared at her.

"No. She's my own wee babby. Smaller than your sister there." He gestured at Chloe, now sleeping on her bed of leaves. John, too, slumbered against Mam's shoulder.

"Where is she?"

Simon gazed off into the darkness. "With her mammy. With her brothers and sisters. Like you."

"I wish my Pa was with us. And my sister, Polly."

"Sure he's in a better place now. Maybe looking down on you."

Nancy turned her face up toward the winking stars and watched them until they blurred. She looked at Mam, but her eyes were closed. Maybe she was praying.

"And sure, ye've no sister but that'un there."

"I do. My sister Polly. You never found *her*."

The caterpillar brows shot up. "Well, then."

"She'll tell my Uncle James what happened to us all. He'll come after us. He's a soldier at the fort," Nancy's voice came out a whisper as hope mixed with fear and pricked her all over.

Simon let out that long breath again. "That would be James Halstead, I reckon. Sure, he might. But you should pray not, for his sake. Else he may soon be keeping company with yer pa."

Nancy did not like this thought and kept her mouth shut, blinked back the tears that threatened to fall.

Simon rose. "Meneshewa! Bring them some cover."

Meneshewa got a deerskin from a pack, roughly pushed it towards Mam, then put the leather cord around her neck again. He jerked on the line, pulled Mam down under the deerskin next to sleeping John. Then he moved farther away to rest, the other end of Mam's cord wrapped firmly around his hand.

If Mam tried to save them in the night, the Indian would know.

Simon pulled Nancy up and led her over to where Chloe was.

"Sleep by your sister. Morning comes early."

# CHAPTER 4

## A Wild Scampering Foray

*The Campaign of Benjamin Logan's Kentucky Militia*
*Into Shawnee Country*

**PelaawiTepeke/Spring Moon**
**Meckacheck**
**October 1786**

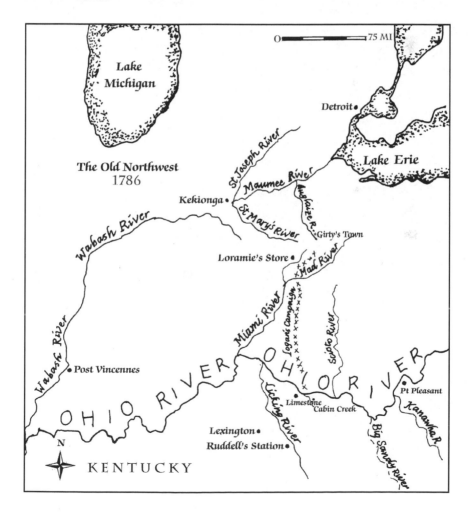

Pelaawi Tepeke crouched in the shade of large oak trees and cooked over a fire pit. Her daughter, Talitha Cuny—known as Priscilla when she was White—worked beside her.

Pelaawi Tepeke's heart filled with pride. They had been together ten summers now. This daughter was now a true Mekoche, a respected healer. Meckacheck, here, was their home.

Talitha Cuny stirred the stew simmering with succulent hunks of rabbit, hominy, and squash. Turnips, beans, and squash still grew in the garden plots beside each cabin while the last of the corn still fattened in the large fields that lay further away. The food might be needed desperately. News had traveled north that Long Knife Clark—George Rogers Clark—was on his way to the Wabash with soldiers. If he destroyed the villages of their friends and brothers, the Miamis, as well as all the other Shawnee towns he came across, the food this village gathered would need to go further, be shared with those who would soon have none.

The happy sounds of children playing rose above the open clearing. The autumn sun lit the meadow, but the air hung heavy and expectant.

Would the Long Knives come *here*?

Most of the able-bodied men of Meckacheck had banded together with raiding warriors of the villages further south and sped to aid their allies against Clark's advance.

While they were gone, the healers went to work, filling their medicine bags for those who would return wounded. They gathered plenty of smelling stick, and sang to the Grandmother as they took bark from the east side of the trees and collected the roots that ran toward the east.

The sun purified these, making them bitter and powerful.

Pelaawi Tepeke and Talitha Cuny, like all Mekoche healers, faced the four directions before gathering these hairs from Grandmother Earth. In thanks for these blessings they offered a tobacco gift to the spirit that lived in the smelling stick, the tree the Whites called "Sassafras."

Medicine women made poultices from the beaten bark and applied them to wounds. They used the tea to keep down fevers. Pelaawi Tepeke hoped these remedies would not be needed.

The warriors were gone three days now. Last night, the smell of burning cornfields drifted up from the south, and Pelaawi Tepeke, along with the rest of the female elders and their daughters, gathered with the others who were left behind. Old Chief Moluntha led them in prayers that Meckacheck, a peace village, be left in peace.

Pelaawi Tepeke's heart hurt. So many had been lost since these wars of the Americans and British. Her people were always caught in between.

Other wise women had arrived at the peace village.

Nonhelema, Moluntha's wife and Cornstalk's sister, known to the whites as "Grenadier Squaw" for her tall stature and fearlessness, was there along with Tecumapease, Tecumseh's sister.

She looked out towards the vast fields of corn. Talitha Cuny's close friends, two other white daughters called Kisathoi and Tebethto were there now gathering corn. She heard the "scritch" of arrowheads being sharpened and saw another of Moluntha's relations, the young Spemica Lawba, who worked on arrowheads given him by those too old now to hunt or fight. At thirteen summers he was not yet allowed to go south with the warriors.

The delicious aroma of the meal brought Pelaawi Tepeke back to the present, and thankfulness for fine day Moneto, the creator, had brought them.

She sang softly, then whispered, "*Da-me*," "Good," as she touched corncakes wrapped in husks roasting along the edge of the fire-pit. Playful barks of village dogs punctuated the sounds of the younger children at play. Older boys shouted as they fished in the nearby stream. Like Spemica Lawba, these were not yet old enough to fight. Among them, Pelaawi Tepeke missed Sinnamatha and Tecumseh, young men the age of her white daughter, who had gone to fight.

Would they return?

Throughout the morning, Tepeke glanced at Talitha Cuny, looking for signs of anxiety or fear.

Did she worry for her friends? There was nothing in her eyes but serenity and contentment. Yet at the ceremony before the Green Corn Festival, when Tecumseh and Sinnamatha danced, her daughter had watched them with interest, her blue eyes brightening when she spoke with them later during the feast.

Yes, it was time for her to marry. Pelaawi Tepeke prayed once more that the young men would return safely, and soon there might be more young children in the village, blessings to her.

The daydream was cut short by screams that stopped her blood. "*Shemanthe*! Long Knives!" rang through the village.

In an instant, soldiers on horseback burst onto the narrow paths between the *wegiwas*. Their swords flashed out at anyone who tried to stop them as they plucked up small children who wailed and struggled to escape.

"Evil, crazy ones!" Pelaawi Tepeke shrieked. How had they come upon them without a sound?

Then through swirling dust emerged—like ghosts—the faces of *Cutta-ho-ta*, "The Condemned Man," also called "Bahdler," or Simon Kenton. This soldier had survived the gauntlet more than once, and even escaped the stake. With him was *Sheltowee*, Big Turtle, whom the Whites called Boone.

Her spirit sank. Those who knew these white warriors, both adopted sons of the Shawnee at different times, knew of their strong medicine and special powers. *Moneto*, The Great Spirit, smiled upon them. Great hunters and scouts, it was no wonder no one heard their approach until it was too late.

She watched with horror as Spemica Lawba attacked soldiers with his newly sharpened arrows. The soldiers cut his bow from him and wrestled him up onto a horse, while he yelled and kicked. There were more shouts and she saw Talitha Cuny racing through the dust.

A young cousin, Blue Feather, flailed about as a scarlet-faced soldier tried to drape him over the front of his saddle. The man grappled with him, holding him down with one hand while wielding a drawn sword in the other. The horse danced in alarm as Talitha burst forward to wrench him free.

"No!" shouted Pelaawi Tepeke, stumbling after to help. The soldier jerked the horse around and swatted at the wriggling child, while Talitha Cuny gained hold of Blue Feather's leg. The horse whinnied and rolled his eyes. Other horses caught his panic, and in the midst of all the havoc, her daughter kept on pulling.

Her heart stopped as through the swirling pandemonium the screaming soldier raised his sword high above her daughter's head.

Talitha, unaware, relentlessly tugged at the wailing Blue Feather.

The horse reared, and the soldier brought the sword down on Talitha Cuny's head with a resounding "Thunk!" followed by a sickening crunch.

She crumpled to the ground.

Screaming and shaking, Pelaawi Tepeke ran closer. She saw a young Long Knife—unencumbered by captives—leap from his mount. He sped to Talitha's side and knelt over her. He pulled back her bloody hair, and then shouted up at the red-faced soldier who was ready to strike again.

The young Long Knife rose and pulled his sword out to ward off any blows from the soldier on horseback. Then he raged at the attacker, "She has blue eyes. Kennedy! Stop! She's one of us."

The blue eyes closed as Pelaawi Tepeke reached her daughter. Soldiers' hands held her back and then dragged her away from her daughter. Then the world closed around her, too.

# CHAPTER 5

## The Girl I Left Behind Me

*Her golden hair in ringlets fair,*
*her eyes like diamonds shining,*
*Her slender waist, her heavenly face,*
*that leaves my heart still pining. . .*

**Polly**

**The Fort**

**October 1786**

Light filtered through the trees. The points of the fort palisades jutted through the morning mist. Polly's heart pounded. She'd made it. She hollered and pummeled the heavy gate, nearly collapsing when it creaked open. She slumped forward into welcoming arms, glimpsed fort horses and Liverpool, Anne Bailey's horse.

And there was Uncle James.

"Good Lord." He crushed her to him in a huge hug.

"Mary Polly. They didn't take you." His hold grew tighter.

"They're gone, Uncle…they took all but Pa, and me. I hid."

As he carried her into the blockhouse, she vaguely noticed more horses in the yard. Their neighbors, the Morrises, must be here, because there was Pluto, one of theirs, and another one—*could it be?* Her Dolly! The mare whickered at her as they went by. The Indians hadn't made off with every horse, then. Somehow the Morrises found Dolly and brought her here.

An excited cry rose up through the air, "One of the Flynns is here!"

Folks hurried up to them, curious and agitated. They clamored to see Polly, but James's voice was stern.

"Leave her be. She needs her rest. She's been through a lot—" his words choked off, and Polly heard murmuring, felt the crowd back away. Reluctant footsteps receded. But one pair continued towards her. Polly opened her tired eyes a crack to see Margaret Morris, their neighbor.

She reached an arm forward to caress her, touched her blond hair, tangled with twigs and brambles. "Oh my dear," she said, tears in her voice.

Pipe in mouth, fort regular Anne Bailey clomped over to join them, looking thunderclouds. She would not be shooed away by James Halstead, whom she had known since before The Battle of the Kanawha at Point Pleasant, a war her husband, Leonard, had also survived. She followed as James gently set Polly back on her feet, and then led her to the women's sleeping area, arranging the cornhusk pallet once more for sleeping.

"Lie down, we'll get you tea and broth," Margaret said.

"Margaret, I'm all that's left." Polly could barely get the words out.

"Shh. I know. Be still. Your poor pa. God bless his soul. You're safe now. Rest."

She couldn't sleep. She heard Anne Bailey send someone for the food, while Margaret stayed with her, holding her hand. Then Uncle James reappeared, Marie DeForest with him. Marie's dark eyes glittered with tears. *How peculiar to see those two together . . .* flitted through Polly's fitful mind.

"Margaret, I'll sit with Polly now," Marie said. She wrapped her bearskin blanket around Polly, then gathered up her fine skirts—too fine for the fort, Mother always said—and sat beside her. She held Polly's head in her lap, and sang a song, but Polly didn't recognize it as coming from the songbooks they so prized. The words were not even

Bridger Public Library

English. Still, it sounded like a lullaby, and Polly fell into restless sleep before the tea ever came.

Anne had an idea. As she watched Polly's eyes flicker into sleep, then tried to whisper it softly to Margaret and James. It was always hard to talk soft with her throat rough from regular whiskey drinking and pipe smoking.

"Clark is taking an army up the Wabash to fight the Miamis." Everyone knew George Rogers Clark, famous Indian killer.

"When the Shawnee skunks from up the Mad River come to their aid, General Logan—with the likes of Boone and Kenton in his regiment—will pay a visit, and strike their villages along the Mad River, all the way up to Wapatomica. With those Shawnee warriors down here helping the Miamis, it'll be easy for the militia to bring back some Injun captives." She blew a puff of smoke from her pipe. "For trade later on. So's we can get back our own." She looked for their reaction, wished she were with Logan. She'd hardly slept a wink last night, between fretting over the Flynns and worrying over the men—many of them her friends—on Clark's campaign.

She glanced at James.

"They won't have made it up to any of the villages yet. There's not even been time enough that they'd be traded off to anyone yet," he said.

Anne thought about the Girty brothers—those traitorous scoundrels—and their trading post at the junction of the Auglaize and Maumee rivers. That was where many captives were taken, then traded to various tribes in the region. Adoption used to be the future for most captive children and many adults, but since the Treaty of Fort Finney, more and more were painted black and marked for the fire. But she also remembered Clark and Logan would not be going so far north as Girty's Town.

Anne and James had both known people who'd been burned at the stake. Simon Girty was rumored to have been present at many of the tortures. Some captives who lived to tell their tales said Simon helped to free them, even ransomed some. During Dunmore's War, he Simon Kenton was one he had rescued from Shawnee captivity and torture during Dunmore's War. But Anne had heard another witness tell of the merciless torment and burning of Colonel Crawford four years ago at the hands of Girty and Captain Pipe, a Delaware chief.

James's face was gray. "I want to go after them." His voice became a whisper. "But with Logan and Clark gone from the area, I can't leave the fort. There's bound to be more raiding." His jaw tightened.

He was right. There would be no chance to follow their trail now. Unspoken, though, was the terrible question: If not now, when? A cold trail was no trail.

There was silence as they reflected on the sad situation.

"John Flynn, bless him." Anne frowned. "Slaughtered just like my Richard. It was Girty. Bloody Irish traitor. And the heathen Old Meouseka." She turned to Margaret. "Your Leonard said he saw them."

"Yes. Leonard was at a distance, up on the bluffs, but he saw eight to ten raiders, including Old Meouseka, and Meshenewa. He thought he may have seen Girty. The Indians got most of the horses. My husband thinks they will split up, take Elizabeth and the children upriver, maybe on the Sciota, maybe the Miami. And they'll take the horses up to the villages."

Anne fingered the hatchet at her waist as she thought of Girty, the turncoat. Once an American, he had started out fighting against the British in the War of Independence. But he had been passed over for a promotion, and the bitter taste was eventually strong enough to send him into the arms of the British Loyalists and their Indian friends. He went over to the enemy while on General Hand's ill-fated Squaw Campaign of 1778. Well, one could hardly blame him for leaving during that sorry mess, but he had been a scourge to the frontier ever since. After his desertion Hand offered eight hundred dollars for

Girty's scalp. She'd heard it was up to a thousand. She'd like a chance at that, but then again, she'd just as soon scalp him for free.

Anne's first husband, Richard Trotter, was killed at bloody Point Pleasant more than ten years back, and ever since then Anne had carried a gun, could shoot better than most men. She also dressed like a man, in buckskin shirt and breeches with hatchet and knife at the waist, and long rifle on her arm. She'd once overheard Elizabeth Flynn warn her children not to spend much time around her, but they still flocked around her when she came to the fort. Even Polly. She was fond of them and wanted to help.

"What will become of Polly?" asked Margaret. The Leonards had several children of their own already.

James lowered his eyes. "She can't stay here. I can't leave one her age on her own here, with so many soldiers. If I'm called out, it might not be safe." As he said this, Anne thought he stared over at Marie DeForest just a moment too long and too hard.

She groaned as she sat down on a nearby barrel and puffed on her pipe, pondering. Smoking always helped her figure things out. She cast a kindly look on James. "My William's at Moses Mays', over to Augusta. Charlotte will have Polly on. Like a companion. They can use help over in that big house."

James flinched. Everyone knew Moses Mays was wealthy, owned plenty of acreage and could use more help on his properties. He dealt in guns and horses, the commodities that most interested Anne, too. But many also remembered some bad blood between John Flynn and Moses over horse dealings. Was James afraid this would be held against Polly? And if James was worried about soldiers at the fort having their eyes on Polly, he might be even more wise to worry about Moses Mays, considering some of the reports she had heard regarding his philandering ways. Would Polly be out of the frying pan and into the fire? Or—she puffed again, could be all that talk be just idle gossip? Plenty of that around here.

Margaret spoke. "James, you know we'd love to have her. But after what's happened to John and Elizabeth, and the children, I want us—and all our own—to just leave this God-forsaken place. This dark and bloody ground," she murmured. Her eyes flashed at them. "That's what Leonard says the Indians call it. But that's what they're making of it."

Silence once more.

"All right, then," Anne exhaled. "She'll go with me, over to the Mays'."

She addressed Margaret. "Leonard can ride with me." Besides fighting in Point Pleasant, Leonard had been a scout later, in the War for Independence. Anne did not need him. The truth was, she had had her own adventure with the Shawnee long ago, almost been caught while out scouting. She'd had to leap from her horse and hide her own self in a log, just like Polly. She'd held back her laughter as the Shawnee, setting to rest a spell, sat on the very log where she'd hid. They'd taken Liverpool, so she had gone after them. After nightfall, she took him back. When at a safe distance, she'd let loose a dreadful howl of triumph that echoed throughout the woods.

Since then she'd heard that the Shawnee thought she was "tetched." Thought she was in powerful possession of magic or some such. They called her White Squaw and believed she could not be hurt by bullet or arrow. Yes, Polly Flynn would be safe with her.

She grunted as she rose from her seat and patted James on the shoulder. "It'll be fine, James. I'll make sure she's well taken care of."

# CHAPTER 6

**Nancy**

**Kettle Town**

**October 1786**

Rivers everywhere, and finally they were on the great one, the O-y-o, Ho-he-o, Ohio—the different tribes had several names for it. Grand rushing river, it sang them to sleep on the bluffs that first sad night.

Next morning, the Indians led Nancy and her family on foot down to the riverbank where Simon and Meouseka pulled canoes from the underbrush. Two Indians stayed up on the bluff. They stood there a spell, watched, then rode off with the last of the horses.

Now Simon had the rest of them split up into the two canoes: John and Mam with Meouseka, and Chloe and Nancy with Simon. In this strange place, she once more thought of home and did not want to get into a boat that would take her farther away. But her home was gone. All that was left of it was poor Polly.

*If the Indians didn't catch her.*

But Nancy soon was distracted by the pleasant slap of the waves against the birch canoe, the splash of the birds as they dove and splashed in the river, hunting fish. On shore she spied bear catching fish for themselves, and elk and deer grazing.

She heard voices raised in song—a different language yet than English or Indian—and the paddles beating in time: The *voyageurs*. Those fellers paddled the rivers in boats loaded down with furs packed in big wooden trunks. They did all kinds of tricks while rowing; she saw one hopping, jigging, and singing over the oars while the others paddled.. The men wore colorful suits of clothes and smiled at her with white smiles out of furry, bearded faces. It was hard to keep Chloe in the boat when they passed by.

She thought one of the boats had a little one napping in it—she'd caught a glimpse of a small figure lying down near the front seat. She protectively put one hand on sleeping Chloe's leg, and felt for her corn doll lady in her apron pocket with her other. "What's that baby they got in there?"

"What?" Simon peered over at the *voyageurs* and gave a snort. "*Le petite homme*. The Chippewa call him *wonakonjaa*. He is 'little man,' and helps to make the canoe strong."

"How come we ain't got one?"

"We do not need a little Frenchman in our boat to keep it strong. Maybe these Frenchmen do. Many of these lads come from a faraway place to the north called Montreal. They have their own name, too, for this Ohio: *La Belle Riviere*, the beautiful river."

After awhile, Nancy fell asleep, but her growling stomach awoke her. She hoped Simon would give them food soon. She had seen some when they set out, stored in packs under the boats. But Simon waited until they came to where the Ohio joined the Big Miami. There the two Indians they had last seen on the bluffs met up with them again, and they finally stopped to eat.

Meouseka handed out chewy dried up meat mixded with berries. It had a smoky taste but was not bad. He also fried some fish he'd caught. After the quick meal, they were back on the water, floating down the Big Miami to a point where more rivers met and mingled. When the rivers disappeared underground, they met up with the Indians with horses, then all went by horseback, this time the short distance to Kettle Town.

After traveling along such a mixed up trail, Nancy knew it might be hard for Uncle James or anyone else to ever find them. Canoes do not leave tracks. Still, Uncle James was smart. He might find them yet.

She had to believe.

Kettle Town was not much like what Nancy imagined a town would look like, but then she never had seen any town—let alone an Indian one— before. Above the river there was a clearing with tall oak trees towering over it on the south and west. Hazel brush bloomed along the banks in bright October colors. There were a few cabins with pelts and bundles of other goods stacked alongside. Wisps of smoke rose from outdoor cook fires and some cabin chimneys.

A man who looked like Simon burst out of one hut, an Indian woman close behind.

He stopped short when he saw Nancy and her family. "You've brought guests." Well, it didn't sound as if they were welcome guests from the tone he took. Nancy had never known guests to arrive like Mam and John with their hands roped together. Meouseka had done that, had them on a lead like Pa did with the horses. He carried Chloe in his free arm. Simon just had hold of Nancy by the hand.

The Indian woman looked at them. She had a cold hard face, real mean. Then Nancy saw she was not a true red Indian. She was white, but dressed like a squaw, in deerskin leggings and a long belted blouse of faded blue material. Her eyes were blue, too, and her hair the color of dust. She wore it in the Indian way with one long braid down her back.

Simon took the man's hand. "Seamus, me brother." He then turned to the angry faced woman. "Hello, Bets. I see Logan did not run you out. Meneshewa brought news that the general and his men have destroyed the villages along the Mad."

Seamus looked at Mam as if she was to blame.

"My family had nothing to do with that. You need to let us go back," she begged.

He laughed. "Go back? You've got to be joking." He turned to Bets. "Did you hear that? They'd like to go back to their homes."

Bets reached right out and pushed Mam with her greasy old hands.

"Stop it," said Simon. Bets glared at him, but kept her paws to herself. If Simon hadn't tightened his grip on her, Nancy would have hauled off and kicked her.

"What about all those from around here who no longer have homes to go to? Who cares about *them*?" Seamus shouted and laughed, but not a happy laugh.

From his wide mouth spotted with dark teeth came the smell of whiskey, an odor that often drifted off the soldiers at the fort—and even off Anne Bailey from time to time. Seamus looked a lot like Simon, was more like Simon magnified. A larger, brighter, nastier sort of Simon.

They began to talk Indian. Simon had taught her some on the boat, but she could not understand any of this.

"Get her out of my sight," Seamus finally said to Meouseka, switching back to English and tilting his head at Mam. Meouseka, with Chloe still clinging to him and fiddling with his earrings, tugged on the rope that held Mam and John together and pulled them away. Chloe laughed, happy to be out of the canoe, and happy to have Meouseka bouncing her around again.

Simon's grip on Nancy grew tighter the farther her family was pulled from her. He held her back with Seamus and Bets by their cabin. A shadow passed over her heart and she panicked.

"No!" She stomped on his boot, managed to twist away and race towards Mam. Mam grabbed her hard and hugged her.

But Simon came from behind and dragged her away. "Sure, you'll be seeing her again." She looked into her mother's sad gray eyes. "I love you," she whispered. Then Simon tugged her rudely, wrenched her back around.

"Where are they going?" A part of her was pulling away, floating off with them. She wriggled out of Simons's grasp enough to watch them stumble down a path twining between the cabins leading to the riverside. In spite of the rope tying him to Mam, John had turned himself backwards. His limp had grown worse over the last few days, and he hobbled as he stared at Nancy, sucked his thumb again as he grew small and smaller in the distance.

"Ah, they'll be havin' a rest. But you, I told you I have a wee lass that shares your name. I'll be after bringing you to see my own Nancy Ann and her mammy."

"But I want my own mam."

"No." His voice was hard like that cruel old brother's of his.

Through tears she tried to hide, she saw that Seamus squatted beside a cabin with casks and other items perched around it, stacking bales.

"Seamus is me brother. James, they call him sometimes. Catherine and Nancy Ann will be up this way." Simon pointed towards a rise where there was a cabin with smoke curling from its chimney.

He pulled her up in that direction. Lifted her right up under the arms and pushed her forward even though she dug in her heels, tried to turn back towards Mam. At the cabin, he pushed open the door and called. "Katie!"

And then a surprise: A woman rose up from before the hearth. She'd been tending a small baby who lay on a pallet. She looked like an angel. Nancy had never seen someone so beautiful, prettier even than Polly's friend Marie DeForest. Simon looked older than Pa, but Katie looked to be not much older than Polly. She had the same black sparkling eyes like Marie, but her skin was fair, save her cheeks. They were a rosy color that grew even pinker when her eyes lit on Nancy and Simon. Her long hair, the color of a shining copper kettle, hung down and gleamed in the firelight. It was loose, not braided, like that on'ry old Bets. She wore a dress that looked like cloth, but Nancy could tell it was made of very soft deerskin, with beaded decorations.

"Katemeneco," Simon said to the woman, and Nancy reckoned she had both a white name and an Indian one. Katie came to him with her arms all stretched out for to hug him, and he held her tight, pressed her head on his chest and kissed those pretty locks of hers. Seemed he forgot Nancy was even there.

The baby gurgled.

Katie turned towards the young'un, and it stretched itself out, then quietened down and snuggled into a fur blanket.

"Who is this?" Katie's cheeks crinkled up with dimples as her lips curved up into a smile, Her voice was like music. She sounded like she was from France, like Cruzatte, the Frenchman who sometimes played fiddle tunes at the fort.

Simon patted Nancy's shoulder. "Here's a stout-hearted lass, named Nancy like our own babby." He walked over to where the baby lay and gazed down at it kindly.

"Nancy." She liked the way it sounded when Katie said it. Katie touched Nancy's tangled hair, untouched by a comb for days.

"So. Another Nancy. And haven't you a sweet face like our own dear baby?" She tilted Nancy's head up towards hers. "Your eyes are like pieces of the sky." Then she looked at Simon and talked Indian.

"No!" was the loud and gruff answer Simon made to whatever she was after. Then, "We already have a Nancy," he said more softly. The baby stirred.

Katie looked down at the floor, a dirt floor with designs someone had carved into the surface, around the edges of the room. Mam did that sometimes at the cabin. Katie slipped her soft arm around Nancy again.

"We must clean you up. I have some clothes here that I know will fit you."

All tuckered out now, Nancy slumped down near the fire and watched that sleeping babe while Simon talked more Indian to Katie. What could she do to find Mam? Would they ever let her go?

"Nancy *Og*," said Simon to her, using the name Old Grandda called her that meant, 'Young Nancy.' "You be a grand girl and watch me young one."

"And Katie, I know you'll watch over this one." He nodded her way as he started out the door. "I've business to attend to."

She rose the next morning in a clean shift, with a clean body and washed hair, braided now, and saw Katie feeding her baby. There was no privy, but she went to a private spot outside the cabin to make water, then came back in to find her own dress, clean and warmed by the fire, along with her pinafore. She reached in the pocket. Was her doll still there? It was. Someone had removed it while they washed her dress, then replaced it for her, safe and sound. The scrap of blue cloth had been stitched into a real dress. A tiny bead, like the ones on Katie's dress, held it closed in the back.

Nancy dressed in silence, then moved to Katie for help fastening the back of her own dress.

"I'm going to see Mam now. And Johnny and Chloe."

Katie did not answer.

"Then I'm going to find Simon." Simon had to let her go back to her family.

Katie sighed, had a strange expression on her, but would not talk. Nancy realized it was worry she saw in the dark eyes.

She couldn't breathe, felt like to burst. Desperate now, she pushed out the door and ran through the small village, searching high and low. Her heart pounded with each empty step.

They were gone.

Mam, Johnny, Chloe. Simon was gone, too, as were the Indians who had traveled with them this far. She was truly alone with no one left to her. The thought made her sick and wild. When she found someone to question, it seemed like they could not understand her through her panting and tears. Or maybe they didn't speak English. Many either answered her in Indian or French, or wouldn't answer her at all, acted almost like she was invisible.

Now a dog followed her. And she noticed a crow had decided she was worth watching, too. He flitted from tree to tree, black eyes glittering, cawing at her, staying right beside or behind her. Just that one crow.

"One for sorrow," the rhyme sprang into her head. Anne Bailey back at the fort always insisted it was magpies in the rhyme, but in these parts everyone said crows. Well, she surely had grief now, so that crow could just leave her be.

Emptiness filled her up. She walked slowly back towards Kate's cabin, her surroundings a blur, her stomach hurting as she tried to catch her breath.

As she came close to the Girty cabin, she saw Bets near the door-way. The sight of the cruel one gave a brief focus to her thoughts. Once more she wanted to kick her or yank that long braid out, but she knew that would not do.

Bets squatted among a bunch of pelts. There were more bundles here now than yesterday, and two young *voyageurs* stood by, trading. She could tell them by their bright clothes, their big shoulders.

When the *voyageurs* gave Bets a bundle, she did not use the fancy canoe cups that hung from their belts, but measured whiskey into the lid of a copper teakettle, and then poured it into their cask, a lidful for every pelt in the bundle—beaver skins, from the look of them. Bets interrupted her task just long enough to give Nancy an evil eye. She grunted something that sounded like, "Gone," and the voyageurs turned, noticing Nancy for the first time.

They were not much taller or older than she was. Maybe Polly's age. The shortest one had merry black eyes like Kate. His red hat hung from his head like a large stocking with a tassle on the end, and his long shiny black hair trailed down below the hat. The dipper dangling from his waist was carved with flowers, hearts and fish. A tiny beaver head formed the handle. He said something to his friend in French. They both looked at Nancy and laughed., but not in the mean way Seamus had.

The smaller one said, "*Bon jour, Madame*, Why so sad today?"

He seemed kind. Nancy started to say, "My Mam," but her throat clogged up and smoke from nearby cook-fires stung her eyes. She put her arm across to wipe them.

Just then, Kate arrived with her baby. The *voyageurs* straightened up and turned serious. Kate scolded them in more French talk. They glanced again at Nancy, this time without smiling and joking, and the smaller one took notice of the dog that had followed her over here.

He reached down to it and held up its paws. It was a boy dog, Nancy could now see. "Well, your little man is quite happy today," he said. Humming a tune, he pretended to dance with that hound.

"He's not mine. He doesn't even know me. Nobody here knows me."

"What is that you say?" He gazed with surprise from Nancy to the dog, then lifted the dog up so that his muzzle was beside his ear. The dog licked him and squirmed. "That is not true. He tells me you are his best friend." He leaned his head next to the dog's muzzle again. "His only friend."

"*Monsieur Chien.*" He made that dog's acquaintance. "I am Jean Baptiste. And this is my friend, Henri."

The dog was much smaller than Lafy—Lafayette, the fort dog. Thinking of him made her touch the scar forming on her hand. A keepsake. It had healed a lot in the last few days, even if it was the only thing getting better. It seemed years since the accident with Lafy and the boiling soap kettle. She even missed Lafy now.

"What is his name?" she asked Jean Baptiste.

The *voyageur* leaned his ear to the dog's mouth again. "Oh. He says you are to decide that for him. He is tired of going without a real name."

The dog had fur the golden color of fallen leaves. His ears, which pointed up, had a brown tint on the tips, his muzzle of the same brown.

Katie's baby laughed and squirmed as she tried to reach out to him.

Jean Baptiste held the pup close to Nancy. "What is my name?" he pretended it asked.

Nancy's sore heart split open a crack as she looked at the soft brown eyes and friendly face. She reached out a hand to touch the golden fur. "Scout. I'll call him Scout."

# CHAPTER 7

## The Big House

**Polly**
**Augusta, Rockingham County**
**November 1786**

Golden flames softly sputtered and spat in the huge fireplace in the great room.

"Polly, please fetch my shawl dear?"

In spite of the warmth, Charlotte Mays always seemed to feel a chill. "Yes, Miss Charlotte." Polly rose from the stool where she sat with her needlework and went to the fancy chest where Charlotte's wraps were kept. She removed the fine wool shawl and brought it to where Charlotte reclined on the sofa and bent to arrange it around the thin shoulders.

"Thank you." Charlotte's voice was barely above a whisper.

If people were birds, then the women at the fort would be chickens in their little hen house—busy, poking around in the garden patches, chasing after their chicks. Anne Bailey might be a raven with all her carrying of messages back and forth. Marie would be some beautiful show bird. Maybe a peacock? But it was the males that were the attractive ones in the bird kingdom. Polly would have to think more on that.

Here in the mansion, Charlotte would be a dove. A gray mourning dove, quietly beautiful. Not that fiery beauty of Polly's friend Marie, but a soft, fine beauty.

Polly shivered. The glowing fire warmed her, but thoughts of Pa and the others swiftly chilled her to the bone, brought out gooseflesh on her arms and the back of her scalp.

She sat on her stool and tried to focus on the sampler. The Tree-of-Life pattern was difficult. The thread was slippery, her stitches uneven. One part of the linen was damp with tears, try as she might to stop them from falling.

At least Charlotte left her alone for the most part, trapped in her own grief.

"She lost her only child a year ago," Anne had told her on the journey here. It was Moses, the husband, who wanted a female companion for his wife, someone to draw her out while he was so often away.

"Aye, she has her own sorrows, and illness, too, from what I hear. Ye may be just what she needs." Anne had clucked her tongue.

So here she was.

There were other women, of course. Venus, the female house servant, for one. But as a slave, she was not to be considered a proper companion. She could not read or converse about things that might interest Charlotte. Polly could read, at least, but considered herself as poor a companion as Venus in every other way.

A log thunked. and she glanced up to see Venus load more wood onto the fire.

Polly turned back to Charlotte. "Is there anything else I can bring you?"

"Perhaps you could read to me?" The question came out with a soft sigh.

Venus's back stiffened. The servant often seemed angry with her. Polly had never been in a household with slaves and was not used to it. Was Venus upset she had to wait on someone of no account, like Polly? Someone who was not fine like Charlotte?

Or did she wish *she* could read? Would Charlotte have any objections to Polly teaching her? At home, Mother had taught Polly—and even Nancy—to read from the Bible and *The Farmer's Almanac*. She would ask Charlotte some time when Venus was not about.

Polly went over to the delicate desk where Charlotte kept several books. "Which would you like?"

"*Robinson Crusoe*, I think." This was one of Polly's favorites, too.

She sat beside Charlotte on the sofa and began to read. She found a coincidence. Today the story focused on Crusoe teaching "his man Friday" to read. Venus lingered over her tasks, fussing with the tools along the hearth, listening, though Charlotte did not appear to mind or even notice.

Charlotte dropped off to sleep before Polly finished. Then Polly tucked the shawl securely around her and returned the book to the desk, setting it on top of *The Castle of Otranto*. They had finished that one last week, and with this fine mansion for comparison, Polly began to imagine what a real castle was like, though admittedly, this was nothing like Otranto, except in size. Of course, she had yet to find a dungeon.

Marie herself had stayed at a plantation before and tried to coach her on life in The Big House, once she knew of Polly's destination. She taught her how to speak so that she would not appear a common and unschooled country bumpkin. Yet it was hard to shake off the feelings of a country mouse. She wore an orphan shroud, felt lost—like the girl in the palace of Otranto—alone among strangers.

Oh, how those times with Marie seemed a lifetime ago.

She went to the front door to look out at the sky, breathe in the fresh air. In spite of cold damp November, she longed to be outdoors. Dolly was in the stables where Polly had been allowed to keep her for her own use.

She took a woolen jacket, an old one Charlotte had tired of, from a hook near the door. Charlotte's cast-offs were better than anything Polly had ever owned. Even the house servants here had better garments than most folks back at the fort.

In spite of Marie's coaching, Polly could not get used to wearing a linen cap like the one Charlotte wore, but she tied on a straw bonnet. She made her way to the back of the house, out past the garden and the small coach house to the barn and stables. Caesar, a male slave, worked on a forge not far from the stables. He nodded to her and she returned his greeting as she passed.

As she entered the stables, Dolly nickered in welcome. Next to her was another of the Flynn horses, Ringo, a sorrel with a star on his head. Leonard Morris had found him back on the Flynn's improvement and taken him to Uncle James at the Fort. Polly had overheard Uncle James and Moses talk about him, and she understood he was payment for her staying there. It made no difference to the happiness she felt at having one more piece of home here, never mind the reason.

When he brought Ringo over, Margaret had insisted Leonard also bring a packet to Pollly. When she opened the parcel, she found a corncob doll, a carved wooden spoon, and a piece of blue cloth. Leonard had come upon the precious items when looking for a trail that might tell which way the Flynns had been taken. The doll was the one Polly made Chloe, and the cloth was a scrap of quilting material meant for a gown for Nancy's doll. Polly put those small treasures in a special bark box Marie gave her as a going away present and kept them under her bed.

She buried her face in Dolly's withers and blinked back tears. Then she heard the approach of horse's hooves. Moses rode up and reined in Sabre, his stallion, before he dismounted.

"Miss Polly." His gloved hand lightly tipped the brim of his hat.

She swallowed, hoped he would not notice she was near tears. "Hello, Mr. Mays."

Well, if people were birds, not only Marie, but Moses would definitely be peacocks. Even at home he was well dressed, with his powdery blue gentleman's jacket and silky green vest. But more than a bird, he reminded her of a cat, clean and graceful. Around him, Polly felt a shy little mouse. She thought back to what Anne had told her of him.

"He's only twenty-eight, yet he was a major in the army when the war ended. Smart as a whip. And the grass hasn't grown under his feet on that plantation. Got a lot of crops. Got himself an orchard. Lots of stock. You wouldn't recognize the place if you'd seen it when his father John Mays was living."

Anne leaned in. "Now your uncle and your poor mam, of course, would want me to warn you. A roving eye, some say he has, though I've not noticed it myself. Lord knows he'd have a hard time finding a prettier wife than Charlotte." Anne sighed. "Of course, now they say she's just a shell of her old self. Since she lost the child, you know."

Polly snapped back to the present. Moses was regarding her with sly cat's eyes. Waiting on her. For a pounce?

"Would you like to ride, Polly?" His quiet voice was low, silky.

"Yes, please. I'd very much like to." This was an unexpected pleasure, a ride not related to a task or journey.

Moses led Dolly out and motioned for Caesar, to saddle her.

Then he helped Polly up, briefly meeting her eyes. "Enjoy your outing," he said, swatting Dolly gently on the rump.

There were acres and acres of the corn, though tobacco was the main consideration. The vast plantation also was dotted with fields of flax, barley, and rye. Once they were a ways from the mansion, Polly let Dolly have her head.

She galloped out past endless fields when in the distance she noted a speck growing larger and larger. A rider approached from a distance. He wore a broad-brimmed black hat and sat the largest horse she'd ever seen. She slowed Dolly to a walk. The rider looked just slightly younger than Moses. A pair of startled blue eyes flashed at her from under the brim of his hat. He slowed his horse, gazed at her with surprise and shock.

"Hello!" he hailed her.

From a distance she reckoned he might be William Trotter, Anne Bailey's son. But this was not wiry, bony Will, but a grown man with an open, handsome face. Blonde hair curled from under his hat.

Polly's heart pounded. Was it from the galloping? The sudden stop? Or was it because Mother always said she should not speak to strange men? That rule was a hard one to follow in Kaintucke. Especially now that her family was gone.

She nodded at him, making brief eye contact, not allowing Dolly to linger to befriend the huge beast the man rode.

From the corner of her eye, she glimpsed him pull his mount to a complete stop. He had turned in the road to watch her. She urged Dolly into a trot, and after skirting a maple grove, she turned off onto a deer trail that led down into the woods. He would not be able to see her now.

She caught her breath; the thumping in her chest grew fainter.

*Who was he?*

She had never seen him at the fort. Was he one of the Palatines from Mann's Fort? Moses and Will had spoken of this prosperous family. In fact, Will Trotter preferred working for the Manns to working on the Mays's plantation. The Manns owned a large farm and many acres in a settlement along Indian Creek. They lived near a saltpeter cave, operated a forge and gunpowder mill that had supplied ammunition to the patriots in the War of Independence. It was still in operation. Sadly, there never did seem to be an end to the need for gunpowder.

The patriarch, Johann Jacob Mann, was from Kraichgau, Baden-Wurttemburg, a place some called Palatine, located somewhere between the Rhine River and the Black Forest. With place names such as this, Polly wondered if the region they'd left was as grim as that area around the Castle of Otranto.

Charlotte said Johann and his wife, Barbary, were among the large group of Palatines who had started the Lutheran Church on Peaked Mountain.

Polly continued to think on the blue-eyed stranger as she entered the quiet thicket and smelled the angel's share as it hung in the air: that smoky, malty scent drifting from the stillhouse. It was somewhere in these woods, down by the creek. The corn whiskey Moses sipped of an evening was made here and then eventually shipped down the river from Limestone to New Orleans.

She rode deeper into the woods. A calm descend upon her. But in the silence of the forest her peace turned to melancholy soon enough.

"Ca-a-w-w," a black crow called down to her from above, accusing her somehow. The trees closed in on her, and her mind drifted back to the evening of her flight to the fort and the loss of her family. A flood of tears fell. What she would give to have the last day back, to hear Pa tease, to know Mother was concerned for her, to have Chloe in her arms, to hug John? And who would have thought she could miss pesky Nancy so much? Among the trees, she wept until her head hurt and she gulped for air.

Uncle James still hadn't looked for them. Too dangerous yet to leave the fort. The Flynns' trail was now cold. Where were they all? Did they still live? How could she not know? It seemed as if that would be one thing her heart would be able to tell her. But it did not.

Before the journey to Augusta, Polly overheard Margaret Morris murmur to Jenny McBride, "I can't sleep thinking of Elizabeth and the children."

"T'would be a comfort if we knew t'was not Simon Girty who'd been among the savages who've taken them," replied Jenny.

"Yes, but Leonard is sure he was there with the Shawnees. Only think of how Colonel Crawford suffered. The torture that poor man endured before being burnt alive, and Simon right there, watching," said Margaret.

"I've heard tell that since he now has his own wife and children, he begs mercy for women and young ones." Jenny's words were filled with doubt. After a moment of thoughtful silence she whispered, "God bless them and save them."

The forest grew darker. Polly wiped her eyes, turned Dolly, and rode back to the stables.

There, tied by the gate was the huge horse. The stranger was here. Polly's heart sank at the thought of being seen—especially by an outsider—in such a state. She sighed. There was no way to avoid it. She had already been out too long. She should call a slave to remove the saddle, but she would rather do it herself. With little effort she was able to undo it and put it with the other tack.

Her face was sore from sobbing, swollen. Her eyes stung. Noticing a pitcher of water near the smithy, she dipped a corner of her petticoat in it and wet her face with the cool water. It helped.

She took a deep breath, made sure her jacket was fastened, and felt her hair to see if it was still respectably knotted at the back. It was not. She could never fix it herself before they all saw her. She pulled off her hat and combed through her thick blond hair with her fingers before she walked, worn out, up the grand steps to the ornate door of the limestone mansion.

They were all in the great room. Their conversation stopped abruptly when she entered. Her face burned as they all turned towards her in a bright silence. They'd been talking about her. She could feel it.

Moses stood, remembering his manners, and the blond man, sitting with hat on his knees, also rose. Charlotte was more alert than Polly had yet seen her. There was color in her cheeks, and her gray eyes were bright. Polly realized she had never really seen Charlotte smile before, and her smile was interesting—a crooked half-smile. Somehow that imperfection made her even more beautiful, Polly thought. Feeling very shy she turned to greet the stranger.

"Adam Mann, this young lady is Miss Polly Flynn," said Moses.

Adam took a step forward towards Polly and briefly clasped her hand. "I am happy to meet you, Polly Flynn."

And the warm room grew warmer still.

# CHAPTER 8

## I Find None to Remind Me

*"How sweet the hours I passed away*
*With the girl I left behind me."*

**Elizabeth**
**Late November 1786**

She was dying. Snow fell over the autumn hunting camp, and cold crept into her bones. She felt life ebb away, leak out like tears. For the longest time, she had cried no tears, in spite of her deep sorrows and losses. But little Johnny, the only child she had left to her, had finally been taken, too, and then the weeping began. And once it started she could not stop.

Her eyes were dry now. Her whole body felt dry and empty, a brittle, broken twig like those she picked up for the endless fires of the hunting camp.

She was no stranger to hard work. Any woman who spent time working land in Kaintucke had rough hands. But there was respite from time to time: a celebration, a wedding or dance. There was no rest here. She was but a slave now, subject to a cruel Mingo Woman called Black Water. Wood gathering, dressing game and scraping hides filled the days. Time was now one dismal yet painful road. A road she knew must end soon for her.

"*Kanyo okha!* White one! You!" Black Water, her tormenter, hissed at her. "Work!" She grabbed Elizabeth by the shoulders, hard, and shoved her towards the women who worked over bloody hides on a makeshift table. Then she kicked the basket of wood Elizabeth had gathered, scattering pieces across the snowy ground. Elizabeth bent to fetch them up when she felt a whack in the small of her back from the club Black Water wore around her waist.

Breath knocked out of her, she bent, then fell to her knees. Slowly and painfully, she collected the wood again. Her cold fingers hardly obeyed her. She stumbled her way towards the table loaded with skins and carcasses of deer, beaver, and raccoon.

"Elizabeth. You are not well." It was the kind voice of Samson of Africa, who'd once been a slave.

Like she now was. Her head felt so light she nearly floated, but he took her arm, helped her along. She could not speak, her tongue didn't make words, but she reached for his hand and squeezed it in thanks. She doubted she would have survived here without this one strange friend. Strangers in a strange land, together. There was not much he could do for Elizabeth but show her the occasional kindness. In this topsy-turvy world, the women were in charge of the captives' fates, and Black Water was in charge of her. It was hopeless. Samson, free among these people, had already done all he could for her.

After Girty and his bunch took Nancy and Chloe away, she and Johnny had ended up in this village mixed with all kind of folk, mostly Indians from different tribes. Some were Shawnee, but there were also Mingos, Miamis, and a few Seneca. Then there were a few from other tribes whose names she'd never been able to make out. There were some French traders, some married into the different clans. Some here were escaped slaves, like Samson. He had told Elizabeth he had been freed, as an agreement for fighting in the War for Independence, but after the war his master had tried to enslave him again, so he'd run off to these parts.

Strangest of all were the white Indians, some who'd been Indian so long they could no longer talk English, or spoke it very poorly. Lord knew she'd tried hard to communicate with them when she could escape Black Water's cruel eye. Most of all, she had hoped to find at least one who would help her Johnny to remember his real name. Here they called him "*Quetaske*," for One Who Limps.

Samson had promised her he would not let Johnny forget his name.

She regarded her surroundings once more. This camp where they now worked was a day's journey from the village on the Sciota—or Sciota-cepe, as the Shawnee called it. She would struggle here while winter deepened, until the Pleiades, called The Seven Sisters by the Shawnee, appeared. Then they would go back to the village for the winter.

But Elizabeth knew she would not last so long. Surely she would draw her last breath in this cold bloody spot, too exhausted for any more travels or trials.

Samson helped her hobble to the worktable, made of large stumps and huge split logs. She tried to straighten herself up. Samson guided her towards Red Squirrel, his wife. She was one of those white Indians, young with pretty blue eyes.

Blue. Like Nancy. Like Chloe. Elizabeth swallowed, trying to work some wetness into her dry mouth. She tried to focus on the work before her, but all she saw was a foggy vision of her lost children. All gone now. She took a hide from the pile and began to scrape fat away with the bone knife set before her.

Still those children appeared before her while her numb fingers fumbled at their task. She knew they weren't really there. An old French woman had taken Johnny in trade for jug of rum. For that she should be thankful. She had seen the black paint being readied for him, had been here long enough to know that was the sure sign Johnny would have soon been burnt as a sacrifice. He was too small and lame to be much account as a slave, and the Indians weren't in a rush to adopt any crippled or weak ones. The French woman saved him with her rum, but God had sent her, of course. He had finally answered at least one of her prayers. Perhaps scraps of gratitude were the only things Elizabeth had left to give, spent as she was.

How she missed Johnny now. In the weeks before he was traded away she had managed, a miracle again, to steal a few moments with him each day. She needed him to remember. His sisters, his father, his mother. English. That he might one day be able to tell someone who he really was.

The river of tears that flowed out of her had been for all of them. Rivers, rivers. In her hazy mind, they floated down a river. A river, a pool of blood dripped from the hides onto the ground below her. A crimson growing stain. Elizabeth stared at it, mesmerized.

She heard the soft voice of Red Squirrel in her ear. "Watch out." Elizabeth turned too late to see Black Water loom up before her, and once more she felt the brunt of the club as she melted down into the blood.

She awoke in the cabin of Samson and Red Squirrel. From far, far away, she heard the voice of the healer known as Otter Woman.

"She will die anyway," the medicine woman muttered." I heard Coyote howl at midnight." Through fog, Elizabeth heard a pot clank, then a steam scented with strong herbs filled her nostrils. Her eyes cracked open enough to see a gourd dipper filled with hot liquid thrust towards her dry lips. Samson looked on. She tried to sip the bitter tea, but choked as she swallowed. She laid her head back down upon the furs piled up as a pillow. She recalled the Shawnee belief that a coyote that cried at midnight was really a shape-shifting witch casting a spell over an unlucky one. Her own self, she reckoned.

Her eyes opened slightly again. She took in the bearskins that covered the lodge door. The edges of Samson and Otter Woman blurred in the pale winter light that leaked in through the smoke hole above the fire in the center of the lodge. Peaceful in here. Much better than the hovel Black Water kept her in.

Along the walls, dogs softly snored on pallets piled with furs. The murmuring voices of Samson and Otter Woman faded, and Elizabeth felt herself floating and lifting. Her tired limbs grew light, the air bright. She heard her husband, John, sing that familiar song:

*"I'm lonesome since I crossed the hill*
*And o'er the moorland sedgy*
*Such heavy thoughts my heart did fill*
*Since parting with my Bessie*
*I seek for one as fair and gay*
*But find none to remind me*
*How sweet the hours I passed away*
*With the girl I left behind me."*

He came out of a wood bordering a green meadow, smiled wide at her. And didn't it look just like the meadow at home on Cabin Creek on a bright summer day? His dark hair shone in the sunlight. His blue eyes danced.

"Ah, Bess, I'll leave you behind no more." His smile grew more tender as he made his way to her, reached for her hand.

She smelled his living self and her body yearned towards him, only to feel the tiniest twinges and tugs on her apron strings: those lost children floating near, pulling on her, light as butterflies.

He came closer. "Bess, it's time to go." He kissed her gently on the lips, and the butterflies released her. Together they rose, flew upward. Yonder.

# CHAPTER 9

## Seven Sweets

*In their cooking, those of the Palatinate*
*Always try to balance seven sweets with seven sours...*
Barbary Mann's Cooking Tips

**Polly**
**Late November 1786**

The nights were hard. Plagued by dreams, nightmares, haints, as some might call them, she couldn't sleep. Nancy had always been the dreamer, the one who woke others with her talking in her sleep. Next day she'd remember the visions, tell them of the strange worlds she'd visited, the odd creatures they'd all turned into. Nancy was gone, and now it was Polly's turn.

Sometimes the dream started out fine. Last night she had entered a golden haze, and they were all there: Mother, Pa, Nancy, John, Chloe, and herself. Talk and laughter filled the air, but then the glow became a gray mist. Her family drifted away toward a dark wood and Polly tried to follow after, called to them in vain. The words wouldn't leave her mouth, try as she might. And then her family all faded away into that black forest just as she awakened, and she'd be left snatching at shadows.

The only thing worse than having those dreams would be when she no longer had them, could no longer see them at all.

She sometimes envied Venus her chores. She actually had more in common with the work-filled life of the slave—especially with the chore-ridden days at the fort and on the improvement—than she had with Charlotte's life.

Now things were different, though. In some of her free moments she had been teaching Venus letters in the big kitchen. And though she continued to read Charlotte the Crusoe tale, work on the sampler, and ride Dolly, those things only filled a bit of her day. There was still plenty of time for grief to eat at her heart.

The day always had one bright spot, however. Adam, the blonde man who rode the big black Hanoverian Holsteiner horse called Schwarzie came nearly every day since that first time she met him. He'd be in the Big House when she returned from her ride. She listened, as over bourbon and Moses's tobacco, the men discussed horses, the gunpowder mill, and shipments of various sorts. They talked whiskey, tobacco, muskets, and more, as the women sipped hot cider. Charlotte lounged on her cushions, and Polly continued to struggle with her sampler.

But every now and then during a lull in the conversation Polly looked up to find the eyes of both men upon her, the light green cat eyes of Moses and the bright blue eyes of Adam Mann. At such times, Polly would quickly lower her head, try to ignore their gaze.

During one such lull, Charlotte herself, always more talkative and lively when Adam was around, asked, "How is your Elsie?"

Polly jerked, pricked her finger with the needle.

*Your Elsie?*

Adam set aside his glass and smiled broadly. "Elsie is good." It sounded like "goot." He had grown up speaking a language Polly thought was Dutch, so foreign sounding words often crept in. His eyes danced in the firelight. "She is my mother's little shadow." Though he answered Charlotte, his eyes were on Polly.

Confused, Polly's face grow hot. As if reading her mind, Charlotte said, "Elsie is Adam's little daughter."

He was married! And had a daughter. Her face burned even more as she tried to focus on a particularly difficult section of her pattern. She was angry at herself for feeling so embarrassed and awkward. Why *shouldn't* he have a wife? He had to be ten years older than she, even if he was still young and handsome and had manners. Polly thought he might be like one of those gentleman farmers Marie had told her about. Those ones that lived back east where Charlotte came from. Was it Baltimore?

Charlotte again faced Adam. "How long is it now that Mary's been gone?"

The smile faded from Adam's face. "Dead these past three years."

Charlotte's gray eyes clouded. "So Elsie must be four. She lost her mother at such a young age." She aimed a delicate hand towards Polly. "You know, Adam, Polly has practically been a mother to her younger sister, Chloe. She is even younger than Elsie—" Charlotte stopped short. Must have seen the shock on Polly's face at the mention of her lost sister in front of a stranger.

"I am sorry, Polly," she said. "You both have had great losses. We all have."

Now it was even worse. Through the sting which threatened tears, Polly saw Charlotte pretend to search for something in the bottom of her tea cup. Then with a bright, birdlike movement she sat straight, the crooked smile lighting up her face.

"Adam, when is Wintering In at Mann Station?"

"Friday next. And my mother would be honored if you all would come." Adam answered quickly, apparently relieved that the talk had turned to happier subjects.

Moses continued to gaze into the depths of his whiskey glass. Perhaps both of the Mays had strange concoctions added to their drinks.

This time it was Charlotte's face that flushed—with pleasure—at the invitation. Polly marveled once again at how the presence of Adam Mann seemed to raise folks' spirits, in general

."Moses! Did you hear? It's already that time. How wonderful."

Charlotte addressed Polly. "The Manns have a delightful Wintering In. You'll come with us this time, of course."

"Yes." Adam beamed. "I have told *meine Mutter*—mother—about the new guest here at the Mays'. She says, 'The more the merrier.'"

Polly tried to smile at the hopeful face. She surprised herself, managing to find her tongue and blurt out her acceptance, "Yes, I would love to come," just enough so they could hear her.

That night, excited dreams crowded in amongst the troubled ones. A party! There had been many celebrations at the fort, but Polly had never been to a party without her parents. Her feelings were confused as sadness mixed with excitement and anxiety. The Manns were Dutch and "had different ways" according to Charlotte. Yet Polly was eager to meet Adam's daughter, to see Adam.

The next afternoon he arrived at the stables just as Polly was ready to dismount. He easily leapt from Schwarzie, his huge black stallion, and wrapped his reins around a nearby post. "Let me help you, Polly."

"Thank you." The loathsome blush crept back onto her cheeks. How red was her face? It was already flushed with cold.

He reached his arms up for her, and as she leaned towards him her cloak fell open. He grasped her from beneath the cloak, and she felt a shock and tingle as the strong hands circled her waist.

He stopped midway, held her suspended, perched against Dolly's back. He gazed into her face, and she wanted to fall into the pools of his clear blue eyes. He slowly lowered her until her head reached his chest. Their eyes locked.

He let go. He took off a glove and touched her cheek with the back of his hand. "You are cold." His voice was low and husky.

Somehow, she relaxed into trust. Tightness fled from her limbs, and she felt surrounded by warmth, the warmth of the nearby animals and the warmth and kindness of Adam.

Schwarzie nickered, and Dolly answered.

Adam glanced at them. "I will put them away. You can go ahead to the house. If you want?"

Polly answered, shy. "I'll wait to walk with you."

He grinned at her, then quickly went to work unsaddling Dolly. He wondered, did she enjoy her ride today? Was she looking forward to the gathering at Manns' Station the following week? He talked of the delicacies that went along with hog butchering, the fiddling and dancing that would follow the feasting.

As they walked up the path to the big house, Adam told her about the brothers, cousins, nieces, and nephews who would all be there. He began to explain their language and ways to her.

She knew that the Manns came from Palatine in the early 1700's, but wasn't Palatine where the Dutch came from? And she had met some Hessians who had stayed in the country after the war, and weren't they Palatines, too? Their speech sounded all the same to her.

Adam asked, "Surely you have heard of General Von Steuben, George Washington's chief of staff?"

"Yes. My Uncle James had his Blue Book—the drills. Tried to use them with the men at the fort but could not get too far. And..." Polly paused, "I remember Uncle James telling some story about the general...that he wasn't able to—that he could not curse?"

Adam laughed. "*Ach, ja, meine Liebchen*, he could curse. Just not in English. My brother has heard him curse in French and Deutsch and then send his translator off to swear in English at the 'stupid American soldiers.'" He took her arm. "Anyway, he is a fine example of our people." His eyes twinkled.

He continued the story on the Manns of Indian Creek. "Many call us Palatines, but really my family comes from the Palatine *und* the Rhineland. People think we are Dutch, and because so many of us lived in Pennsylvania, they say we are Pennsylvania Dutch. Sometimes they call us the 'Gay or Fancy Dutch' so people can tell us from the

Moravians and Mennonites—the 'Plain Dutch—who do not hold with all of our music, and dancing, the designs we make in our homes. We Lutherans—and Reformed—are the Fancy Dutch. Though Lutherans are more fancy than the Reformed, I think. We are the ones who love song, music and beauty," he said. He touched her cheek lightly with the back of his hand.

"Beauty like this," he murmured, and the touch turned into a caress.

They were at the door. He pulled back, stood straight and finished his lesson: "And they only call us 'Dutch' because we speak *Deutsch*—sounds just like 'Dutch.'"

Adam kissed her hand and bid her good night.

That evening Polly dreamed sweet dreams.

# CHAPTER 10

## Prairie of the Dog

**John**
**Indian Village near Prairie du Chien**
**Late November 1786**

She brought him back to the hunting camp not even one full moon after she had taken him. The old woman did not speak English, but French and sometimes Indian, as they journeyed along. It was better than silence, and some of the time he could make a good guess at her meaning.

But no one was at the hunting camp. So on they walked to the village on the river, where he hoped at last to see Mam again.

No one greeted them at his return. But at least they didn't get out the black paint.

The old French woman took him to Black Water, but she screeched at them and wouldn't let him see his mother. So the old one took him to Samson who could talk French and English and all kind of Indian tongues.

And then everything was different once more.

# CHAPTER 11

## Himmelsbrief

### *Letter from Heaven*

**Polly**
**Indian Creek**
**Late November 1786**

As their coach finally rolled to a stop at Mann's Station at Indian Creek, Polly sniffed the air, invited by a delicious scent, the spicy aroma of roasting pork. And then a sea of Manns, Millers, friends and neighbors descended upon them. She met many Palatine relatives: Adam's uncle, George Mann, on his father's side, along with another uncle on his mother's side, the Millers. As numerous as the Manns, some had traveled quite a ways to be here for the gathering.

After introductions, some of the men wandered off to compete in shooting contests near the smithy. Others sipped ale or rye and smoked pipes as they lounged on benches or stumps near the blazing bonfire that cut the chill of the autumn afternoon. A few inspected the latest stock, the foals, calves, lambs and pigs born that spring.

Women cooked or laid the feast on trestles of split logs.

While Charlotte dazzled the Mann and Miller men, Adam quietly led Polly away from the crowd towards a garden path where a woman in a linsey-woolsey dress covered by a snowy apron herded two small girls. The ties to her bonnet fluttered about their rosy faces.

"*Meine mutter*—my mother," Adam explained.

*Großmutter* Barbary chased after the children, waving her pinner at them as if they were so many chicks. Here was a grandmother hen—if ever there was. The children called her "*Großmutter,*" or "*Oma,*" and Barbary Miller Mann basked in the role.

"*Mutter*! I have a guest for you."

Barbary's face lit up and she threw out her arms in welcome. A sparkle glinted on her cheek and Polly was surprised to find they were tears—as she grasped Polly's hands.

"I am very pleased to meet you, Polly."

"Pleased to make your acquaintance, and much obliged for the invite." Marie had taught her some genteel phrases, but Polly found herself saying words Ma had trained her to instead.

Adam bore a resemblance to his mother, had the same blue eyes. Though Barbary's English was heavily accented, Polly sensed intelligence, a sturdy wisdom. It seemed as if Barbary could see right through her.

The children grabbed onto *Oma's* apron strings. "Up!" they shouted.

"You want to meet Polly, too?"

She was introduced to Adam's daughter, Elsie, and his sister Elisabetta's child, Liza. They both were christened "Elizabeth;" it seemed every other female child on Indian Creek was named thus. It was a mercy that most of them went by nicknames, because upon hearing her lost mother's name, Polly could not help but feel a cloud of grief surround her.

But the cousins pulled on her and drove away her sad feelings. As she gazed into their lively faces, she saw that not only did the two children share first names, but since their parents had married each other's siblings, they even looked alike, as double cousins often did. With their dark eyes and hair, Polly thought they bore more resemblance to the Maddy's than the Manns'. She had met William Maddy when she had been introduced to some of the men. His dark and dour countenance had been the only sour note so far this day.

A young fellow who was perhaps the opposite of William Maddy trotted up just then, cheeks glowing.

"Polly, this is my cousin, George Miller," Adam said.

George Miller looked to be a few years younger than Polly, close to her sister Nancy's age, and reminded her of a younger Adam, having the same open honest face and apparent good humor. He took her hand and began to raise it to his lips when Adam snatched it away.

"*Ach du! Aus mit du!*"

George only grinned.

"Take these to the kitchen for me?" Barbary pointed at a basket of cabbages in the nearby garden patch.

"How can I refuse *meine besten Tante?* She's my favorite aunt," he said with a wink to Polly and Charlotte. "*Meine Tante ist the besten* cook in Virginia!" he called as he carried away the basket.

"I vill tell the women you are here." Barbary went towards the kitchen, a spring in her step. Adam chuckled as his nieces continued to latch onto Polly, their new plaything, until Barbary returned carrying the empty vegetable basket.

"*Meine mädchen, genug*. Enough, young ladies!" The girls reluctantly released their hold. "Take Miss Polly to meet *die Schwestern*," she said to Adam.

"So far you are popular with both the Mann men *and* women. But you have not met the sisters—*meine Schwestern*." Adam gave a low whistle. "They are the tough ones."

Polly glanced up, worried, and then saw the twinkle in his eyes.

"*Ach, du*." Barbary thumped Adam with the basket. "He is joking you." She led the two granddaughters back towards the vegetable patch.

Polly watched as wide-eyed, they listened to their grandmother's instructions: "Now *wir machen Kohl Slaw. Meine* cabbage heads vill gather more cabbage for coleslaw," she heard as they trotted away.

Obviously, there would be no shortage of food at today's feast. Over the smell of the roasting meat wafted the malty scent of bread, and the sweet aroma of baking apples and pumpkins. As Adam brought Polly into the kitchen she marveled at the recessed oven built into the huge fireplace. Loaves of bread and platters of baked apples, sauerkraut, roast pork, and the main dish, the *Saumagen*, waited to be carried out to the barn for the feast.

Her stomach rumbled.

Adam plucked a piece of *Saumagen* or *Seimaaga* and placed it between her lips.

It was a concoction of bits of potato and pork sausage mixed with cabbage, onions, caraway seeds and other spices.

"It's good," she sighed as he took a piece for himself.

"*Ja*, after we butcher, ve clean the pig's stomach, put in the sausage, and ve roast until it splits. Then ve put the fresh butter on. *Meine Schwester* just churned this." He gazed around. "Where are they? Elisabetta!" he shouted.

From the summer kitchen came a group of women. They patted the golden braids that peeked out beneath white bonnets, smoothed their aprons.

With surprise, Polly realized that perhaps they were as nervous to meet her as she was to meet them.

Like Barbary, they seemed happy to make her acquaintance. She met Adam's sister Elisabetta, and his brother Jacob's wife, Mary Kessinger, as well as a young wide-eyed creature named Lizzy Stigard, and several others. Polly could not begin to hope to remember all their names.

Adam's younger cousin, George Miller, burst into the room, cheeks bright from the cold. He pulled Adam away to help set up more trestles, and the women clucked around Polly.

She was surrounded by warmth in the comforting room, large, but still cozy with its decorated cabinets and hutches, its ornate *Frakturs* and the colorful *Haussegen*. The women led her around and explained.

"House what?" Polly paused before some fancy script painted over the doorway.

"*Haussegen*. That means house blessing." Elisabetta read to her, "*Der Segen Gottes Kron dies Haus.*" 'That means, 'the blessing of God crown this house.'"

In Polly's mind flashed St. Brigid's cross, the cross Grand-da, Old Patrick, Pa's father from Ulster, hung over the door to their cabin. Yet that blessing had not kept the Indians away.

Elisabetta distracted her, telling about the wrought iron hardware that made up the door latches and hinges. They were worked at the Mann forge under the cliff across the way. Each was lovely, taking on fanciful shapes of hearts or flowers called tulips.

Polly's eyes lit upon the long rifle hanging on the wall, what the British called "Widowmakers" in the late war.

"My pa had one of these. I reckon most men did who served in the war. But Pa's rifle wasn't fancy like this."

The weapon gleamed in the light reflected from the glow of the fire, and light that danced from the pinpricked designs on many tin lanterns perched round the kitchen glinted on the intricate brass design inlaid in the cherrywood stock.

Adam had returned and stood beside her, watched her as she traced the carved design on the gunstock with her finger. "My father made that. He grew up on a farm, but many where he came from trained as blacksmiths. He made all of this," he waved a hand at the etched design, and then at the ironwork decorating the kitchen in general. His face was shy and proud at the same time.

The strains of a fiddle drifted through the door and they both turned to listen. "But we waste time here." Magically the notes wove themselves into a reel. As Adam took her hand, Polly noticed the women all seemed to beam at him as he asked, "Dance with me, Polly?"

The blood moon hung in the tall oaks, beyond ripe: a plucked, promising orb. Guests took well-deserved rest on rag rugs spread under several trees. As Adam led Polly out to dance, leaves crunched, and laughter and spirited conversation in both English and *Deutsch* filled the air. Family and friends of the Mann family danced in the clearing before the house while the fiddler sawed out tunes and clogged on a half-door taken down from the barn.

Adam spun Polly around, and from the corner of her eye once more found the baleful gaze of Elisabetta's husband William Maddy, father of young Liza and brother of Adam's late wife. She stiffened momentarily, and Adam quickly turned to see the cause.

"*Ach*. It's Poor Wilhelm. Sour Bill."

"Why does he look like that?"

He laughed loudly. "Because that's how he *does* look. Unfortunately. Much of the time." Then in a kinder tone, "He misses his sister, and he wants everyone to suffer with him."

Polly, with her own recent losses, could sympathize. "But she's been gone a long time now, hasn't she?" Three years certainly seemed like a long time to *her*. Shouldn't William be healing by now? She hoped that three years from now she herself would not still feel that shroud of pain that hung about her—albeit a shroud she occasionally shed, especially around Adam. At least William had not lost his entire family, as she had.

"Yes, she has been gone these three years now. He could surely honor her memory in other ways than making faces at you. Or me."

She was silent. William *was* married to Adam's sister. It was she herself who was the outsider. With the familiar pang, Polly again thought of her mother, her own Elizabeth, and imagined her mother would caution her to mind her own business if she only she was here.

The dance finished, Adam led her to a small carpet under a maple tree. On the way, he grabbed drinks from a tray of pewter on a nearby sawbuck table. The fiddler struck up a sweet air as she and Adam sat down to finish their conversation.

"He wants me to mourn for her still. They were very close."

What could she say to this? Adam took her hand and gently stroked her fingers.

"Do you still miss her?" Her curiosity outweighed her anxiety that Adam might still love another.

"I cared for her. And I miss her for Elsie's sake. She was a good woman. She tried many times to have a baby, but could never carry a child to term." He shrugged his shoulders. "No use. The midwife told her not to try again, but she insisted. And that is how we got our Elsie." His gaze drifted towards his daughter, who sat at the feet of her grandparents, watching the dancing with enchanted eyes.

The fiddles went into a frisky tune.

Adam's face brightened. "*Ach*!" He only occasionally reverted to Deutsch phrases around her, though he lapsed in and out of the language with Elsie and his family. "It's 'Hunt the Squirrel'! Let's dance!"

Polly returned to Charlotte's side when she next had a chance to catch her breath, and noticed Moses promenaded with Lizzy Stigard, who seemed unable to follow his conversation, acted as if she could not understand his English.

Baby Adam stirred gently has he slept on Charlotte's lap, and "Big" Adam left the side of William Maddy, whose glum face had brightened up during his conversation with his former brother-in-law, to come over to them. As he drew near, Polly found herself a mix of emotions. She wondered with excitement: Dare she now think of him as *her* Adam?

Adam's words about his wife had stirred up wild feelings within her and she willed them to calm, while at the same time Baby Adam's restlessness increased. Charlotte pointedly focused all her attention on him, as Adam paused beside them.

"Polly, the fiddler will soon quit for the night. Let us dance one more," he said as he drew her to him. Always the gentleman, he looked to Charlotte and asked, "Charlotte, may I fetch you anything?"

"No, I am quite happy here with my Little Adam," she replied, with the hint of a naughty smile and an encouraging look at Polly. "Enjoy yourselves on this lovely evening."

Instead of leading her out to dance, Adam cupped her elbow and led her away from the party. He carefully plucked one of the tin-punched lanterns hanging from a nearby tree branch, and took her into the shadows of the great barn. As soon as they were out of view, he pulled her closer to him. She inhaled the smoky vanilla scent, and her head seemed to float, intoxicated.

"Polly," he began, and stared into her eyes as if he would find answers in them. He opened his mouth to continue, but instead of speaking, swiftly brought his lips onto hers, moving his hands to her face, capturing her head in his hands while he kissed her mouth again and again, ever more deeply.

She breathed in the taste of him, and her will to behave properly, to resist, melted away. A wave picked her up and carried her. She felt herself dissolving in his arms. Then he stopped himself, gazed into her eyes, the light from the blood moon and starry lantern reflecting in his own.

"Polly." He named her as he touched her lips with his finger, "I know we have not known each other long, but I feel that I know you, that somehow I have always known you." He took the hand he held in his and placed it gently on his heart. "My heart is yours." He paused, glanced downward before raising his head and locking eyes with her. "If you want it."

She opened her mouth to respond, but he spoke again before she could say anything. "I want to be a husband to you."

Speechless, her head spun. Marie had led her to believe there would be many stolen kisses, many flirtations, before she would meet the one whom she would wed. And Charlotte, great belle that she had been, had been courted by many—both military officers and gentlemen.

Before she lost her family, Polly had wondered about boys she met and sometimes asked herself questions about some of the handsome soldiers at the fort. But since she had met Adam, his face was the one that appeared to her whenever she pondered her future. Was this dizzy rush the way courting and marriage worked?

"Polly," he repeated, sounding uncertain. "I don't want you if you don't—if you couldn't—love me." The words trailed off. "I want us to love each other, to want each other." He paused, searched her eyes. "I hoped you did," he said, and hesitated, "care for me."

The joy she had been afraid to let loose sprang forth. She squeezed Adam's hand in hers, stood on tiptoes, and whispered, terrified and thrilled altogether, into his ears. "But I do, Adam, I do care for you." And she kissed him lightly, shyly, beneath the ear.

He wrapped her tightly in his arms. Relief and happiness flooded their embrace. Then he kissed her again. And again: her hair, her eyes, cheeks, nose, chin, and neck. He lifted her up off the ground and spun her around, somewhat as he had swung his sister, Elisabetta, when he had danced with her earlier in the evening, but definitely different. And unlike the sister who had scolded and slapped at him, when swept off her *own* feet, Polly clung to him for dear life, eyes blissfully closed, a smile on her lips as she relaxed into the strong arms of her future husband, Adam Mann.

As they shyly walked back to the others, Adam said to her, "My mother knew."

"What?"

"My mother said you cared for me."

"You asked your mother about me?" Her face burned in the cold night air.

"No. But she told me. You will be family, after all." He draped a possessive arm over her shoulder. "Or so she hoped."

Polly wondered at this close-knit clan. She was not used to seeing grown up men share their thoughts with their mothers. Even boys like her brother Johnny seldom did. She had never even met Pa's mam, long dead before Polly was born. Pa. Who would give *her* to Adam? And what would she have to offer? What would Old Jacob think, the patriarch who apparently was so concerned with the wealth of his son's potential brides?

"What of your father?" she asked, trying to hide her anxiety.

"Him!" Adam sounded scornful. He stopped in his tracks and cupped her chin in his hands. "My father loves a pretty face almost as much as he loves money. And yours," he said as he leaned down to her level, "is most certainly a pretty face." He kissed her again, lightly.

"As you can see, the Mann family does not lack for earthly goods." Adam's statement was not boastful but matter-of-fact. "He will be happy to have you in the family."

Polly's head swam. Such a short time ago, she was a—well—a mostly dutiful daughter. Then suddenly, in the near blink of an eye, a homeless orphan. Now she would be a wife with a ready-made family and daughter close to the age of her youngest sister? Dare she hope to truly belong once again?

"I will ask your Uncle James," Adam said with confidence.

Her eyes widened as he explained.

"I ride to the fort next week. As soon as possible, I want you as my wife." This time he punctuated the word, "wife," with a hot kiss against her throat. Though once more thrilled by his touch, she was suddenly aware of the crowd of folks not far away from them, anxious lest anyone see this open affection.

He saw her discomfort, and his face became serious. "I do not want you at the Mays Plantation, not with Moses there. I see how he watches you, and my sister told me stories about him tonight." He frowned darkly. "Things I had no idea of. He has behaved improperly towards many women. There is even rumor of him being with one of his slaves in a way he should not be."

Polly's eyebrows rose.

"Yes, Venus. There are tales of a child."

At Polly's shocked expression, he hugged her close. "He will know better than to interfere with you. As soon as possible he will know that we are to be married."

Fear and excitement rippled through her, and excitement won.

She raised herself upon tip-toes to embrace him once more. And then they re-entered the glowing circle of guests.

# CHAPTER 12

## Marie

**November 1786**

She thought she'd sketch the creek behind the fort, or read her novel if her fingers got too cold. So she sat beneath a tree and worked, but she couldn't capture the creek, and before she knew it, her pencil had drawn James Halstead. She snapped the book shut.

She slumped back against the trunk. Lafy, the fort dog, leaned against her, pushing his snoot up under her hand.

"We miss them, don't we, *mon ami*? The Flynns?"

He groaned in response.

"*Oui*, even the madame, who did not approve of me so much."

She rubbed his ears, and suddenly he pricked them up. The air held a hint of tobacco. A twig cracked and they heard a cough and a snort.

Anne.

Anne Bailey crouched, then creaked down beside them, smelling of leather and smoke, wood and tobacco. She puffed on her pipe.

"Out here on yer lonesome?"

"I wanted a little fresh air. Tried sketching, but it's too cold."

Anne's eyes lit on the book and before Marie could grab it, she'd flipped it open to the sketch of James. She tilted her head, squinted. "I'll be. That's a fine likeness of Captain Halstead!"

"Well. It's not really done yet." Marie found herself embarrassed, a truly unusual feeling for her, and couldn't think of a blessed thing to say.

"Hmmm. I'm surprised you'd feel like drawing him so nice after he the way he lit into you gals awhile back."

"Pooh. That was nothing." But it was *not* nothing. It had definitely been something. Her mind wandered back to the summer day when she first made meaningful acquaintance with James Halstead.

The sun was out, the air crisp and cold. In the clearing just beyond the fort palisades soldiers played ball, wrestled, and lounged about. Every once in a while a whoop or holler rang out as the women busied themselves with the chores that came along with fort living.

Marie, bored to tears, watched others go about camp chores. Elizabeth Halstead stirred her wash-pot over a fire. "When the cat's away, the mice will play," she heard her say to Polly as she laid a hickory basket in her arms. "But I bet they won't be caught playing out there when your uncle returns." She'd clucked in disapproval at the sporting of the young men.

James Halstead, a veteran of the late war and captain of the fort, was hunting with Polly's pa and some others. Marie knew the men liked him, though sometimes the youngest soldiers complained he was too strict.

Elizabeth's comments gave Marie an idea. She spied a rifle and necessary pouch that someone had laid down in the shade of a tree, then hissed to Jenny McBride who was headed back towards the fort with a vegetable basket.

"Jenny! Here!"

With Jenny on the lookout, Marie concealed the rifle in her skirts and hid the pouch under the vegetables. Then they made their way back into the blockhouse. Once inside, Marie paused to get a strong grip on the gun. As she rearranged her skirst, she heard Mrs. Flynn tell Polly take Nancy and John fetch in some vegetables.

That was good. Polly would not be involved in Marie's prank, should anything go awry. But nothing would go wrong.

"Mice will play, indeed. *Chacun cherche son chat les souris dansent*," Marie murmured, She urged Lucinda up the stairs.

Once above, she revealed her plan. Lucinda gasped in horror, but Marie only smiled. She rested the rifle butt on the floor, and commanding Lucinda to hold it steady, carefully measured powder from the horn into the charger and poured it down the muzzle. She pulled a greased patch of linen from the pouch and laid it on the muzzle, and finally placed the ball of lead on top of that. With the palm of her hand, she started the ball and patch down the barrel, then tamped them into place against the breech with the hickory ramrod. Then she dribbled a little powder into the flashpan, pulling the frizzen down over the top.

She placed it into the loop, cocked the hammer, aimed for the sky, and fired.

All hell broke loose. Folks froze a moment, then panicked. Babies wailed, mothers called out for their children, and the men scurried every which way.

Marie laughed so hard tears streamed down her cheeks. Beyond the palisades, the soldiers continued to scatter like chickens with their heads cut off, in a hurry to gather their weapons and get back in the gates. But they'd been shut. Some dove into a pond, while others headed for the bushes. A few pounded at the gate, hollering.

Marie wiped her eyes and clutched her middle, calmed down enough to find out what was happening below. Elijah Branch, an old veteran of the French and Indian War who'd been cleaning his musket in the shade of an oak tree not far from the blockhouse—lucky he had not seen them, she thought—limped to the gate and unbolted it.

"Shots come from *in here*," he grunted as he tried to admit the men in an orderly fashion.

"You done it?" one of the militia asked, on his face the awe turning to anger.

"No! I ain't the one that done it. Nincompoop." The old one swatted him with his musket. "Git back out now and round them other fellers up and fetch them back in here."

Then Marie heard a voice beside her.

"What happened? What's so funny?" It was Polly Flynn.

As if in response, there was an angry voice downstairs. James Halstead. Marie peeped out the loophole and saw his horse, Apollo, then heard a stomping on the stairs.

"Those shots came from up here." James glared at them, his eyes flashing from one to the next, then resting on Polly.

"I never thought I'd need to tolerate this behavior from my own niece." Two red spots flamed in his cheeks. Marie stepped forward while Lucinda gaped and goggled.

"Polly had nothing to do with this. I did it. And you should be glad I did, because now you can see how poorly prepared we'd be if there was a *real* attack."

James, speechless, glowered at her, then found his voice. "And *you* should be glad if you're not whipped for this. Whose musket did you have, anyway?"

Marie had avoided his gaze, ducked her head. "I don't know. I borrowed one. No one knew I had it. I already put it back."

By then Mr. Flynn was up the stairs, and a couple of soldiers with Lucinda's mother. She took hold of Lucinda's arm and said, "You better not be a part of this!"

"Lucinda is in no trouble at the moment, Mrs. McBride," James said. "But I'll be much obliged if you will escort  Miss—" He'd faced Marie and the spots on his cheeks burned brighter—"DeForest, is it? —downstairs to await an interview with me."

And suddenly the dull afternoon blossomed into luminous color.

Jenny McBride was clearly relieved that the shenanigans had not been her own daughter's idea. She plucked at Marie's sleeve, "Now come along, lass," she said, and led her downstairs while Lucinda skulked behind.

As Marie descended the stairs, she heard Polly receive a warning from her father.

"Sure it's a good thing you weren't involved in this, Mary Polly."

His next comment was aimed at James. "And it won't do to whip the lass, Marie, James," Mr. Flynn had said. "You know who her father is." Everyone knew her father was an important trader.

"I don't give a fig who her father is," James responded, steel in his tone.

"You can't whip her!" Marie realized with surprise that this last shout echoing off the walls was from little Miss Polly.

Jenny pulled her into a storeroom that had a table and chairs, and soon there came the sound of loud footsteps approaching. And James Halstead was all hers for a few moments.

Well, there'd been no flogging. What started out uncomfortable (for James at least) evolved into a nice long chat. Afterwards, Marie was happy to note that James looked more like the one who'd been whipped. She was only sorry that after that incident when Polly had sassed him, Polly and James seemed to avoid one another. But Marie didn't avoid James, or any opportunity to talk about him with Polly.

One day soon after, they stood together to watch the men shoot targets while James coached them. "Has your uncle had a wife?" she asked.

Polly raised her eyebrows in question. "A wife?"

Did Polly even know how handsome he was? Tall and lean, his broad shoulders filled out his light buckskin coat—made of soft elk hide. The pale color contrasted pleasantly with his dark skin, tanned from so much time in the sun. Tiny lines around his startling blue eyes crinkled as he chuckled at something one of the men said to him. Yes, he was a bit older than her. His wavy light brown hair had strands of gray. Marie reckoned he might be around forty. She nodded.

"No. He's never had a wife."

"A sweetheart then, surely."

"I don't know," Polly had mumbled. "Maybe back in Pennsylvania, before the war. He was a surveyor then."

"Hmmm," Marie said, continuing to gaze at him. Then she smiled her most charming smile. "Do you think I could get him to help *me* with target practice?"

Anne continued to smoke, reaching over to pat Lafy every once in a while. "Well. I don't blame ye fer missin the Flynns. It's quiet here without them. But Polly's doin' fine where she is. Lots of good folks up that way to take an interest in her. I bet you'll see her before too long." She put out her pipe and rose.

She winked. "I won't tell the captain about yer pitcher, neither."

# CHAPTER 13

## Neeshematha

### *Little Sister*

**Nancy**
**Somewhere Along the Miami River**
**Early December 1786**

Shortly after she found Scout, she had been handed off to a new Indian woman, a kind one who cared for her ever since they arrived at the new village. All of them had such long names and this woman, too. She was called Pellolly Tobaccy, or some such. This meant Spring Moon, but Nancy called her Becky, for the "Tobaccy" part. Becky didn't seem to mind.

"Soon you have a new name for me. Special name," she said. "Then no more Becky."

Every morning they wandered down to the river, and Nancy took the plunge with a few womenfolk and the other Shawanese girls around her age. But today felt different. It was just another cold day in a long line, but the air crackled. The crow that had followed her since Kettle Town sat in a tree, waiting, and then another flapped down beside it, and they both perched there. Quiet. Something important was happening. Mam used to say an old rhyme about crows: "One for sorrow, two for mirth." Maybe this day would be a better one than when that first crow had showed up on its own, when her real mam had been taken away.

Becky and her cousin, Prairie Deer—whose Indian name sounded like "To Wash Coats"—led her along the pebbled shore to the river's edge. Prairie Deer's name fit her. Not the washing coats part, but the part that meant she was like a deer, graceful and high strung. That made her almost an opposite of Becky, who seemed stout-hearted, strong, and steady.

Scout, gold fur on his back standing on end, paced the shore, anxious, as Becky stripped off Nancy's ragged dress and the pinafore, torn to shreds now. The fabric fluttered briefly, a raggedy flag, before it took flight, yet another bird, and then dropped down to drift away into the river. Nancy watched the pieces float away and sink. Her old life was further away than ever.

She shivered. The women took her hands again and together the three waded into the icy current. The cold water stung, though their hands were soft as they scrubbed her with tiny stones and shells scooped up from the river bottom. Her skin tingled and her spine hummed, too, as she listened to the soft song the women sang as they washed her. It was a kind of magic. Rainbows prismed off the water drops that clung to the pebbles and shells before they dripped back down into the water like tiny gems. Becky pulled her out of the water, wrapped her in a soft hide, and rubbed her dry. As they walked to the long council house in the middle of the village, Scout pranced beside them, happy now.

They were somewhere in a loose line of Indian towns clumped along the river for miles. One town was big, called "The Blackberry Bush" in English, but something else in Shawanese. That was some rich town, where many supplies from the British up in Detroit—what that *voyageur* Jean Baptiste called Fort Pontchartrain du Detroit—came in. Detroit was filled with cousins of the Mekoche clan of the Shawanese. They had stopped there for a spell before ending up here.

The small village was a pretty place, up on a hill that peeped out over the river. Cornfields stretched out across the bottomlands, and fields of tobacco, beans, and pumpkins— mostly harvested by now— spread out as far as the eye could see. As they walked through the village to the council house, the bells on the Shawanese horses chimed faint on the wind. Nancy spied one that looked like Dolly, Polly's horse, and was hit with a lonesome pain in her heart. But the fat cows who mooed hello at her as they walked past their pen, and the warm hands of the women guiding her along, helped her shake off her sorrows.

At the council house, they went to a platform in the center. Just like the smaller *wegiwas*, fur and hide-covered benches lined the walls. Some sat there while others arranged themselves on the floor.

Becky now tended the burn on Nancy's hand, as she did each day. From her medicine bag she drew some salve of slippery elm and bear's grease and rubbed it in. The wound was healing, the edges of the ragged map of Ireland no longer red. Instead, the scar had a silvery cast.

"You will soon be like new," Becky beamed and waved her hand around them. "Look at your new sisters!"

Nancy glanced up to find that the longhouse now brimmed with the women of the village. All eyes were upon her as Becky and Prairie Deer brought a new suit of clothes from a woven wooden box.

They dressed her in a long calico shirt, pulling it together in front with a silver brooch. This was overlaid with a skirt of blue trimmed with white ribbon. Best of all were the leggings. Bright ribbon decorated the hems, and there were tiny silver bells stitched along the edge glinted and sang. Nancy remembered Becky had traded for the blue fabric at the post at Fort Detroit.

There was yet another new pair of moccasins, fancy with sparkling beads and colored porcupine quills. Nancy's face flushed with pride and happiness. Becky smiled at her, touched her head, and began to braid her hair into one long tail like hers, trailing down her back. She pulled a small paint pouch from the larger bag she wore around her middle, revealing some small shells and pieces of bone that held colors in the hollows. Becky dipped a finger in the crimson color and painted Nancy's face and the part in her hair braid.

Nancy felt all eyes upon this New Nancy, and once more she was proud and joyful. But something nagged at her, pricked her underneath the happiness. Who was she anymore? What did this mean?

Then Prairie Deer began to sing in high, thin voice. She sang a long song, and the women cried and wailed. Then the melody changed and tears dried. A white Indian woman reached a hand out to her and said in English, "Moneto has sent you to be our sister. You will be a blessing to us. May you be happy as long as you live."

Becky turned towards the crowd. "My child," she announced. "Now you are *neetanetha*, my daughter." She hugged Nancy to her.

The women laughed, shouted and clapped.

Becky placed her hand on Nancy's shoulder and addressed to the smiling crowd once more. "This is our sister, *neeshematha*. Her eyes are like those of my lost daughter, Talitha Cuny. Her hair is like our lost sister, Tebethto. And her smile is Kisathoi's, our other sister who disappeared in the raid. She will walk in their ways and be a sister—*neeshematha*—to all of us." Then she tied a Mekoche medicine pouch around Nancy's waist. She leaned down and gazed into Nancy's new red face and said, "Now I am *neega*, not Becky. *Neega*. Your Shawanese Mother."

There was a feast that evening: boiled jerky, baked fish, stewed squirrels, squash, venison, roasted pumpkins, succotash, and two kinds of cornbread. Nancy sat and ate with the other young girls. Some white boys a few years older than she had also been adopted into the tribe. They chased other boys or sat separately, with the men. Nancy caught the eye of White Buffalo, who was not a white Indian in spite of this name, but the son of Prairie Deer. He fashed her a wild smile as he raced after one of the new boys while older people feasted, danced, sang, and played music near the blazing fire.

Two young men, Big Fish and Tecumseh, had traveled with Nancy and the group that brought her away from Girty's Town. Big Fish loped over to sit beside her, squeezing out the youngsters surrounding her. Scout crouched close to Nancy, growled as Big Fish pushed his way in. Big Fish, whose name sounded like Sidney Natha in Shawanese, flicked a finger at him, "Little Sister, *neeshematha*, you are now one with us! You must learn to speak our language. We start with most important word, '*Sinnamatha*,' which means Big Fish."

"I already know you. And I know your name."

There was a whoop above her head. "Ha! She told *you*, Big Fish!"

Nancy looked up to see Tecumseh's scarlet leggings. Her eyes lit on the fancy tomahawk pipe and silky otter-skin pouch that hung from his belt. The war club that usually dangled from his waist was not in sight tonight. A woolen mantle hung from his broad shoulders, covering his linen shirt.

Like many others, he had painted his face red for the feast. Through the crimson he had traced a line that let his own skin show through. This ran from the top of his forehead to the tip of his nose. Then it curved out from the nostrils to each ear, dangling with silver hoops. His lobes were not split like many of the Shawanese men.

Though the Indians in this village wore their hair in many different ways, from shaved heads with scalp locks to heads covered with turbans or scarves, Tecumseh's hair was unusual, too, in that it hung loose around his shoulders like a thick black mane gleaming in the firelight.

Nancy knew these two boys—or were they men? —were older than Polly. They were lots taller for one thing. But after the long trip they had taken together from Girty's Town to Detroit, and then back here to Blackberry Blossom—well, Meckacheck—in Indian words, they were like friends or cousins to her.

She realized she had missed them; they had been gone a spell hunting while others visited in Fort Detroit, but now they were back for the festivities.

'Of course he would think *he* is the most important thing for you to learn about," Tecumseh continued. "Big Fish! Do you know why he is called this?" he asked Nancy. He did not wait for her answer. "Because he is one slippery customer!"

Big Fish Sinnamatha gave Tecumseh a playful punch and then turned his attention towards Nancy. "Little Sister, you are lucky. No gauntlet for you. For me when I became one of The People, there was *long* gauntlet. This one made sure of it," he said, pointing at Tecumseh. "Two or three people deep, it was."

Tecumseh nodded reluctantly, as if he didn't really want to admit Big Fish had won any contests or shown any bravery. But as Tecumseh continued with the story his voice grew proud. "He was twelve when he was adopted. Slippery as a fish when he ran that gauntlet. No one could touch him. But *my* name is the name you want to learn."

"I already know your name, too."

This time it was Sinnamatha's turn to hoot.

Tecumseh shot him a warning glance, then proceeded. "Yes, I am called Tecumseh, but do you know what it means?"

Sinnamatha leaned in and began to whisper to her in English.

Tecumseh grabbed him by the shoulder and threw him back. "See how he tries to cheat? I am Shooting Star. Blazing Comet." He struck a pose, looking as if he would pounce. "I am Panther, crouching for his prey." With this he fell upon Sinnamatha and they began wrestling again. Scout let out a yelp as they rolled onto him, then barked before he latched onto a leg, joining in the fun.

"Stop!" Sinnamatha pried Scout off his leg and pushed him back towards Nancy. "You can't teach her if you keep attacking me," he told Tecumseh. "Anyway, your *whole* clan is the Panther." Then he turned to Nancy, "*Neeshematha*, he's nothing special. All of his brothers are panthers, too."

Scout looked on from Nancy's lap, softly growling warnings as Tecumseh continued to wrestle Sinnamatha.

Through grunts, Tecumseh continued. "My mother saw a falling star when I was born. You know that. My sister told you. And Grenadier Squaw—Nonhelema —told of it in the Winter Tales." He accented each sentence with a punch.

Nancy remembered hearing of Grenadier Squaw. She, too, had been taken away wounded after the raid on *Neega's* village. Nancy nervously rubbed the medicine pouch *Neega* had given her.

"Enough," laughed Sinnanatha. "Yes. Brave Panther attacks Poor Fish. That should be his name." They stopped fighting and fell away, both chuckling as they gasped for breath.

As she continued to finger the soft hide of her pouch, Nancy felt a familiar shape. She reached in to touch the cornhusk doll Polly had made her. She was an Indian now, with these strange new brothers, but she still had a piece of home. *Neega* must have saved this for her? Becky was not Mam, and she never would be. But *Neega*, another sort of mother, she could be. She was kind to keep her doll safe.

She gazed around to see many white people here who were not red like Tecumseh and Becky, but like Sinnamatha, like *her* now, they dressed like Indians, talked Indian and *were* Indians. What happened to their old selves? What happened to their white folks?

"Do you still have a white mam?" She asked Sinnamatha.

The two friends stared at her a moment, and Sinnamatha grew serious. "Yes. And a father. Jean Baptiste told me they were once held in Fort Detroit, but they have long since been redeemed. I do not know where they are now."

She let out a soft sigh. "I know I have *Neega* now, but I still wish I knew where my white mam was. Or my sisters. I have a brother Johnny, too." She glanced at the group of young boys sporting near the fire.

"Little Sister, we are now your family," said Tecumseh. "If your white family is dead, you must let them go on their path. Do not keep them here."

"Pa is dead, but Mam—"

He cut her off, but his voice was kind. "Spring Moon— PelaawiTepeke, who you call Becky— is your Shawanese mother. *Neega*. She has already been so good to you," he said, his brown eyes warm. "Look at this!" He jingled the bells on her hem as he turned to Sinnamatha. "Have you ever seen such fine adoption clothes?"

Tecumseh turned back to her. "Your *neega* also has lost much. We all have. My own father I lost when I was six. Have you heard of the Battle of the Point?"

"Yes." She remembered Anne Bailey's stories about the battle of Point Pleasant, what she sometimes called Dunmore's War. It was the battle where she lost so many friends. "There was a lady from the fort, but she dressed like a man, and her husband died there. She sings the story. When she drinks lots of whiskey."

Tecumseh seemed surprised again. "My father died there, too," he said, and was quiet.

"I thought Cheeseekau is your Pa?" Nancy had seen Tecumseh and Sinnamatha with an Indian named —Cheeseekau. They stayed in his lodge.

"No, he is my brother. But he cares for us all like a father. Your Neega will care for you like that. She had a daughter, Talitha Cuny, taken from her when Logan came to our village." His dark eyes briefly became even darker, then brightened to warm her light ones. "They think you have eyes like hers. Our other sisters, Tebethto and Kisathoi—white Indians like you—disappeared during the battle. They are the ones who taught me English." He gestured towards Sinnamatha. "And we taught him Shawanese when he came. I am sure you will be a quicker student than he."

"Hey" —warned Sinnamatha.

Tecumseh's voice turned sad. "No one has seen them."

So it was true. Everyone had lost some family. Maybe they would be a new family together.

Sinnamatha's face also lost its grin, but then he joked, "Doesn't Tecumseh speak good English? He talks like a white man!"

Tecumseh went to pounce upon him once more, but Sinnamatha Big Fish raised a hand to ward him off. "Tebethto and Kisathoi taught him English first, after they were adopted, then he learned more from me. But *he* taught me how to speak the language of The People, Shawano. Now we will teach you, *neeshematha*. We need a sister."

# CHAPTER 14

## Two for Mirth

*One crow for sorrow*
*Two for mirth…*

**Polly**
**Augusta**
**December 1786**

Two crows bickered on a tree branch outside her window. She started, her heart leapt as she heard a rap at the door. Polly jumped up from her Tree of Life sampler. *Could Adam be back with the written consent from Uncle James?*

She made her way to the door, eager and anxious, feeling her legs tremble slightly beneath her.

She opened the door to find Venus. Was there a glint in her normally gloomy eye?

"Master Adam downstairs," she said and stepped aside.

"Thank you!" Polly squeezed a dark hand and sped down the stairs. Her heart pounded, she nearly flew, glimpsing a flash of pale blue—Charlotte's skirt—as it disappeared into the sitting room. She was relieved and grateful Charlotte would give her some privacy with Adam.

He stood waiting in the hall, his face brightening at the sight of her.

"I have it." He tapped his jacket just above his heart, then reached into his vest pocket, pulling out a folded paper. He waved it with a flourish.

His eyes never left hers as he slowly and carefully unfolded it. He cleared his throat.

"I, James Halstead, certify that as the guardian of my niece, Mary Polly Flynn, I hereby give my consent to the marriage of Mary Polly to Mr. Adam Mann, this Fourth Day of December, 1786. Signed, James H Halstead. Witnessed by Leonard Morris."

He folded the leaf up and returned it to his vest. Then he pulled her to him. She drank in his scent again, relishing the sweet aroma, a smoky vanilla overlaid with the smell of the outdoors: pine and snow, fresh air. Adam's jacket was cold, but the heat from his body warmed her as he clasped her to his chest. She leaned in, listened to the thrum of his heart. Then she spied Charlotte, head bent over a book, through the sitting room door. As if she felt Polly's gaze, Charlotte looked up and smiled. "I couldn't help but hear," she said, and rose to meet them.

"Such happy, happy news."

Venus clinked through the hall just then, bearing a tray of crystal goblets filled with wine. As Moses was not about, Charlotte alone stood hostess to bestow upon them good wishes. As Venus offered a glass of wine to Adam, Polly once again noticed the bulge beneath her apron and could not help but cringe. The talk about Moses and the slave and a baby coming *could* all be only rumor. She tried to convince herself of that as she took a seat beside Charlotte on the settee.

Adam moved a stool that he might sit beside her, then reached for Polly's hand. He traced soft lines along it.

"You are welcome to stay the night, Adam," said Charlotte. "It is late already."

"Thank you. I appreciate that." His waited until Venus was out the door, then grinned as he added, "Or Miss Polly and I might bundle. You know it is the custom in many of our Palatine households."

Moses entered the room, and at Adam's comment he shot a quick look at Charlotte. Was it a warning?

Polly felt like the child in the group. Had she heard of bundling before? It sounded slightly familiar.

"No bundling in this house," Charlotte said. "*We* are not Palatines after all." She directed a steely gaze towards Moses, then murmured to her lap, "Though it might be better than some of the practices that are rumored to go on in this very household."

Moses looked down, a faint scowl on his face

Adam squeezed Polly's hands, bringing her thoughts back to him. "So, no pretty *Fräulein mit grüne Augen* to keep me warm tonight, then," he said. He reached up and gently pushed a stray curl behind her ear. Polly had come to know that "*grüne Augen*" were green eyes, and she lowered her lashes over hers.

Moses bristled. "Surely your mother, Barbary, would not have allowed your sisters to engage in such practices." But there was a question in his lofty tone.

*Hoity toit*, thought Polly.

Adam looked up, confused. "*Ach*, no. Not *meine Mutter*." He winked at Charlotte, which seemed to irritate Moses further. "But Mary Kessinger. Her parents couldn't wait for a husband for that one. Her mother welcomed *meine Bruder* Jacob to bundle."

"No wonder there are three small ones so close in age," Charlotte's muttered.

And then Polly remembered what she had heard of bundling. Only the Palatine families allowed it. While courting, a suitor would spend the night with his intended bride, in order to get to know her better. They would be separated only by bundling bags, which were some kind of pillow coverlets. Sometimes they might even use a board, or other sorts of barriers to divide the bedmates.

Polly blushed at the thought. Moses's face took on a peevish expression. He wiped his hands on his damp trousers and said, "I am going upstairs. To change," he said, and stalked off.

"Yes, change would be nice," Charlotte's voice was soft again.

Adam ignored their exchange and stared deeply into Polly's eyes, almost as if Charlotte were not there. "I do have another surprise for you. One you may like better than bundling."

"I beg your pardon?" she asked. The past year made Polly wary of surprises, and she felt a familiar anxiety scratch at her chest, in spite of her new hopefulness.

"It is true your uncle cannot come."

Well, that was not a surprise. She reckoned Uncle James could not leave the fort at present, anyway.

Charlotte focused on her fancywork. Polly also knew by now that Miss Charlotte was a fine actress who most likely was simply hiding her interest and would not want to miss this bit of the courting going on right before her very eyes.

"And that is the surprise—that Uncle James will not be here?" Polly was hard pressed to hide her disappointment.

"The surprise is that perhaps my pretty Polly will still have some friends from the fort to watch as she becomes the beautiful bride." He sent another wink to Charlotte who looked up just in time to smile in return.

Polly's glance was questioning. Who could possibly be coming from the fort?

"Should we leave a surprise for our Polly, Miss Charlotte?" Adam asked.

Charlotte smiled and Polly begged, "Tell. Please?" She pressed Adam's hand more urgently.

"It is so hard to refuse her. He faced Charlotte, pretended to ignore Polly's pleas.

He finally turned to her, laughter in his eyes. "Since you are so insistent," he said. "Anne Bailey is bringing the young *Fräulein*, Marie DeForest. Though your neighbor, Leonard Morris is the official witness to your uncle's consent, the *Fräulein* Marie also insisted to be there to watch him sign. And Mrs. Anna Bailey says she will like to see her son, William Trotter, and she will like to celebrate your marriage— our marriage—with you. And the young lady Marie said nothing could keep her from attending you on your happy day. She also said that Anne was as good an escort as any soldier would be."

"That she is." Charlotte's laugh rang out.

Polly's heart pounded. "Marie? Here?"

"Yes." Adam addressed Charlotte again. "I hope that is acceptable, Miss Charlotte, for them to stop here before they proceed to Mann's Fort for the wedding?"

Charlotte responded with delight. She dropped her needlework and clapped her pale hands. "It will be lovely."

And after all the talk of setting up bedchambers and bundling, it turned out Adam did not stay after all. Moses returned in fresh clothes, and the two men left to discuss some business with the gunpowder mill. Apparently it was of the utmost importance, for Adam left shortly thereafter. But before he did, he stole a moment alone with Polly. There was a miserable look on his face.

"Polly, I know the best surprise of all would be to have good news of your mother—or sisters and brother. I am sorry. No one at the fort knows where they are. Though there are rumors of some captives being taken as far north as Fort Detroit."

The British held Fort Detroit, nearly a world away. Polly pondered this news.

"I am sorry," he repeated, his expression sympathetic, then pulled her in close to whisper, "Soon we will make another family. But we will not give up on the return of the others."

Polly's mixed-up feelings returned after Adam left. Yes, she had not enjoyed being controlled by Mother and Pa, back at the fort, back in the other life. But now things were spinning so far out of her reach. Not all of it was bad. But how could one life disappear so completely, and another one appear so quickly in its place?

Mam sometimes said, "When God closes one door, he opens another." Was this what she meant? Polly felt as if she were standing in a passageway—albeit a grand one, as grand as Charlotte's Big House—between two doors, two worlds.

Surely what she felt for Adam was love. But even that feeling was out of her control. Sometimes her body even felt as if it were no longer her own, but his. Would she be happy in this new life? And had Mother and Pa ever felt this way?

Surely *not*. Their whole lives had been made of nothing but hard work. Worry clawed at her again. Her heart raced, and her hands shook slightly long after Adam left.

When Polly returned to the parlor, Charlotte said, "Let's look at that gown again."

Charlotte had ordered it special from her own dressmaker in Baltimore. She gave directions to make it a size or two smaller than her own petite size so that it would be just right for Polly. What a surprise this gown had been, yet another of the happy ones.

It was of damask silk, the palest of green, like a June apple, and had alternating dark and light lines of pink broken by tiny bouquets of pink rosebuds. Charlotte herself had stitched the fantastic vines and flowers on the lovely pocket to be worn just over her petticoat.

There was a hat, straw, covered with creamy silk. A ribbon pattern, fancy yet delicate, decorated the brim and the crown, and wider ribbons of ivory silk dangled below, to tie beneath her chin. The light colored neckerchief was done in a chain stitch, worked in the same light green silk thread of the gown. Polly's wedding slippers were fit for a queen, of the cream silk satin of the hat.

Beside it lay the wedding shirt Polly worked on for Adam. Not long ago, a packet had arrived containing the pieces of a linen shirt and a letter from Barbary, instructions for how to make it translated into English script by Barbary's daughter-in-law Mary, Jacob's wife. It was nearly done, and far easier to sew than the sampler that waited to be finished down below stairs.

Charlotte spied it. "Hmm…it's coming along," she said, examining a seam of the shirt.

Then she gathered up the dress once more. "Let's have Dorcas fit you one more time," she said. More and more, Venus was kept to the downstairs while Dorcas gained more experience above. "I wonder if this still needs to be taken in a bit more at the waist?"

Gangly Dorcas soon answered the bell, proud as punch to be called to wait upstairs once again. Polly suspected she lorded this new advancement over Venus when not in view of her mistress. As she was pulled and prodded into the gown, Polly felt like she'd never get used to being dressed by others, and tried not to flinch at the poking and pulling. The excitement over the new finery conquered her discomfort, and the evening passed in a blur. Nearly feverish, she was shocked to find herself looking happily forward towards the future.

That evening she was just about to drop off to sleep when she heard a soft knock at the door. There stood a figure in night-cap and dress, looking almost like a child. For a moment Polly thought it was her sister Nancy, rising to wake them with one of her night terrors or visions. Or was it her shade or haint?

No, it was Miss Charlotte.

"Would you mind if I sat with you, Polly?" Charlotte perched on the edge of the bed. "You won't be here much longer." In the flickering candlelight, her face had a sad cast to it. Tonight she was the gray dove.

She examined the room as if she had never seen it before, then fixed her eyes on Polly. "I will miss you, Mary Polly. You've hardly been here, but now I feel like I have always known you. You know, you are like the sister I never had."

She stared into her lap, mournful, then glanced up suddenly. "Oh! I am so happy for you. Never be mistaken about that." She brightened, took Polly's hand. "It is clear Adam Mann loves you. All young wives are not so lucky in their husbands—especially out here," she added.

Polly steeled herself. Was Charlotte going to tell her tales of horror the like of the Castle of Otranto, or the one about Blackbeard? As the days had gone by, Polly had come to realize that surprisingly, Charlotte did not just love to read frightful tales—or have them read *to* her. She loved to tell them herself. Dreadful tales—likely to stand Polly's hair on end—of pure young brides with cruel and vengeful husbands. Once Charlotte had adjusted to the thought of Polly's betrothal, she had recollected and recounted these alarming tales with glee.

When she tired of those, she'd start in with another new favorite topic: Army officers. Polly was not sure if Adam's visit to Uncle James is what started it all, but lately Miss Charlotte had mentioned that on both sides of the late war, men—especially the officers—had camp wives, or "cousins," they often called them, and second families borne of these women. Charlotte hinted that Moses himself had had a camp wife. She did not mention the somewhat obvious, the possible reminder of of another of Moses's infidelities right here in Venus, each day blossoming a bit more with child.

Well, so the rumors flew. Though Charlotte did not speak of the unborn babe or slave wives. Yet. Thankfully, the topic took another turn. Instead of warnings about Adam, who had also fought in the war—having a secret family somewhere—Charlotte had this to say.

"Adam was a good husband to Mary Maddy, for all her faults. And the way he regards you," Charlotte's voice trailed off. "Well, it is quite clear he will cherish you as a husband should. Oh, yes. Adam is too much of a gentleman to tell you, I am sure, but Mary was a harpy."

Where had this train of thought come from? Had Charlotte been tippling this evening?

Charlotte's glance sharpened. "You poor lamb. I bet you do not even know what a harpy is. And I know I may sound unkind, but she was a bit of a scold. Tried her bossy ways out on Adam, but they didn't work. Too much his own man, even at the young age he was when she hooked him. The soft and gentle grave dove that embodied sweet Charlotte was turning into a lively magpie this evening! Or was she a mockingbird?

"He didn't want to marry her."

At Polly's horrified reaction, Charlotte softened her tone.

"Oh, no, Polly. Nothing sordid. Adam is an obedient son, like most of these Lutherans. And actually," she mused, "I'm sure he would have married one of his own background—you see how he loves his mother and sister—if only there was one to be found. Mary Kessinger's beautiful sisters were all taken." She laughed again, but not cruelly.

"Now those two, Mary Kessinger and Adam's brother Jacob," she said in a conspiring tone, "That was a love match. No one needed to urge *them* to marry." Charlotte's voice grew wistful. "Three sons in six years. The Mann menfolk have passion. It should surprise no one that she is with child again *now*. And maybe you, too, soon, my sweet."

Polly felt curious and uncomfortable at the same time.

Charlotte patted Polly's knee as if sensing her unease. "Well, I just wanted you to know, as a second wife, that Adam's match with Mary Maddy was not for love. His father, Old Jacob *would* have interest in that damnable gunpowder cave, and better one of his sons with ownership in a gunpowder mill—than one of his brother George Mann's sons."

Charlotte caught herself. "Don' t fret, Polly. And don't imagine that Adam fancies you because you are the only choice. There are more girls from his homeland available here than there were five years ago." She looked at Polly with something like respect or admiration. "You know, I think he *is* in love with you. I have seen how he looks at you." She sighed. "I, of all people, recognize that look very well."

Polly fidgeted. Charlotte sometimes read her ladies magazines aloud while Polly did her fancywork, and much was made of true love. If Moses came within earshot, he scowled and left the room as quickly as possible, often slamming a door behind him. Then Charlotte would chuckle and arch her perfect brows, smile her crooked smile.

Charlotte exhaled a long thoughtful breath, lost in deep thought. "My father thought Moses and I well suited for each other. He hastened our match. And I did think I was in love with him. How dashing he was. All those balls during the war. The never-ending dances. But I was blind."

"Don't say so, Miss Charlotte. It is clear he cares for you."

"Is it?" The somber gray eyes searched hers and her lips rose again in the uneven smile. "No matter. Times are changing. Even were you not an orphan, young people now have a far greater chance at making a love match."

Charlotte shifted and Polly hoped she would leave now.

"Ah, Polly. I did not mean to burden you. Your friends are arriving tomorrow, and you will need your rest. I find I am much more of a sister than a mother to you, though I came here hoping to give you a mother's advice—on how to be a good wife."

Polly thought back to a particularly puzzling bit of marriage advice Charlotte read her last week. A sage pronounced that though a wife's prudence and virtue would certainly gain a husband's esteem, esteem alone would not make a happy marriage. "Passion was the key," the wise one proclaimed.

And passion must be that feeling she had when her heart wanted to burst when Adam kissed her. Maybe passion described how she sometimes felt likely to melt beneath his touch.

Charlotte finished. "Be a kind wife, Polly. Men seem strong, but are easily wounded by things we would never imagine. I'm sure it looks as though Moses and myself never once felt passion, but once there was something there. Love or something very like it. She pressed Polly's hand, gently. "Let Adam know you desire him—as he desires you. That, too, will make him happier than you might ever imagine." Charlotte's half-smile flickered in the candlelight. "And from how you look at him, that just might not be too much of a chore."

At the door she paused, caught Polly's eye. "You don't mind about the bundling? That I wouldn't have it in my house…"

Polly started. "Oh no." She found herself blushing and was grateful for the dim light. "Adam made mention of that just to tease me, I know."

The crooked smile played on Charlotte's lips before she said, "Don't be too sure about that, my girl."

# CHAPTER 15

**James**

**The Fort**

**December 1786**

The ax glinted through the frosty air and struck the log with a satisfying thunk, cr-r-rack. The muscles in James's back and arms strained and stretched. He found the pleasant pain to his liking, too. Splitting wood was one task that took his mind off his troubles, and the fort in winter could always use fuel. Oh, he still hunted; of course he was needed for that. It just wasn't the same without John Flynn by his side with a wink, a song, and a story.

He sometimes felt John watching, felt the sharp eyes look over his shoulder, guide him on. He knew he wasn't there. James knew soldiers who claimed they still could feel a limb that had been taken off in battle, and he wondered if this feeling that his dead brother-in-law and friend was there beside him might be the same, He heard John's voice in his head as he continued to make kindling.

*"It's gentry who're now moving on into Lexington and Louisville. Boone and Kenton say lands are claimed by fancy officers of the late war. And some of them are already quite wealthy; now they're after more, want new and bigger mansions built."*

This is where John would give him a knowing look. *"And don't they say the rich appreciate good breeding? I'm only the one who'll help them with that."* Here would be the wink. *"When it comes to horse breeding, of course."*

Yes, if there was one thing John had known, it was horseflesh. Flynn, excited to hear of the racing now taking place on Market Street in Louisville, had raced a horse there himself two years ago. Now all of John Flynn's dreams of horse breeding and homesteading had gone up in smoke and flames. His family was scattered, his home in ruins, and his horse herd just a remnant. The Shawnee had most of them.

The pile of cut wood grew larger, and so did the lump in his throat. He was lonesome not only for his brother-in-law, but his sister, gray-eyed Elizabeth. James, along with Leonard Morris, a fine scout, had tracked the raiding party that had carried Elizabeth and the children as far as the river. Then they had to turn back. Raiding continued in these parts, and James could not desert the fort now to make a longer search of it. His sister, his nieces and nephew, were as lost to him as John Flynn.

There was one bright spot: Polly. His niece Polly had survived. And just last week James had been visited by the man she would soon wed. James knew immediately that Adam Mann cared deeply for his niece and was happy to sign the letter of consent, relieved that Polly would be safe and cherished.

But he missed her, as well as Nancy, John, and Chloe.

The other thing he seemed to have lost lately—though it was a welcome loss—was his foolish pride. Marie DeForest was not the flibbertigibbet he had imagined. She had been nothing but kind and helpful since the incident at Cabin Creek. He'd sometimes find her watching him, catch a look of concern on that pretty face before she quickly turned away, shy all of a sudden.

She was supposed to be at Post Vincennes. Her trader pa had sent one of his clerks to take her down there to some friends in the French community, but she had refused to go. She had approached James as he was cleaning his rifle after the fellow left.

"Anne said she'd take me to Polly's wedding." Marie's skin was flushed, and her dark eyes flashed, as if she dared him to argue with her.

James barely heard her words. Her beauty sorely distracted him. He gathered his thoughts together enough to say, "I thank you kindly for being such a good friend to my niece."

Marie's color deepened, and this time it was she who seemed at a momentary loss of speech. She tossed her head. "Well. I just thought you would like to know, is all." She'd lowered her lashes—that shy look again—then thrust her chin up, held herself high like a queen as she gathered her skirts and swooshed away.

He could not help but grin as he'd watched her. Then, aware that others were watching *him*, he'd quickly wiped off his smile and focused once more on his weapon.

He talked briefly with Anne and Marie before they left for Mann's Station. Leonard had rounded up one more of the Flynn's stray horses, a fine gelding named Hercules, and James brought him to the women before they left. Hercules would make a bit of a dowry for Polly, not that she'd need any, judging by the eager glow in Adam Mann's eyes.

The two women were a rare sight: Anne in her buckskins, outfitted with long rifle, hatchet, knife, and necessary. She wore her old broad-brimmed hat, and her long wavy hair, glinting with silver strands, hung loose.

Marie could have stepped out of a fashion plate of one of the magazines he'd seen her reading. She wore a riding coat of dark blue twill, with matching skirt of an unusual style, split up the middle, he reckoned, as she had been known to ride astride. He'd heard his niece explain when his sister Elizabeth had asked about the strange cut. "She says if it is good enough for the Dauphine in France, Queen Marie Antoinette, it is good enough for her."

Anne and James loaded packs onto the horses while Marie watched them, bright eyes sparkling from under a black felt hat quivering with black and blue ostrich feathers.

Anne grabbed James in an awkward hug before she mounted Liverpool. Marie's face was serious.

"Goodbye *Monsieur* Halstead. I will give your love to Polly." She gave her horse a little kick and wheeled onto the trail. Anne followed close behind, almost like her page, leading Hercules.

James watched as they dwindled into the distance. His heart danced a little jig as Marie turned round, smiled at him, and waved her gloved hand. *"Au revoir,* we will return soon!" rang across the wind.

# CHAPTER 16

**Marie**
**The Way to Mann's Station**
**December 1786**

Marie was excited. A *soiree*! She was eager to reflect upon the fun to come and think her private thoughts, but that was not to be. My, how Anne Bailey loved to talk.

"Now, being a military man, James Halstead may have told you some of this. There are some famous patriots in the Maddy family. Them's the family that Polly's man, Adam, was married into before. The Maddys. Adam was married to Mary Maddy, and she has a brother, William, who is married to Adam's sister Lisabetta. And the uncle of William and Mary Maddy on their mother's side is Robert Morris."

Marie looked at her blankly. She hoped this ride was not to be a long and boring genealogy of the late wife of Polly's husband-to-be. The poor woman was *dead*, after all.

"Robert Morris is their famous uncle, brother to their mother, Ann. Now yer lookin' at me like you don't know what that means, but he signed both the Declaration *and* The Articles of Confederation. Now he serves in the Congress of the Confederation. And to hear his kinfolks, the Maddys, tell it, Morris practically financed the late war, as well."

Marie knew little of the money matters of the late war with the British—except that there never seemed to be enough for horses or fine uniforms such as the French wore—and held her tongue, eager for Anne to finish.

"The Maddy family came from Liverpool, like myself." Anne paused a moment as her horse nickered. "No, Liverpool, I ain't talkin' to ye. Yer just named after my old home place."

"Anyway," she continued, "Ann Maddy—that's the mother of the dead wife—her father was involved in shipping after he arrived in this country. Later, he made another fortune in tobacco. He was real rich by the time he was killed in a crazy accident. Hit by the wadding of a ship's cannon." Anne's grin was grim. "This is what some folks would call ironical on account of the cannon was fired in the man's honor, you see."

Anne stopped a moment to relish Marie's horrified reaction. "So afterward, Ann was what they call a rich heiress. She married a soldier, and they had ten children, including William and Mary, Adam's late wife. After the war, Ann's new soldier-boy husband drowned in the Shenandoah River—another sad accident." Anne drew her flask out of her pocket, slowed her horse and held it out to Marie. "Care for a dram?"

"*Oui.*" Marie thought she might need several drams to make it through the complicated tale of *les miserables.* She took a healthy swig and handed the whiskey back to Anne, who took an even healthier one before she continued.

"The widow Ann, loaded down with her share of the family wealth, left her children— the late Mary and her brother William— in the care of relatives and came out here on her own to claim the property she had coming to her through her husband's military service. That property was the saltpeter cave which is now owned jointly by the Maddys and Manns."

Finally, something to do with Polly. Polly had written to Marie about the smithy, the rifle-making, and the saltpeter mines that were all concerns of the Mann family.

"This widow, Ann, traveled alone?" Marie asked. Because of her Indian and French heritage, Marie was not as fearful of travel as most white women. And traveling with Anne Bailey, The White Witch, eased any other anxieties. That Ann Maddy traveled alone with neither of these protections indicated a lot of courage or little sense.

"Yes, she has more in common with me than just her name and birthplace." Anne took another gulp of whiskey. "On her journey here, as she traveled over the mountains, she spied a cabin where she stopped in to see if she could stay the night. There was no inns or forts along that trail. The settler, or should I say villain, who lived in that lonely place thought Mrs. Maddy had money with her by the fine horse she rode, the clothes she wore, and the supplies she had with her. The next morning, he kindly offered to lead her himself to the path that went her way, and she gratefully accepted his offer. However, the rogue took her up onto a deserted bluff in order to rob and kill her."

"*Mon Dieu!*"

"Yes. And here is the part the Maddy family is so proud of. Ann asked the blackguard to turn his back for modesty's sake—because she had the money concealed on her person. And when his back was turned, *she* pushed *him* off the bluff. She not only saved her own skin, but her family's riches, to boot. She still lives by that place, with her son James, near the caves."

"That is almost like the song, 'Pretty Polly,' *Monsieur* Flynn liked to sing," Marie mused. With her escape from Simon Girty and his fellows, perhaps their Pretty Polly had something in common with the Maddy family after all.

Anne pulled on the flask once more, then held it out to Marie. "Adam's dead wife—Mary—was a lot like her mother. She was the oldest gal in her family, older than Adam by six years. Tough and strong-willed. But bearing a child—that's what killed her."

After this morbid announcement they rode quietly for a while. Anne had successfully ruined Marie's chance for a pleasant ride filled with reverie. Instead, she began to wonder where *they* would be spending the night?

"Anne, another sip of your whiskey, *s'il vous plait?*"

# CHAPTER 17

## Three Crows

*One crow for sorrow*
*Two for mirth*
*Three for a wedding...*

**Polly**
**Mann's Station, Indian Creek**
**December 1786**

The next day the much-awaited company arrived: Anne Bailey on Liverpool, and Marie on her own handsome mount. Another dark horse trailed along on a lead behind Anne: Hercules. Leonard Morris had discovered another of Pa's horses roaming the improvement and had brought him in to Uncle James, and now he was here at Mann's Station.

Anne wanted to sleep in the barn near Liverpool, so Polly walked with her down to the stable while Venus slowly traipsed ahead with the lantern and blankets.

"So, with that piece of fine horseflesh, ye'll have some dowry after all," Anne said with pride.

"Dolly remembers him." The horses nuzzled each other over the walls of the stall, whickering softly.

"Anne, have you heard anything—about the rest?" Polly stumbled on the words, almost afraid to hear an answer. Anne, with her traveling from fort to fort, was likely to know even more than Uncle James.

"Lass, I wish I had good news for you. Your family was taken when Boone and Logan—Kenton, too, were on their own campaign up into the villages. The Shawnee that took 'em had no villages to return to and went off on the run. So now, those scoundrels what carried them off will have ended up even further north. Where the British can protect them," she said, disgusted.

Then her face brightened. "But in those raids, Boone and them took a lot of prisoners. Even the Warrior Woman." Anne paused to explain, "She's that giant-like Indian woman what goes by the name Nonhelema. Also, they got a feisty young'un called High Horn—Spemica Lawba is his Indian name. Said to be some relation to Chief Moluntha. General Logan has him."

"And funny thing. I hear they've taken to one another, Logan and the boy. Might be adopted already. But anyway, the Shawnee want them back. There is rumor there'll be a trading of prisoners in the spring. At Limestone."

Polly's heart leapt. Would she see her family again?"

"Mind, no one knows what white prisoners will be traded back. This'll take some doing. But one never knows." Anne exhaled deeply. "Those savages ain't predictable." A blast of tobacco smoke billowed from the clay pipe as Anne pondered the situation.

Finally she said, "Yes, lass, ye'll soon have a family of your own again." Was that a tear Polly saw glistening in Anne's eyes—or was the smoke making her eyes water? "I know it's not the same, with yer mum gone and all. But it's more than some folks have. And ye've found a fine husband in Adam Mann. Those Dutchmen make good providers. And they ain't gamblers." She dragged again on her pipe, then jerked as if bitten by a flea.

"I wisht I could've got a game in with Moses," she said, as looked around as if expecting him to suddenly appear in the stables, cards and all. "Ah well. Maybe Caesar," she smiled hopefully, then yelled over to the slave who was fussing with the blankets, "Venus, I'll fix my own nest!"

She faced Polly again. "You get back to your friend, Marie. I'm fine out here with Liverpool and these'uns. Go on now, git."

A few months ago Polly would never have dreamed she'd owe thanks to Anne Bailey. Now there was a lump in her throat as Anne turned away towards her cozy bed in the straw.

"You be a good girl and sleep well tonight," she called as Polly walked back to the house.

As Charlotte and Marie visited in the parlor, Polly saw Marie snatch at something. When she noticed Polly's curious look, she thrust it behind her back, but a part of it trailed onto the ground. Some sort of blanket.

"What's that?"

"Well, I guess it makes no difference now," said Marie.

She plucked up the fabric and carefully displayed it on the settee. Charlotte stood up, too, helping to arrange it.

Tears filled Polly's eyes. It was a quilt. The medallion quilt she had so wanted to work on that fateful autumn day that now seemed a million years ago. The day she lost everyone.

It was lovely. There border was a dark blue of the same fabric she had set aside to make dresses for Nancy and Chloe's cornhusk dolls. The rest of the quilt was a pale ivory, its layers stitched through in delicate patterns contrasted by the colorful pattern of the Tree of Life in the center.

"It's beautiful." Polly swallowed, hardly trusting herself to speak. "You had barely started when I—"

Mercifully, Marie interrupted her. "Yes, this is the chintz appliqué from one of the panels I brought from Philadelphia." She pointed at the medallion. "Charlotte tells me this is very like the design you have been working in your sampler."

The sting of tears melted away, and Polly nearly choked, trying to laugh and cry at the same time. "No." She turned to Charlotte, "Not so very much, anyway."

Charlotte kindly ignored the outburst. "You all did exquisite work," she said as she examined the stitches.

"Well, we gave it our best," Marie said. "You know the girls at the fort had never worked with chintz applique. So, I think it *is* nice," she pronounced. "Our love and best wishes to you are worked into every stitch, *mon ami*," She hugged Polly to her.

" Ladies, it's late," Charlotte announced. "I will leave you two until the morning. Good night."

Charlotte had insisted they travel in a coach, though Polly and Marie would have been happy to go on horseback. They'd left Augusta two days earlier for the journey to Mann's Station. Though the road was better than the one that led to Cabin Creek, it was rude enough that Caesar had to continually dismount, ax in hand, to chop away obstacles. Each time he did, Polly's stomach clenched. Would Indians attack them? This trail appeared to be quiet; the violent warpath was westward in Kaintucke, but one never knew. Would she be carried away like the rest of her family and never see Adam again?

Marie had traveled this way many times with her father the trader, and displayed no fear. As time wore on, Polly was able to admire the fine carriage they shared. She sunk back onto the fine pillows and tried to enjoy the conversation.

"Is Moses not with us?" Marie asked, dark eyes darting towards the servants who followed.

"He stays behind on tobacco business. But he'll be joining us in time for the wedding," answered Charlotte. "On Sabre, he can travel in a day what will take us all of two days."

"Is that young servant Dorcas?" asked Marie, pointing towards the smallest figure, bundled in many layers, who with two other slaves rode the horses that made up most of Polly's small dowry.

"Yes." Charlotte sighed. "I did not want Venus to try this road in her condition. She will take care of things at home."

Marie's eyes widened. Even Marie had guessed that Moses must be the father of Venus' unborn child, and normally flirtatious, she had avoided the man, confided in Polly that she did not trust him.

Polly gazed out the coach window, momentarily lulled by snow flurries that drifted down throughout the afternoon. Her mind flitted back to the snowy day before they left on their trip. Soft flakes had sifted down during that day as well. Polly and Marie had been on their way to give some orders to the kitchen when they had spied out a shape—couple—pressed against an outbuilding. Quickly the male figure released his grasp on the female, and they saw it was Moses with Venus. Venus scurried towards the fields and Moses headed in the direction of the stables.

Marie had sighed. "*Mon Dieu*. That man. Lovely as this all is," and here she had waved her hand at the elegant mansion and property, "I am so happy you soon will be leaving. I do not like the way he looks at you. Or *me*."

They each retreated into their own thoughts. Polly drifted off only to lurch awake and notice the woods outside the coach windows were dark. Before long she spied the lights of an ordinary where they would stop spend the night. The three ladies would share a room while Dorcas slept outside their door. The male slaves stayed in the stables. The forty-one-cent hot suppers of roasted chicken with root vegetables and corn cakes warmed them and were better than Polly expected. And though Marie and Charlotte got a bit tipsy on the shampaign that was served, they made it to their room upstairs without incident, where Polly fell into a blessed dreamless sleep.

# CHAPTER 18

## Christmas

**Nancy**
**Miamitown**
**December 1786**

As time went on, Nancy learned that the village they lived in was but a bead on a string of Indian towns strung along the edges of the rivers and lakes. All together they were known as Miamitown, named for the Miami Indians that had once lived there.

Nancy hoped to see Tecumseh again. His sister Tecumapease lived in their village, so Nancy counted him on to return for Midwinter Festival. But a hunter, one of Tecumseh's Kisopoko cousins, returned with bad news that squelched her hopes.

"Tecumseh's horse fell on him. He was chasing a buffalo when the beast turned and spooked his horse. She fell and now his leg is all broke up. He and Big Fish and Cheeseekau might not be back for many moons. They are treating the leg and have made a camp where they will stay while they wait for it to heal."

Becky and some other women raided their medicine pouches and gave generously of salves and other remedies. The Kispoko gave his sincerest thanks before he rode off to rejoin his wounded cousin.

Other excitement awaited. The largest of the towns near them was called Kekionga, which meant "Blackberry Patch." A huge trade center, some still called it "French Store" for the French who had the first trading posts there. All kinds of folks came from nigh everywhere and Nancy looked forward to having Christmas there.

In Kekionga, Christmas was not but one day, but many days. Becky had cousins scattered throughout the villages, but the ones she most liked to visit were in Kekionga. Prairie Deer was some kind of relation of Becky's, so she and White Buffalo went along with them, and even White Buffalo's pa, Standing Elk. Of course, Scout went, too.

Bright Wing, Becky's favorite kin, lived there with her husband, Henri, a French trader, and their two little ones, Petit Henri and Belle. To Nancy it seemed they lived in a halfway world. Half white people ways and half Indian ways. Their cabin looked as if someone had mixed the house—the home of her white family at Cabin Creek that was no more—together with an Indian *wegiwa*. Yet it was richer than either. There was a big fireplace, but not of stone, like at Cabin Creek. This one was made of clay and straw. The trammels on the hearth always held pots bubbling with tasty meats and stews.

Around the cabin were beds, same as in lodges, layered with skins and fancy wool blankets. Near the hearth sat a large brass kettle for washing, then a copper kettle for hominy, and a hominy block. The shelves against the walls were stacked with wooden bowls, tin cups, spoons of horn and pewter, and all kinds of baskets. The family ate meals at a long wooden table with benches.

Nancy surely did appreciate that happy house. She held wee Belle, who had bright black eyes and smiled while pulling at Nancy's braids. Petit Henri was about the size of Chloe. Chloe. The lost name stuck on her tongue like a burr. She had to drive her thoughts away from them: Chloe, Mam, John. Polly. It hurt less if she let them fade.

Petit Henri spoke baby Indian and French, and taught Nancy French words, though she still remembered some that Jean Pierre, the *voyageur*, had taught her.

"*Chien*," little Henri said, in his low husky voice, pointing at Scout. Then he'd stumble towards the dog on his stout little legs and come away from him with clumps of golden fur in his chubby mitts. Scout bolted away now, whenever he saw him coming.

"Becky says Kekionga is a big town, but how many folks live here?" Nancy asked White Buffalo one cold morning. Once in awhile Polly shared tales of city life with Nancy, stories she had heard from Marie DeForest.

"Yes. More than three hundred here," he said, proud of it. "Did you not see those houses? What do you call those big ones? Ah. Mansions," he said, answering himself. "Some of stone, brick, or wood. With real glass windows and stair steps. " Like many Indians, he was very interested in stairs.

On Sunday, after they had been there nearly a week, Nancy woke to the sound of bells. She jumped up, peered out the window of the loft where she slept and saw three boys walk slowly through the village. They rang bells, like the ones the Shawnee horses wore back in Girty Town.

She climbed down to find Bright Wing, dressed in white people's clothes, setting out corn cakes on the table. She laid them out alongside fat slabs of bacon and a jug of maple syrup. The little ones were dressed and Henri had pieces of corn cake stuck to his lips and syrup on his chin.

"What's that?" Nancy asked, pointing towards the sound of the fading bells.

"It is call to prayers," Bright Wing whispered. Prairie Deer and Standing Elk still slept on a bed against the furthest wall. "We will go. Henri wishes it."

White Buffalo came down from the loft, rubbing his eyes.

"I'll come, too. I have never been in a church."

Nancy kept silent. She did not want to admit it, but she could not remember if she had been in one. She knew a priest had baptized her, but that might have been at home. They took turns washing up with warm water from the brass washtub, put on their best outfits, and gulped down their victuals. Nancy wore her adoption clothes, with a warm overcoat made of bearskin.

They followed a small stream of folks—French, Indian, Scotch, British, and African—through powdery lanes to the home of one called Mr. Barthemie, who held weekly prayers there.

So, really, they still weren't going into a real church. Inside the cabin, people crowded together and one named Payet or Payee, called Father Louis by most, said prayers in a strange language while. Some folks talked along with him in their different tongues and counted from strings of beads that had crosses dangling from them.

Nancy remembered Old Patrick, her granddad, had those same beads and sometimes sat the children on his knees to help them learn to pray. But Mam didn't like it. She never really cared for those prayers with the beads. The Rosary. But she did know "Our Father" and that one of "The Lord is My Shepherd."

It all took a long time. Old Louis led most of the prayers in an high quavery voice. Soon Nancy's knees were sore from kneeling on the hard floor. They were at the back of the cabin, so no one saw or thumped them when White Buffalo poked her and blew on her neck.

But there were some good parts. A feller with yellow hair got up and played a fiddle, and another one joined in with him on a flute. There was singing, even some songs in English, and that was real pretty, too.

When they got back to Bright Wing's home, there was more delicious food on the table: roast venison along with succotash and baked sweet potatoes.

Henri had gone to Fort Detroit on trading business, and Standing Elk went along to take care of some Shawnee business. They would be back by Christmas day. White Buffalo sulked at first, for he had wanted to go along, but Prairie Deer refused him. "Next year you will be old enough," she said. Nancy was glad White Buffalo's pouting time was short. It might get lonesome without him around, but if he was around, it wouldn't be fun if he turned out to be sulky, like Polly could be. Ah, she wouldn't let herself think of Polly nor Chloe. Forced them out of her mind.

During Christmas, important ladies of the fort held tea parties. Bright Wing got to go because Henri was a well-known trader there. So Becky went, too, and took the babies, leaving Nancy and White Buffalo free to roam. Nancy now realized that Indian children rarely stayed home to work. They got to rove out and play on their own, though older girls and boys did learn to do the same chores as their parents.

A nice thing about White Buffalo—in spite of the fact that he was a feller and all and nearly of the age when he would just be learning from the menfolks—he treated her kindly and seemed to like having her as a playmate. She sure did appreciate that.

She and White Buffalo bundled up in jackets made from woolen blankets, and put thick woolen stockings on under their leggings. Scout pranced by their side, as they trudged through the snowy paths of the village. They stopped short when they spied a strange sight on a pond on a frozen marsh. Scout sat on haunches, ears up.

"Sccrrriiittcchhhh…" rang out into the air.

"What's that?" asked White Buffalo.

""I don't know." The ice shone like a mirror in the sun, and in the middle of that looking glass, people with strange shoes on their feet slid round and round. Some linked arms and nearly flew across the ice. Others raced together, or flung each other around in long chains till some spun off the ends, hollering.

There was more than one group. Towards one end of the pond, British in red coats—officers, White Buffalo said—held sticks that had a curve at the bottom. They hit a buckskin ball back and forth. Sometimes they kicked it, shouting and clapping when it hit a post on either end of the playing area.

At the other end a group of Indian women played a similar game. But their sticks and ball were decorated with paint and beads, and there was more laughter at their end of the pond. Above the entire glassy surface merry shouts floated on the cold breeze, the many languages mixed together.

"I would like to do that," said White Buffalo.

"Me, too," whispered Nancy, eyes wide.

They moved closer through the tall frozen marsh grasses and saw that the shoes the people wore had some sort of sharpened bone on the bottom.

"When we get back, let's ask Bright Wing. Maybe we can join? Maybe tomorrow." White Buffalo was wistful. Excited, too, he squeezed her hand before casting a last admiring look at those swirling figures.

The sky grew dark and they made their way back to the cabin, where a small dinner of savory stew and warm cider awaited them. They told about the people on the pond.

Becky smiled at Bright Wing. "Skaters," she said.

Then she and Bright Wing spoke in Shawnee, and Bright Wing said, "Shinny."

Bright Wing walked over to one of the platform beds bordering the walls and reached under to pull out two sticks, decorated like the ones they'd seen at the pond. She also hauled out a basket that held a beaded bag and two strange bones. The bones were from a horse's leg, she told them. They had been flattened, had holes on the ends, threaded through with leather strips. Bright Wing showed them how to tie them round their moccasins. She sat back as she finished, and held up her foot.

"Skates," she said.

There were sticks and bones for two people, because Bright Wing sometimes played on the ice with those gals, and Henri with the men.

White Buffalo's face lit up. "Can we try tomorrow?"

Nancy jumped up and down just thinking about it.

The mothers said yes—*was Becky her mother now?* —and Nancy wondered when the winter months had ever been so fun. Then she felt a twinge and missed her lost family again. If only they were here to skate, too.

That night there were no bad dreams. She drifted into a vision of sparkling ice, and heard the faint shushing song of skate bones as they sliced silvery patterns into her sleep.

# CHAPTER 19

## *Hochsheitstag*

### Wedding Day

**Polly**
**Mann's Station on Indian Creek**
**December 1786**

At last the day arrived.

The "Fancy Dutch,"—Palatine Lutherans like the Manns—loved a party. And though winter was the marrying season in the territories, it was rare for these "Fancy Dutch" to wed in the week before Christmas.

However, the minister in Roanoke, a Miller of Barbary Miller Mann's family, was willing to make an exception. Since he wished to be back in Roanoke in time to hold Christmas Eve services, Polly Flynn, and Adam Mann, would marry on the shortest day of the year, the morning of St. Thomas Day, December 21st.

This feast was widely celebrated along the Rhine, that distant homeland of the Manns and Millers. Thus, Polly and Adam's wedding would include St Thomas Day doings from the Rhineland. One cousin would recite poems for St Thomas Day while another—the one who had been last to rise from bed—would be forced to wear ears and play the part of the *dumm Esel*, or lazy donkey.

After the wedding ceremony, but before the evening's dancing began, they would enjoy *Rittburgische Hochzeit*, or Rittberg Wedding Feast. They would sup on a fat little *Weihnachter*, or roast Christmas Pig. The Palatines believed that if one ate well on St. Thomas Day, one could expect to do so for the rest of the year.

One cousin would recite poems for St Thomas Day while another—the one who had been last to rise from bed—would be forced to wear ears and play the part of the *dumm Esel* or lazy donkey.

The Mann women were excited to teach Polly their wedding customs.

"*Ja, und Gott helfe mir*," Polly repeated after Barbary. That meant, "Yes with the help of God," and it seemed the right answer to many of the questions she'd be asked—including the ones the minister would have during the wedding ceremony.

"*Und deine Fuß*," said Lizzy Stigard, a neighbor and good friend of Adam's sister and sister-in-law. "*Fuß*," she repeated, pointing to Polly's foot. Mary Kessinger Mann, Barbary, and Lizzy Stigard all stared at her shoe.

"Dine what?" asked Polly.

"Oh." said Mary. "She means that during the ceremony you will feel Adam's foot— *Fuß*—on the hem of your gown. While you are kneeling."

Adam's boot on the hem of her beautiful gown? She raised her eyebrows in question.

"It is our way to show your man is in charge," replied charming Mary. "You know, head of the house. But you show him who is really in charge when you rise up and give him a swift one, here." She pretended a quick kick in the shin at Lizzy, who crumbled and fell.

Oh. It was all a joke. Yet she didn't think she could kick Adam, even in jest, and even if he stood on her skirt.

The wedding finery lay on Barbary's bed for all to admire.

Lizzy picked up a satin shoe. "*Und deine Schuh?*" she asked, looking at Mary once again for agreement.

Mary's face was blank for a moment, then she snatched the shoe from Lizzy, said something in Deutsch—a bit scolding—and put the shoe back on the bed. She turned to Polly. "Now how shall we fix your hair?" Her smile was broad.

Polly sighed. Yes, these Palatines had some strange ways and habits.

As Mary combed her hair, Polly realized she had not seen Adam but once—when she arrived at Mann's Station with Charlotte and Marie.

"Where's Adam?"

Lizzy opened her mouth and received a sharp elbow jab an elbow from Mary.

"Lizzy, did you say he is helping William Maddy mind the kettles at the mines?"

Polly's face fell. *With William Maddy? At the saltpeter kettles?*

When Polly had visited Mann's Station at the Wintering In, Adam had given her a tour of the saltpeter mines and the gunpowder mill. The stench near the kettles was nearly overpowering; the haze above tinged the air with a putrid odor. William Maddy was overseer, spending plenty of time with the foul aroma. Perhaps there was more than one reason for his sour countenance.

The smell, Adam told her, was hard to remove from one's skin and clothing. The only way was repeated bathing in strong herbs.

An anxious pit blossomed in Polly's stomach. Would Adam be ready in time? Would he have time to scrub away the stink?

Mary hummed contentedly, unaware of the worry she caused Polly. Polly gazed distractedly in a hand-mirror as Mary braided her hair into several plaits entwined with silk ribbons. She wound them around Polly's head, then plucked cherry blossoms from a branch—the *Barbarazweig* or St Barbara's Branch—that bloomed in a nearby jug. Adam's mother was named after St Barbara. In their homeland, unmarried girls cut a cherry branch, and brought it into their homes on the fourth of December in hopes it would bloom on Christmas Eve. If it flowered then, that lucky girl might be the next one to marry.

Mary glanced at Lizzy. "Sorry, Lizzy. This branch has already bloomed, and it is not yet  Christmas Eve. So now you must wait another year for your chance with *Monsieur* Michel."

Lizzy, enamored of a French widower who had fled to this part of the country after having fought in the war against the British, ignored the teasing and held out a wreath woven of green vines. "*Ja*, I have my own branch. And it is not yet in bloom. I think, *ja*, on *Heiligabend*, it will."

Mary arranged the blooms and delicately perched the wreath on Polly's head, like a crown.

"Now, if your groom is a little smelly from the kettles, you just sniff these blossoms."

Polly did not have time to respond, attracted by the sound of deep voices downstairs. Men, greetings, and backslappings.

In a silken fog, she was led downstairs. She stood before the Manns, the Millers, the Mays, dear Marie, and several friends and neighbors. Her legs as if they would barely carry her to Adam's side. Her smile was weak when she finally found the courage to face Adam in front of all the guests.

But his eyes were warm and his smile bright as he reached for her hand. "My Polly."

She saw he was wearing the wedding shirt she had made him under a new dark waistcoat and vest. Silver buckles shone on his shoes, and his wavy blonde hair rippled in the firelight.

Pastor Miller greeted her kindly, though in her state of fear and excitement, she would later not recall a word of what he said.

Somehow she managed to speak the foreign phrases at the right time. "*Und Gott helfe mir*" —*And God help me, indeed.*

He was definitely helping her through this day. He, or some good angels.

She smelled the familiar hint of vanilla, not the putrid odor of the saltpeter mine, when Adam leaned over to say, "Do you know you have to kick me now?"

The rest of the morning passed in a blur. The ceremony was followed by the feast, and throughout the day more Miller cousins arrived with more friends and neighbors. Along with Polly's joy and wonder—how could she have imagined a day like this just a short while ago?—there were flickers of sadness. So many kin for Adam, none for her. But at least Marie was here.

And oddly enough, Polly was even grateful old Anne Bailey had come. The late-rising cousin who played the part of *"dumm Esel,"* — the lazy donkey had— attached himself to her. He in his donkey ears, and she in her buckskin garb with weapons at her waist, made a striking pair. Anne swaggered to the door with her young companion, soon was joined by George Miller and Simeon Jarrell.

"Sure I'll have a tommyhawk contest with you lads." At this announcement, a few of the older Mann cousins jumped up to follow, either to join in or stop bloodshed.

As she stood beside her new husband, sipping a glass of cider, Polly surveyed the crowd. Johann Miller, Adam's Uncle, was there with his Huguenot wife, Barbary Mauzy, and their ten children who ranged from nineteen years down to a one-year-old baby. Chatting with them was he who made Lizzy's heart flutter, Joshua Michel, the Frenchman who had come over to this country with Lafayette's comrade, Rochambeau, and fought for the Americans at Yorktown. Not wishing to return to Paris, he had fled out to the territory after the war and now called himself Joshua Mitchell.

Pollly and Adam both noticed Joshua had a hard time keeping his eyes off Lizzy Stigard, who was nearby playing with one of the Mann children.

"Ah," Adam murmured. "It appears he does care for our Lizzy."

At that moment, Charlotte strolled over to meet them, a sleeping Baby Adam nestled in her arms. She followed their gaze. "Hmmm," she said, her crooked smile lighting up her face. "It appears that there may be another wedding soon."

Sawbucks had been set up in the barn just as they had been at the harvest party, and people milled everywhere, some snacking on leavings from the feast, others refilling their mugs of ale. Children played in the corners, or scampered near the bonfire that burned outdoors. A huge fire also crackled in the fireplace at one end of the barn near where a fiddler played and a few couples danced.

Most of the Palatine immigrants first made living quarters in their barns and then built their homes. As a result, the structures were often nicer than many of the cabins Polly had seen back in Kaintucke. Like the cherry blossoms, warmth and love flowered in the cold December air.

Sixteen-year old Michael Miller clung to the side of young Dolly Smith, while neighbor Isaac Estill, whose father was killed at Point Pleasant, flirted with Elizabeth Frogg. She, too, had lost her father in the battle.

A brief cloud passed over Polly as her eyes lit on one guest who sat alone: sixteen-year-old Bess Graham. Until a year ago, she had been an Indian captive. Her father had finally located her and paid a large ransom. But she'd lived among the Indians eight long years and had not yet adapted to the white world. Her hair hung in a long plait down her back, and tiny silver hoops dangled from her ears. On her small feet she wore a pair of beautifully beaded moccasins.

Polly's stomach lurched. Would that be her sister Nancy in eight years? Adam conversed with a William Trotter, Anne Bailey's son, and Polly, drawn to speak to Bess and ask of her life among the Indians, began to move towards her. Just then the fiddles struck up a tune, and Adam, pulled her back to him.

Above the din, Anne's raspy voice rose in song. She regaled the Miller and Mann children in a whiskey-soaked version of "The Battle of Point Pleasant." Not exactly the best choice for a wedding day, but the young ones' eyes were wide and their faces beamed with pleasure.

The fiddler announced a new dance.

Adam and Polly joined the couples, and Polly relaxed as they spun around the floor.

When young George Miller grabbed her for a dance, Adam took the opportunity to partner with his daughter. Little Elsie had been dancing—in awe—with Marie DeForest, but when Adam waltzed away with her, another Miller cousin quickly claimed Marie. As Polly watched Marie's graceful steps she thought back to the dancing lessons Marie had given her at the fort, such a short time ago, though it now seemed as if years had passed.

Her feet were sore, and a lace needed tightening. George Miller danced Polly over to a table that held kegs of ale and jugs of rye. For one so young, he was an outrageous dandy and flirt. "Would you like a drink?" His eyes glinted with mischief.

"I'd be much obliged." She smiled at him.

While he fetched the cup, she bent to tighten one of the ribbons on her slipper, and in a flash was surrounded by George's brothers and another neighbor of the Manns, the young rascal Simeon Jarrell.

"Here, I'll help you with that," said Simeon, more polite than usual. He bent down, loosened the shoe, then took it clean off and ran away with a shout, the other boys scampering after him.

The whole crowd watched, hooting and hollering. Then Adam was at her side with Elsie.

"My shoe!" Polly watched it disappear with the boys.

"*Ach. Bruder* Jacob put him up to it."

Sure enough. Simeon proudly carried his trophy to Jacob, who held it aloft with a smirk. He reached in his pocket and produced a coin for Simeon.

Lizzy Stigard rushed over, cheeks flushed. "*Das ist vass* I vant to tell you before!"

Adam turned to Polly. "I need to get a bottle of wine. Luckily, *meine Mutter* had her cousin—Pastor Miller, bring some with him from Roanoke."

"What is happening? Will they give me back my shoe?"

"This is one of the customs from our old country. In order to get your slipper, I have to pay *meine Bruder mit* a bottle of wine." He sighed. "After all, I did the same to him at his wedding."

Adam left her to speak to Pastor Miller, who listened with a grin, exclaimed in Deutsch, and thumped him on the back. Then the minister disappeared into the snowy night, coming back a short while later with a bottle which he thrust into the air with a hoot before presenting it to Jacob.

The music stopped and everyone watched as with a bow and a flourish, Jacob returned the shoe to Adam, who then made a great show of carrying it back to Polly. He knelt before her, and gently fitted it back upon her foot, to the loud clapping and shouting of the crowd.

Adam then lifted her—just as if she were as light as one of those shampaign bubbles—and carried her out the door to Schwarzie. The horse, already saddled, waited patiently for them, great puffs of fog coming from his breaths.

Adam settled her on the horse and leapt up behind her. Together they rode away through the cold night while silver stars watched them make their way to their new home together on Indian Creek.

# CHAPTER 20

## Silver Pond and Silver Man

**Nancy**
**December 1786**

They skated again the next day, were skittering across the icy pond before the snow came down thick. Bright Wing helped them at first while Becky and Prairie Deer stayed home with the little ones. The mirrored pond was empty.

Nancy thought it funny when White Buffalo—looking just like a buffalo calf—couldn't keep those wobbly legs under him. Soon his leggings were coated with a layer of snow and ice, like thick white wool.

Scout seemed to think he, too, could skate. He hauled out after them and slid off on his side, amazed. Still he kept on follwing, yipping at their strange heels before he stopped to rest a spell.

Nancy's biggest surprise was that she was better than White Buffalo at this sport.

"How can you go so fast?" He sighed as he straightened and tightened up the laces on his skates once more. Bright Wing had wound them not only around their feet, but up their leggings. Still they slid down from time to time, and then the blade liked to keel over.

Nancy helped him up, and then kept a hold of his hand to keep him upright. Together they glided across the ice, and he relaxed enough to flash a grin at her. In his dark face, his teeth shone white as the snow around them. And Nancy loved the glitter of his bright brown eyes.

"Next time we should bring the sticks, Talitha."

It was a fine idea.

She got to thinking as they spun around. Polly was the lucky one who always had gals her own age, or even older, like Marie DeForest, as dear companions. There never was a girl Nancy's age for her to latch onto. John and Chloe were fun to play with, but not quite the same as someone you chose—or who chose you. But now there was White Buffalo, one she might dare to call a friend, a feller who seemed to enjoy being around her even if she was a gal, and even if he was nigh eleven and she was only eight.

"Your face is almost as red as mine," White Buffalo said.

His English was getting better. She held her gloved hands up to touch her numb cheeks and nodded.

"Maybe we should go back," he said.

She did not answer, distracted by a delicious scent. "Mmm." she sniffed the air. "Do you smell that?"

White Buffalo pointed at a cloud of smoke, then he took a whiff. "Someone is baking. Let's go see. I am getting tired and hungry, anyway."

They took off the skates and followed their noses up the hill. The fragrance led them to a brick house, with a sign outside that read, "Perrault's Bakery." The delicious scent invited them in. They opened the door to find an old Frenchwoman kneading dough on a counter while a younger man shoveled loaves in and out of a long oven with a wooden paddle. More baking tools hung from racks attached to the ceiling, and on the counter, fresh loaves cooled in baskets.

Nancy turned to White Buffalo. "Now I am starving."

He licked his lips. "Me, too."

Then she recalled they had no coins or trade items.

They startled as the door opened behind them and a man with yellow hair and English clothes entered.

"*Bon jour*," he said, closing out the cold.

As they returned his greeting, Nancy noted a frown on his face.

"You do not speak French, do you?"

"A little," said Nancy, in her own tongue. She had been learning a lot of French in Henri's cabin, but still could not understand when Henri spoke to Little Star or the voyageurs.

"But you are English," he said, showing surprise as he eyed her Indian clothes.

White Buffalo took her hand. "We are Shawanese," he said.

Nancy found herself liking her hand in his and enjoying the sound of "We."

The man's blue eyes widened a bit further. "Hmm. Well, my friends the Shawanese call me Shawneeawkee. I am the Silver Man." He held out his hand. He wore several shiny rings on his fingers and silver bracelets on his wrist. He pointed at a gleaming pitcher on the counter. "That I made," he said in Shawanese. "My English name is John," he added in English.

Nancy stared. "You're the feller that played fiddle in church. Well, at old Mr. Barthelmie's. And you got the same name as my pa. And my brother." The English words flew out of her mouth like strange birds.

White Buffalo frowned.

"I mean, that *was* my pa and my brother that was called John. When I was white. When I was American."

The words nearly stuck in her throat. There was still a slight wrinkle on John Kinzie's forehead, but his eyes were kind.

"Well there is one thing I can see that you both are, and that is hungry. And these have led you here." He tweaked their noses. He spoke French to the baker, and Perrault handed a basket of bread to the old woman, who pulled out a small loaf for them while John Kinzie gave Perrault coins.

"*Merci*," he said. He turned to the children. "Come."

Outside, Scout sat waiting eagerly by the door, licking his chops. John Kinzie gave him a crust of bread which he wolfed it down in a flash.

They walked a few feet to a wooden building with fancy writing on a sign. Nancy could not read it, but saw it hung from a rod with a golden ball at the end. John Kinzie opened the door and ushered them in.

"You are here for Christmas, I think?"

They nodded.

He frowned. "Today was not my best day for playing fiddle at mass. That Henry Hays kept us up at the Abbots all afternoon, courting young Betsy, nigh until mass was ready to begin." He waggled his eyebrows. "All I had was coffee until kind Mrs. Rivarre offered us roast turkey for dinner, when mass was done."

"I sure do like that fiddle, anyhow," Nancy offered.

"Me too," said White Buffalo. "And the flute."

"Too bad you are not older, little one," he said to Nancy. "You are a woman after my own heart."

That was strange. Nancy's cold cheeks grew warm. She was a little girl, not a woman. John Kinzie was a funny man.

He waved his hands towards his cabinets. "I have made many fine things for Christmas. People bring their silver to me, and I make it into whatever they want." He walked through a little hinged door that led into his workshop, right behind the counter.

All was very tidy. There was a hearth and bellows, and all manner of tools lined the wall. Silver hammers lay scattered on a workbench, along with different sized anvils, pliers, and shears.

John Kinzie opened a cupboard door and sliver light spilled out.

Nancy and White Buffalo's mouths fell open.

"Yes. I made these goblets and plates," he said, and handed one down to Nancy. White Buffalo and she held it together, carefully. They gently traced the raised vines and flowers that decorated the rim and stem. After they passed it back to John Kinzie, he took down a shiny wooden casket. He opened it to show off fancy thimbles, sliver beads and hoop earrings like the Shawanese wore in their ears. There were also shimmering brooches and rings with fine carvings twined into them.

John pulled one out and handed it to White Buffalo. "I learned how to make things like this when I was younger than you," he said. His voice dropped to a whisper and he sounded as if he was giving a secret away. "I ran away. To Quebec. Before that, the parents, they sent me to a bad school. So I run to Quebec, and there I learn all of this."

"Perhaps you would like to learn? I am very busy all up and down this river. I could use a helper with all the work I have to do."

White Buffalo looked at Nancy, not sure if he understood. Sometimes they needed to translate for each other.

Nancy spoke up. "He doesn't want to. Mister Kinzie. This is all real pretty, but White Buffalo wants to grow up to be a warrior like his pa, Standing Elk. Don't you, White Buffalo?"

He nodded. Then he looked at the ring once more, held it up before Nancy's eyes. He took one of her fingers and slipped the ring onto it. "There. Now you are a fine lady, Talitha." The fancy ring was way too big and slid all around. She laughed and twirled it, then held her finger up for them to admire.

"Ah, married so young," said John Kinzie, pulling a sad face. "And poor John Kinzie has yet to find a wife."

Nancy handed the ring back, though she wished she could keep it. Then she spied his fiddle hanging on a peg on the wall. She jigged up and down. "Play us a song!"

He took down the fiddle and started up a sad air.

"No," shouted Nancy. "Play us a good happy one. 'Pop Goes the Weasel.'" John Kinzie stopped plumb in the middle of the slow air and went into a fast jig. Nancy grabbed onto White Buffalo and they linked arms for *allemands*. John Kinzie smiled and made more silly faces as he fiddled, tapping away with his feet. Then he went into "The King's Head."

Their faces were red and they soon broke a sweat with all the clothes they still had on from shinny.

John Kinzie put the fiddle back. "Enough fun for now. Poor John Kinzie must get back to work." He peered out the window at the fading light. "Before it is too dark."

He opened the door to them and made a little bow. "It was very nice to meet you both. And I look forward to seeing you on Christmas Day."

The next day was Christmas Eve. They watched in wonder as tall soldiers decorated a spruce tree high on a bank near the home of Madame Rivarre. The men sang a beautiful song in a strange language. The melody softly wafted over the town.

"Hessians," Henri explained. He and Standing Elk had returned from their trip to Detroit. "They were hired men of the British. These stayed on after the war. It costs so much to get back to their own country, and anyway, why would they go?"

Once when she was feeling sad, Henri had sat down beside her and said, "*Cherie*, you will get used to your new life. I myself am from France, though I lived in Montreal before I came here. I do not ever wish to return. You must learn to love your new life."

Nancy was beginning to realize folks around here came from all over, some from so far across the sea they would never see their old homes again. Perhaps she was not so different from others after all.

The children watched that afternoon as the Hessians made the tree special with all kinds of ribbons and candles. They even hung nuts from the branches. That evening, there was a procession over to Mr Barthelmie's place and a Christmas Eve Mass, As they walked to the service, they could see the Hessians' tree glowing in the darkness and heard their carols.

"Why aren't they coming?" asked Nancy.

"They are Lutheran," said Henri. "They have their own prayers."

At the mass, Father Louis said many prayers and songs. John Kinzie and Henry Hays made music again and led singing. White Buffalo came; everyone came but Prairie Deer and Standing Elk, who wanted to stay at home.

The crowded house nearly steamed with wet heat, in spite of the cold outside. Still, it was a treat to be there and Nancy was sorry White Buffalo's folks missed it. Small boys dressed in robes sang in sweet voices. There was a couple dressed like Mary and Joseph, that holy pair, and they came in carrying a baby. An angel and a shepherd boy followed right behind. They laid the dear little baby in a manger, while the little boys sang, and the whole place glowed from all the candlelight.

Then the group knelt before the babe in the manger and the everyone went still.

And a strange thing happened. The angel looked out at her with Polly's face. And when the shepherd boy leaning on his crook looked up, she saw John. And sure enough, when Mary and Joseph glanced up from that babe on the straw with curly golden hair like Chloe's, they had Mam and Pa's face. Mam's eye cried a tear when she spied her, but when Joseph—Pa—caught her eye, he winked.

All the air went right out of her. She felt as if she'd been punched right in the stomach, tried to keep from falling down into the crowd. White Buffalo was pulling her up, and she heard Henri say, "She is much too hot."

As they led her from the packed room, she looked once more at the Nativity. But all the folks playing parts were strangers. None were her own.

As they made their way back to the cabin, snow drifted down in soft feathers. White Buffalo wanted to run and slide, to pretend they still had skates on their feet. But like Mary with that baby Jesus, Nancy wanted to ponder some things in her heart. Quietly.

Could it be her old family was happy somewheres else? In her vision—for surely that was all it was—they looked very happy. Henri had told her once that some people called "saints" got messages from God in chapels or other holy places. And Becky said Moneto spoke to some of the Shawanese, also.

*Was God giving her a message on this holy night?*

Back at home, Henri heated up hot chocolate. Pewter mugs in hand, they all sat around the table by the fire and Henri sang French Christmas songs for them.

The celebrations went on and on. After Mass on Christmas Day—with all kinds of fuss like the night before—there was a feast at Madame Rivarre's. Once more, on account of Henri being such an important trader, the whole family was made welcome. There was roasted venison, wild turkey with stuffing, raccoon, rabbits, roasted chickens, and a roast pig. At the end of the evening, servants came out with a huge fiery pudding. Those who waited upon them were the only unhappy looking folks. Becky said they were not Shawanese, but Pawnee, and often the Pawnee around here were used as slaves.

White Buffalo and Nancy sipped a honeyed rum punch dotted with raisins, while others sipped on drinks called "shrubs," from sparkling goblets like those made by John Kinzie. They frequently raised their glasses to offer toasts to the health of King George, though Nancy could not make herself wish that rascal well.

Just when she felt she might fall asleep from all the feasting, John Kinzie pulled out his fiddle and struck up a reel. A British captain and his lady started off the dance, and others soon jumped in. Even some of the Indians bounced up, adding some steps from a corn dance. Nancy latched onto White Buffalo and they, too, joined in the fun, leaping and stepping till the music stopped.

# CHAPTER 21

## Bleigießen

**Polly**

**Indian Creek**

**Silvester-New Year's Eve 1786**

They gathered around a pail of water set on the cold stone floor of the porch kitchen. A candle flickered in the chill air. The women waited, held their breath. It was just the three of them: Polly, Mary, wife of Adam's older brother Jacob, and their neighbor and friend, Lizzy Stigard. Polly looked on, stomach fluttering.

"Here," said Mary. The ball of lead she plucked from her pinner pocket had no doubt been pilfered from the shot pouch of her husband Jacob. She daintily placed it on the spoon Lizzy Stigard held near the taper.

Lizzy carefully shifted the spoon till it was directly over the candle. Up shot a flash of blue and orange before the flame settled back, melting the lead into a small dark pool in the hollow of the spoon.

"So now, we gently..." And here Mary cast Lizzy a threatening look, "Drop it into the water."

Lizzy frowned, then concentrated hard as she carefully tipped the gray liquid out. There was a soft, "ploosh," when it fell into the water and hardened.

This was yet another custom of the Palatines. If you made a *Bleigießen* on New Year's Eve, called *"Silvestri"* by the Palatines, you might be given clues for your future. Her sister-in-law and Lizzy had insisted she join them in the game while the rest of the family chatted or dozed before the warm hearth in the big kitchen.

"Now we must fish it out," Mary continued, glancing at Polly with a smile. "And we will read your fortune."

Mary eagerly snatched the utensil from Lizzy, grinned again as she flourished it for a moment, and then spooned the piece out of the pail.

Once more they held their breaths as Mary lifted the lead lump up to the light.

Lizzy gasped. *"Ein Säugling,"* she croaked.

"What?" asked Polly. Was a *Säugling* good or bad? Whatever it was, this *Säugling* didn't look like much.

Mary placed the warm piece in her hand. When Polly held it up close, she saw it was like a tiny baby. A boy—there was a small bump just below its middle.

Polly's face burned as they both stared at her.

*"Güt Gluck,"* said Mary, with a smile.

"Is it true?" asked Lizzy, blue eyes glowing huge in her pretty, plump face.

Mary laughed. "Lizzy! Surely she can't know yet." Then she turned and fixed her own blue gaze on Polly. "It's only been a week, after all." She smirked and added, " A week of lo-o-o-ve," drawing out the word. *"Liebe, meine* Lizzy."

*"Mein Gott,"* said Lizzy, glancing down and crossing herself, her face as red as Polly's.

Children's shrieks, laughter, and the scrapings of a fiddle floated out from the kitchen. The clock must be counting down the minutes; the family resting and talking in the kitchen had come back to life.

"We should join the others," said Polly.

"But I need to see *my* future," proclaimed Lizzy, startling them with sudden liveliness.

Mary afforded Lizzy none of the solemnity she'd given Polly. Instead, she began to whistle, then sing a song Polly knew as "There's a Hole in My Bucket, Dear Liza," but that Mary called *Lieber Heinrich*.

"*Wenn der Pott aber nu en Loch hat, Lieber Heinrich, Lieber Heinrich . . .*"

Lizzy glared as Mary unceremoniously dumped Lizzy's lead in the pail.

Her *Bleigießen* looked like nothing at first, but turned a certain way it began to resemble a French *fleur de lis*, so Mary said.

While the two argued about what *that* meant, Polly's mind flitted back to Mary's comment about her own future, and the week of *love*. Truly it had been. Her face burned again at the thought of it, and soon her body felt warm, too.

Because Mary was right. It had been the most delicious week of touching, basking, stroking. She closed her eyes, and imagined Adam's hands on her again, his mouth lingering on her skin. Her flesh was swollen, tender. Sore. She was a ripe fruit, bruised by hungry lips. She was different than she'd been a week ago, but a *baby*? Could it be?

# CHAPTER 22

## The Way of The People

**Talitha /Nancy**
**Winter/Spring 1787**

Winter wrapped round her, a soft white blanket. By now, she was so used to being called Talitha that she easily answered to the name and seldom thought of "Nancy," that gal she'd left behind on the trail somewheres. She and Becky—*Neega*—left Kekionga after the New Year, and settled back into the rhythms of their small village tucked in along the river called the Maumee.

The dark time of year was a great time for stories of brothers Bear, Squirrel, Raccoon, and more. Becky explained that these tales could only be told in winter when most of the critters slept, for they were vain and liked to hear about themselves. If Squirrel's tale was told in autumn, he might stop off his work of gathering nuts to lie about and listen. And then where would he be? Those animal brothers were a caution.

The men of the tribe were often gone a-hunting. Some of the women went along to scrape hides and dress the meat. White Buffalo hunted with his father Standing Elk. Though autumn hunts provided food for the people, these late winter forays yielded pelts for trade. Right now skins were at their thickest and would fetch the highest prices.

Some in the tribe whispered that trading animal skins for money was not good and would cause problems with these brothers of the fireside tales. Wise ones said these critters were blessed and provided good fortune to the People when they gave their lives for food and raiment. Was it not wrong to trade their hides for money with which to buy goods from the white men? Goods that would make the Shawanese more like the Long Knives? The elders predicted this sort of greed would bring nothing but grief in the end, and the natural world would fall out of balance.

Nancy listened to the warnings as she huddled with Scout and Becky around the bright evening flames. The elders passed on other Shawanese wisdom, too, in stories of her clan, the Mekoche, the healers and counselors of the tribe.

She learned something of all the clans. The Pekowi kept rituals and religion of the People while the Kispoko trained warriors for battle and produced war chiefs. This was the sept of Standing Elk and White Buffalo. But Prairie Deer, White Buffalo's mother, was a Mekoche, like Tepeke and herself. Males did not marry women from their own clan.

The largest Shawanese groups were the Chillicothe and Thawekila. The tribal chiefs and leaders usually came from these clans.

With White Buffalo gone, Nancy found a friend in Dove Trees, a gal just a few years older than she. Dove Trees had been staying with some of her kin in the south, but had returned to the village after Christmas. She too was a Mekoche, a tiny one who seemed quiet at first. But once Nancy got to know her, she reckoned Dove Trees was more like a cawing crow than a tree full of quiet doves. Dove Trees jumped at the opportunity to teach Nancy more words and ways of the Shawanese while Becky, her *neega*, continued to school her in the ways of a Mekoche woman.

Their friendship grew as winter waxed into spring. Soon men returned from the hunting camps and women set out to tap maple trees for sugar. One cold morning in early spring, Becky and Nancy readied themselves for the trip to the sugaring camp with Dove Trees and her mother and several more.

Though it was early spring, together they dressed in their winter clothes. Nancy wore a new robe of black fox fur that Becky had traded from some Wyandottes at Miamitown at Christmas time, while Dove Trees wore a robe of buckskin lined with fur.

Nancy felt bad about the foxes. The heads and faces were still on the pelts, and in spite of their dark colored fur, they looked too much like Scout. But she loved the way the tails hung down in the back, and softly swished against her leggings when she walked.

Under the overcoats they wore shifts made of deer hide soft as butter, and beneath that, a belt held up their leggings, also of deerskin. Between the shifts and leggings, were skirts made of calico, like petticoats. Those had been bartered from the British.

Their overshoes, worn over heavier winter moccasins, were of woven cornhusks, and squeaked on the snowy ground.

When they reached the grove of beeches and sugar maples, Dove Trees said, "You and I will collect the sap and bring wood for the fires." Nancy looked around and realized she was in a place her white folks called a "sugar bush."

"It looks like that tree is smiling," Nancy said, staring at the one nearest them.

A curve had been cut in the trunk and a wooden track placed in it. The sap ran out from the grin and down into a wooden trough and then into a pail.

Dove Trees grabbed her hand. She pulled her to where some finished sugar was cooling in blocks and broke off a piece, pushing it into Nancy's mouth. *"This'll* make *you* smile." It did. The little chunks melted into lovely sweetness in her mouth.

Then Dove Trees grabbed a piece for herself.

When the pails by the trees were full, Nancy and Dove Trees carried the containers to women who tended the large kettles of sap that boiled over the fire. It was hard work, but Dove Trees made a game of sneaking chunks of sugar each time they went past the blocks.

"We had a pot like that at home," Nancy said, pointing to one of the boiling kettles.

Dove Trees was silent for a moment. "I think my father traded for that kettle with some hides from the winter hunt."

Nancy thought back to her home on Cabin Creek, remembered how Simon Girty's Indians took her mam's pot, full of stew and all. Telling that tale would do no one any good, so she kept her sad memory to herself, but was soon distracted as this time Dove Trees dragged her over to a split log table covered with wooden dishes.

"They are ready to ladle the sap!"

They brought the dishes for the women to fill with the hot liquid, and then carried them back to the table, where they would cool. As they carried the pails, Dove Trees pretended to stumble. She spilled a pool of sap onto a clean patch of snow, cried out, then grinned smugly. "Oh no! Now we will have to eat this." Soon they wore smeary smiles of sweet syrup.

Yet Dove Trees about wore Nancy out with all her chattering. One of her favorite topics was of a feller named Spemica Lawba who'd been stolen away by a Long Knife named Logan, a captain or general.

"You know," Dove Trees said, "Spemica Lawba was captured the same time as Talitha Cuny, Becky's first daughter."

This was of more interest. Nancy always wondered about that first daughter of Becky's, the one whom she had replaced, even taking over her name.

"Yes. Many were lost that day. Not only Spemica Lawba and Talitha, but also Kisathoi and Tebethto. They were white Indians, like you."

Becky had told Nancy of these two lost sisters. Though no one saw them carried off by the Long Knives, they had disappeared during the attack on Moluntha's Town, and were never seen again.

"Those were the two that taught me so much English," said Dove Trees. "They taught Tecumseh some, too, but mostly he learned from Sinnamatha—Big Fish."

Nancy missed Tecumseh and Sinnamatha and wanted to hear more of them, but Dove Trees returned to her favorite subject.

"I think when Spemica Lawba comes back, we will marry. Our fathers are not of the same clan, so we can."

"Don't you need to wait till you're older?" Nancy asked.

"Well, we wouldn't marry now, of course. Just get promised." She frowned, thinking. "Maybe you can marry White Buffalo."

Now this was not an unpleasant notion, especially since he was always so kind to her and liked to do things with her. But marry? She reckoned White Buffalo was about eleven years old, but she was only eight. They surely would have a long wait.

"Well, if I ever had to find me a husband someday, I guess I would like it to be White Buffalo. I sure do miss him."

"Well, you won't see him when we get back."

"What?" She had been so anxious to spend time with him again.

"He has made his vision quest, and now he must stay with the men. Work on his *pawaka*. That is his sacred bundle. His totem."

"I thought the sacred bundle belongs to each clan."

"Well, yes, each clan has one. But at your vision quest, your spirit animal comes to you if you are worthy, and then you begin to make your own bundle."

"Can gals have a vision quest, too?"

"Yes! But it is different. When you get so you can have a baby, you go off to a hut, and a spirit might come." Dove Trees' brow wrinkled. "Becky, your *neega*, will tell you. I haven't gone yet, but my mother says I will. Soon."

This was confusing. Nancy knew that babies had an *unsoma*, a good spirit in the shape of an animal, and that was where they often got their names. But a *pawaka* was different. It might be a spirit guide, sort of an angel. But also it might have the shape of an animal. Dove Trees added that when White Buffalo already found his guide. It would help him to know the paths *Moneto* and Our Grandmother had laid out for him.

"And how would those fit in a pouch?" Nancy asked.

"Oh, spirits shift shapes," Dove Trees said. "There's all kinds of magic in the bundles."

Becky's voice rang out, calling them back to work. "Check on the pails, my fine girls."

After several more days of sugaring, they returned to the winter village, their precious cargo packed in birch containers and loaded on horses.

Dove Trees continued to school her as they walked along. "Talitha, we also have many *tipwiwe*, truth bearers or witnesses that take our prayers to the Creator. You have seen people toss tobacco in the fire after a hunt, or during a festival?"

Nancy nodded. Becky had given her her very own tobacco to be used in private thanks—a pinch sprinkled on the ground after gathering herbs, for instance.

"The gift of tobacco is our witness to the Great Spirit, who made us the heart of the earth and gave each of us a piece of his own heart. And we have other witnesses, besides the tobacco gift." She pointed above where an eagle soared in the pale gray sky. "Eagle and hawk. The four winds and stars. The sacred fires of cedar. *Moneto* will one day look with favor on us again. And then we will have our feasts and our weddings without all of these interruptions and wars."

Nancy thought on this. The People sure did want to please the Great Spirit. The Shawanese did more praying and thanking than her own folks did back at home.

"And soon we return to Miamitown to plant, and then we will have the summer festivals to look forward to." Dove Trees set down her basket filled with sugar lumps, plucked out a golden piece and broke it in two, putting half into Nancy's mouth and stuffing the other half into her own. Then mouth full, she hugged Nancy to her, giving her a lumpy grin.

"Talitha, *neeshematha*, There are so many things I will love to teach you."

After they returned to the village, Nancy asked Becky about some of the things Dove Trees had told her.

Becky said, "Dove Trees thinks she has many truths to teach you, but she becomes foolish with all her talk. And then she hides the truth from herself."

"What truth?"

"The heart of Spemica Lawba—you would call him High Horn in your tongue—belongs to Bluebird, the niece of Blue Jacket."

Nancy knew Blue Jacket was chief of the Mekoche now that Moluntha was gone.

"It is well known that Spemica Lawba and Bluebird will someday make a match. *If* they ever return. And it is foolish of Dove Trees to trick herself into thinking otherwise."

"But my daughter, my *neetanetha*," said Becky, giving Nancy a squeeze, "she is lucky to have found a good friend in you."

# CHAPTER 23

## Four for a Birth

*One crow for sorrow*
*Two for mirth*
*Three for a wedding*
*Four for a birth…*

**Polly**
**Indian Creek**
**Summer 1787**

It was so hot. And Polly so huge and ungainly. Midges bit and stung as she hung the laundry out to dry. She rose up to swat them, then paused to watch an angry group of crows chase away a hawk flying overhead in the cloudless blue sky. She bent and stretched, ached, belly swollen, distended. She was no longer that delicious ripe fruit, but a bulging pumpkin on a scrawny stalk. Sleeping through the night was now a distant memory; she never could get comfortable with this great bundle she carried within her.

She sighed. At least Barbary, Adam's mother, would be there to help her when the time came. She'd played midwife before—birthed Jacob and Mary's children, and some of the Miller kin, nieces and nephews. She was eager to get this one, offspring of her favorite son, into her arms soon.

Polly heard a horse's whinny and the clop of hooves drawing near.

A moment passed, and there was another noise: boots clomping up the steps of the stoop out front. She left the doors of the cabin open when she did the washing out back, making it easier to get baskets in and out. She always looked forward to the sound of Adam's footsteps in the short hallway, heading her way. Now that her time was so near, he always came home for dinner with her.

"Polly!"

"Back yonder," she answered.

He stood on the back porch and looked down at her, a relieved smile on his face. Then down the back steps two at a time. He caught her in his arms. She breathed in the scent of the sweet hay fields he had been working in.

"Dinner smells good," He planted a kiss on her damp brow. "Rabbit stew?"

"Yes, and rye bread that your mother brought."

"Let me finish for you." He gathered the last of the wash and draped it over the nearest branches and bushes. Then he circled his arm around—well, what used to be her waist—and guided her up the stairs into the cabin. He sat her in the rocking chair he had built for her when they knew the baby was coming. He gently lifted her legs up onto a stool that she had covered with a needlepoint design, another Tree of Life pattern, mercifully more recognizable than her earlier attempt.

"How is Polly *meine Liebchen*?" he asked, kneeling beside her and tucking a tendril of hair behind her ear.

"Good thing you came just now. I'm likely to faint in this heat. This one kicks so." On cue, there was a tiny but fierce poke from beneath her apron. She placed Adam's hand upon the spot.

"*Ach du lieber Kind,*" he said softly. "This will be a strong one. Our own wee Mann."

Polly smiled. Silly pun she heard again and again. Yes, Adam treasured his daughter Elsie, but he hoped this one would be a son.

She leaned her head over against him, nearly tasted that new mown meadow. This time there was also a smoky scent. "You were at the smithy?"

"Only for a moment. Dull scythe wanted peening. *Meine Vater* was at the forge. And *Bruder* Jacob. I heard more talk of the Great Road."

They sat a spell silently musing upon this sore subject. The new government wanted a road that would go from here'bouts all the way to Lexington. Folks along Indian Creek were meant to labor on the sections that ran alongside their properties. But most along the branch were not in favor of this, though a few of the more wealthy supported it. Those with less money, if they were lucky enough to return after fighting the War of Independence, had to make up for lost tie. They had to work hard to improve their long-neglected properties. And the fighting wasn't over yet. Some who had made it home had gone again to the frontier forts to fight off the Shawnee. There was no time to be spared for laboring on this road.

"So, is it coming?" she asked.

"No one is ready," he said. "But it will come."

Little fingers of fear clutched at her. She did not want work on the road to take him away.

He sniffed. "Don't worry, it is not here yet. But I know dinner is." He pulled her to her feet. "Let's eat."

# CHAPTER 24

## Sheltowee Redeems a Captive

**Boone/Sheltowee**
**Limestone on the Ohio**
**August 1787**

Over yonder it was all over but the shoutin'. Over was the hootin' and hollerin' of last night, but the weepin' and wailin' followed today. Plenty of that there was.

Yesterday they'd drawn up the treaty: He, himself—Dan'l Boone to the whites and Sheltowee to the Shawnese—along with Logan, Kenton, and some others were there on behalf of the white captives. Captain Johnny, Wolf, and some other Shawnese were there for the Indians.

There'd been an all-night celebration round the treaty fire, not far from his own tavern. They'd roasted a steer, an elk the Indians brought, and had corn and bacon on the side.

There was whiskey. Plenty of that, and bourbon. Plenty of carousing around the fire, as well, until a fight nearly broke out over a Shawanese horse, recognized by its former white owner. That was taken care of with a keg of whiskey, too. His whiskey.

He sighed. With Kentucky now a state, the government should surely reimburse him. But he wouldn't hold his breath.

Now he had to bear witness to these long goodbyes, like to break your heart. White women clung to their Indian husbands, weeping to high heavens. Or Moneto, more likely. One real pretty one with an Indian husband was plumb terrified of her white pa, an elderly feller who was stunned to see her shy away from him like an unbroke mare.

Sometimes those young wives even had a babe in arms or a young'un or two in tow. All bearing the signs of Indian blood.

Then there was the rare sight of a white man forlorn at leaving his squaw. Boone figured the most desperate were hiding out in the woods and wouldn't come out treaty or not. He knew how it worked. He'd been a captive—an adopted son of Blackfish.

Well, some of them would be sneakin' back to their Shawanese lodges real soon, he reckoned.

He even felt sorry for Logan, in spite of their past differences. During the exchange, Boone had heard a commotion around the captain. Logan had adopted a lad they'd taken from Moluntha's village up north. Spemica Lawba was his Indian name, and he was a-carrying on. Angry as he'd been to be taken from the Shawanese, he now called himself Johnny Logan, and didn't want to go back to his own kin. His Indian pa had been killed before he'd been born, and though he had plenty of Shawnee uncles, maybe that was why he took so much to his adopted pa Colonel Benjamin Logan.

The one they called Tecumseh—the boy's uncle or cousin— looked on, shocked and shame-faced at the lad's fussing.

Sorriest of all were the young'uns who'd been captured when they were so small they'd never known a parent outside the Shawanese. What was it that Ben Franklin had said? Dr. Ben, was friends with Boone's own cousin. He was known to have expressed wonder at how quick captive white children adapted to life among the savages. Of course, Ben admired those savages a heap, himself: their families, their way of self-government, and way of raising up their children. Boone liked those ways, too, especially after he'd been adopted into a tribe and practiced some of it firsthand. But turn 'em over they must.

All but one. No one had come for her, the blonde tyke, cute as a button and all dressed up in tiny buckskin outfit. Though her white folks, if they were only there to see it, might not agree.

But they weren't here to claim her. No one was. And no one knew who she was. Captain Johnny wouldn't give her up with no one legal to claim her. So, no help for it.

He'd just steal her.

# CHAPTER 25

## Green Corn

**Nancy/Talitha**
**August 1787**

Elders and a few warriors danced around the fire waving cornstalks. When the music ended, the dancers stripped off the ears of corn and dropped them into kettles hanging over the fire. After the corn was done, they fished the ears out and hung them from the four poles, the corners of the square that surrounded the fire circle.

Dove Trees, still her proud mentor in all things Shawanese, pointed to the tall stakes. "Those are the Three Grandfathers, and the Grandmother of the South, *Shawaki*. Some people say 'Four Winds,' or 'Four Directions.'" Scout sat between the two girls, watching with interest as the men spoke over the ears, offering them up. Then they scraped ashes from the fire and carefully buried them, ensuring more good fortune before they finally moved to another fire, the greatest one, to roast corn for the entire village.

Dove Trees put an arm around Nancy and snuggled into her. "Tonight there will be the feast, and dancing."

The ceremony ended, the people broke into groups to visit while the food cooked. Laughter, talk, and the delicious smell of the coming feast filled the air. Relatives from other villages had come to join in the celebration.

Dove Trees looked over the crowd with an eager expression, then poked Nancy. "Look! It's Spemica Lawba—High Horn."

Nancy followed her excited gaze. A boy about the age of White Buffalo stood near a sad-faced woman and Becky. She caught a glimpse of two larger boys—maybe men—walking away, and hoped they might be Tecumseh and Sinnamatha—Big Fish. But they were gone before she could be sure, and Dove Trees was pulling her along, leading her over towards the group.

Nancy groaned. She never could break Dove Trees of the habit of hauling her along behind her, dragging her hither and yon.

"You're back!" Tickled, Dove Trees nearly jumped up and down, as she gaped at the famous Spemica Lawba.

He did not return the greeting. He gazed into the dust until his mother poked him in the ribs. Then he lifted his head all sulky-like and said, "Hello." In English.

Nancy thought back to what Becky had told her about Spemica Lawba and Bluebird. Why would Dove Trees tolerate being shunned like this? Shawanese were proud, trained to never lose face. To be shamed was an awful thing. Death was better.

But Dove Trees only seemed surprised at his rudeness.

Becky spoke up. "This is Spemica Lawba, Tecumseh's nephew. And here is his mother, Snow Lily. She is Chief Moluntha's niece. They were part of our old village."

The boy stared directly at Nancy. "I'm Johnny Logan," he said. "What is your real name, your English name?"

"I am called Talitha," Nancy said, slowly. Indeed, she really did not know who she was anymore. Maybe she was like that half-and-half house of Bright Wing and Henri, made of two worlds. She glanced at Becky in confusion. No one had spoken her English name in a long time. Becky's brow was dark. She was not happy with this talk.

All riled up, the boy shouted back at her. "No! Your white name!"

Scout growled at him, the fur on his back rising in little spikes. Nancy swallowed. It was now strange to look back towards the past. The road that led to her memories was fading, and filling up with new ones. She was starting to understand why the Shawanese never spoke the names of the dead. To name the dead was to call them from the Spirit Path. It was better to leave them on their way.

She nervously clutched the corn doll, Polly's doll, tucked away in her pouch. "Nancy," she answered. "Nancy Flynn."

"Hmm," he said. "You are now Tepeke's daughter." He paused a moment, a sly secret opn his face. Nancy had never seen a boy so ornery and contrary. "I know what happened to the first Talitha, Talitha Cuny."

Becky's eyes lit up and she grabbed him by the shoulders. "She lives?"

He shook her off, pouty. "Yes. She lives. And her head is healed. Her hair covers the cut. But her name is not Talitha now. Her name is Priscilla. Priscilla Estes, though some call her Lilly. Her white brother took her. He was there with the soldiers at the village that day, and he has her, and he took her far away."

Spemica Lawba, Johnny Logan, or High Horn, whoever he was— perhaps he was just as confused as she was about that—seemed quite satisfied with himself now. The women looked about to cry, though.

Nancy—Talitha—was not sure if she liked this High Horn. He acted nothing like White Buffalo. Maybe he should have been called High Horse. Unbidden, her mind flitted back over that murky path to the past, to Elizabeth, her white mam, and the times she heard Mam tell Polly to come down from her high horse. No one said that to this one, but Nancy believed someone ought to.

"I have a white father, Colonel Benjamin Logan," High Horn announced proudly.

Then she remembered. Dove Trees' Spemica Lawba was renowned, his bravery told around the evening fires. During the destruction of Becky's village last fall, High Horn had fought the Shemanese. Though only twelve, he was said to have fought like a warrior. And then he had been taken away a prisoner, along with Nonhelema and the first

Talitha—she who was now known as Priscilla—and many others. He certainly was not behaving like a Shawanese warrior now.

But whether or not she liked him, he certainly was taking an interest in her.

Dove Trees, obviously disappointed to find that Johnny Logan High Horn had turned out so ornery and not a likely marriage prospect after all, grabbed Nancy's hand once. They headed back to the fun taking place in the meadow near the firepit of roasting corn. "Come along," she said. "The games have started and they want us to play."

Later that evening Johnny Logan showed up at Nancy's side once more, as she and Dove Trees watched the Corn Dance.

"Can you read?" he asked her.

"Yes," she answered.

He looked pleased, though she did not know why. "I can read. And write."

They all watched the dancers in silence for a moment when Spemica Lawba interrupted. "Did you go to school before?"

"No."

"Then how can you read?" His face showed doubt.

"My white sister Polly taught me. And my mam. At home. No one went to school."

He looked surprised. "Is Polly here?"

"No."

"Where is she?"

Why should *you* care, Nancy wanted to ask. "I don't know where she is. But I think she hid in the log. She might be at the fort where we used to stay, because we don't have a house anymore. It's burned up."

"Like our village was." Dove Trees was happy to have something to say at last. Nancy knew Dove Trees wanted her to see others had suffered as much as she had when she lost her white family.

Johnny Logan ignored her. "At the exchange at Limestone, Big Fish hid when he was supposed to go back with the whites. I saw his father looking for him. He did not want to go with his white family, the Ruddells." Johnny Logan looked proud as punch. "But someday he'll go back. I know it, even if he doesn't. I learned a lot from the captain."

"Did the rest of your family hide with Polly?" he asked.

"No. My pa is dead. But my white mam and my brother Johnny and my little sister Chloe, well, they were with me at first and then Simon made me go with him, and then Becky got me and adopted me for her own. I think Chloe is still with Meouseka."

"Meouseka!" he blurted. "He was at Limestone, too." He paused, thinking for a moment. "Wait, does your sister have yellow hair?"

Nancy's heart leapt. "Yes. Chloe's got yellow hair."

"I saw her, there at the exchange. Meouseka had her, and no one came to redeem her, but I heard later that Sheltowee took her. I saw her before that. She was dressed like an Indian, like you."

Nancy shook her head, tried to understand. "Who is Sheltowee?"

He groaned, exasperated. "The main one who did the exchange, signed some papers at The Treaty of Limestone. My white father doesn't care much for him, the one called Boone."

For the first time Johnny Logan looked at her kindly. "I don't think your white mam was there, or your brother, else your baby sister would have been with them."

"I know some day I will go back to my white father," he said. His hand clung tightly to a book—given him by his white pa, Nancy reckoned.

He resumed his bossy tone. "It's not so bad as you have heard, Dove Trees. The whites do *not* eat their children. And I liked the school I went to."

He leaned forward. "I'll tell you what. Let's start our own school. Every day we will meet by that oak." He pointed down towards the river, to a huge tree silhouetted by firelight. "Captain Logan gave me some books." Once more he rubbed book he carried with him. "We can read. I don't want to forget how."

# CHAPTER 26

## New Life

**Polly**
**September 1787**

As her time drew near, Polly longed for her mother, Elizabeth. She saw her in dreams, only to awaken and find the arms that enfolded her were Adam's. His voice soothed her, and in the soft tones she heard the Pa's voice as he calmed the mares about to give birth.

"You called for your mother," Adam whispered. He brushed her damp brow with a cool hand. "What can I do to help you, *meine Liebchen?*"

Muddled a moment, she reached back for the vision, tried to conjure up Mother. But the dream had taken flight. Mother was gone. All that was left to Polly was fear of a hard lying-in, and a heart's pounding beneath her moist shift.

"Are you well, *Liebchen?*" He could not hide his concern. Sometimes he treated her like glass. Because of what had happened to Mary Maddy, his first wife, after she had been brought to bed. And because, unlike Mary, she was so young.

"Yes, I'm fine." She touched her twitching belly and laid Adam's hand over it. "It's just, this one wants out."

She was not fine, not really. Her body was no longer her own. And when Adam was off working she now had spells. Panics. What if the child died, like Charlotte's? Or what if she herself died, like Mary Maddy?

Then there was the cussed whispering at the Mann farmhouse. Hushed conversations dwellt on the difficulties of childbearing for young females like herself. Nary a one of them had birthed a baby when as young as Polly. Mary Kessinger had been a bit older than Polly when she wed Jacob. These Palatines, so stout and sturdy, marveled at Polly's frail form. How was it supporting that monstrous belly?

Finally this, and perhaps this thought spawned the haunting dreams: What if she and the babe both survived, only to be snatched away by Indians, like her own family? In daylight hours, the piercing blue of these late autumn skies flung her back to that day nearly a year ago when her whole family vanished. Now at night, not only Mam, but the rest of them, too, flitted in and out of her dreams. Here she'd thought Nancy was the Flynn child to be cursed with nightmares.

Adam distracted her, cradling her back into his arms and gently planting kisses on her neck.

"I will bring *meine Mutter*, tomorrow," he said. "The time is so near, and it will be best if she stays until the baby comes."

Barbary arrived with her usual bustle and young Elsie in tow. She happily clucked around the cabin, helping Polly put by vegetables from the garden's bounty. Then they sat together in the afternoon, stringing leather stockings, and Barbary continued her attempts to educate her in *Deutsch* ways.

When Polly remarked upon it to Adam, he said, "She does that because Mary would have no part of it. With you she has a new chance. All will be done as in the old country."

While Elsie played nearby on the cabin floor, Polly learned. There was a long list of things to be done for the new baby. The devout Lutherans kept many traditions that seemed as superstitious as those of Old Patrick, but honor them Polly would. She would willingly adopt these ways. She needed to belong.

Barbary had brought with her a small wooden trunk decorated with fanciful carvings and filled with baby things. There were new linen clouts and tapes, but Barbary pointed to a soft worn one. "This will be worn first, else the child might be *eine Diebe*. Thief." Her eyebrows rose dramatically, "And then when it is soiled, vee burn it. For luck."

Next, she pulled out a tiny flannel gown. "Now, vir must be sure to put the right arm in this first. And then we take him upstairs to the loft, so he can look upon the world and be success."

Then there was a white dress, long and decorated with fancy work. "Gown *für die Taufe*. Baptism. Elsie wore this, too," she said with pride. Like the Catholics, the Lutherans baptized babies. Though not all Catholics were baptized as babies. Polly remembered when a French priest on his way to Vincennes had stopped by their cabin, and baptized both John and Nancy together. Barbary had made sure here brother, Pastor Miller in Roanoke, would come to baptize this one shortly after birth.

Barbary had something else with her, too. It looked like a scroll, carefully rolled up and tied with ribbon. She gently unfurled it.

"What is this?" Polly asked. The paper was covered with beautiful brightly flourished letters and designs.

"This is Adam's baptism certificate, a *Taufschein Fraktur*. There is his name—" Barbary smiled proudly and pointed to the words "Adam Mann," barely recognizable to Polly in the fancy black script.

Pointing below, she said, "Here are the names of the *Eltern*—elders, parents—me and Johann. This work was done by the school-master at the *Lutheranische* school at the church at Peaked Mountain. That is where Adam went to *die Schule*. The school there. You know Adam's father and his Uncle George helped build that church."

Polly nodded and admired the beautiful document, before she gently rolled it up again. She knew Adam would frame it, and soon it would adorn their wall. She had seen others like it grace the walls of Barbary and Johann's home.

Her mother-in-law pulled a new blanket out of the chest, and added it to the nest that lined the cradle built by Grandpa Johann. This, too, had belonged to Elsie. A highly polished horseshoe hammered by *Großpapa* gleamed from the headboard. It would bring good fortune. This would be one blessed babe.

Elsie tucked a small poppet she carried with her into the crib, and rocked it, humming softly.

Elsie. Polly reckoned the child would come to live with them directly after the wedding, but Barbary had objected. "*Ach.* She is happy where she is. She vill go *mit dich* when she has a *Bruder.* Or *Schwester.* Then she can help."

That day was almost here, and Polly looked forward to having the little one around. Once shy, the child was now attached to her. She was also intrigued with the tiny brother or sister growing inside of Polly, though Barbary insisted the new baby would be found under a cabbage when the time came. Polly knew Barbary was the one who would suffer when the day came that she must part with her tiny shadow.

Polly and Barbary locked eyes and smiled as they watched Elsie sing to her doll. Polly remembered how her own sister, Nancy, bent over little Chloe, rocking her to sleep in the same way. Oh, being with child she was like to weep at the drop of a pin. She quickly wiped away the hot tears lest Barbary see them and wonder.

Well. A four year old could help, just as she herself helped with Nancy and John, and as Nancy helped with Chloe. She must not let her mind dwell on the dark place—an Indian village or grave—that might hold any of her lost family now.

Barbary's babbling drew Polly back to the present. She went inside and brewed up some switchel, a drink made of cool spring water mixed with vinegar, maple sugar, and ginger when they had it, that she sent out with Adam in the morning. She and Barbary sat on the porch, sipping it in the fading sunlight while Elsie gathered wildflowers that bloomed in a small patch of green.

# CHAPTER 27

## Sinking 'Sang

**Boone/Sheltowee**

**Fall 1787**

The money troubles and lawsuits never let up. The folks in Bourbon County felt kindly towards him and sent him to the state assembly, but there was little compensation in that.

Yet he'd found another way to make money. And he was in good company. George Washington himself, and John Jacob Astor, the fur trader, now enriched themselves even further with the trade of ginseng to China.

'Sang, or ginseng, was plentiful. It grew up in the mountains, in the woods among the beech, hickory, maple, and tulip trees. Could live to be a hundred years or more. Ever year of its life, that plant took on a different look. The Shawanese had taught Boone not to take any less than seven years old. One could tell how old the 'sang was by following the stalk all the way to the ground, then reaching down and counting the scars on the stem. Then you dug it up, careful of the roots, washed it, and dried it.

While his daughter, Becky, and her husband minded the tavern in Limestone, he and wife Rebecca and their sons got fifteen barrels loaded onto a keelboat on the Ohio, headed for Philadelphia. Chloe, the little orphan gal he took on at Limestone came along, too. Still neither hide nor hair of kinfolks for her.

Then disaster struck.

Chloe and Nathan kept each other occupied—rough-housed mostly—while the older lads bushwhacked the craft down the river. Rebecca was on the lookout, of course, for submerged logs and branches her sons might miss. But the young'uns often distracted her. And unfortunately the older lads did not have her vigilance. It was up by Point Pleasant, where the Ohio met the Kanawha—accursed spot where Boone himself had seen so many lost in the only real battle of what they called Lord Dunmore's War—that they had the accident. Rebecca and the lads all failed to notice a log hiding just below the surface. They heard a crack, felt a jolt as it rammed them. Water gushed in, wetting their load and they purt near capsized.

But strange as all get out, who should appear on the shore—with others to help lend a hand—but John Vanbibber, the Captain, whom Boone himself had rescued in a snowstorm years earlier. After his shock at this strange reunion, Vanbibber was only too happy to pay back the good turn. He and his family helped haul the soggy load in to shore, then welcomed them to hearth and home where they sat a spell, visited a few days while the 'sang dried out.

Boone asked after kin for Chloe, as he always did when he met up with folks who lived in these parts. Vanbibbers knew of none, and told him of their own recent loss on account of the Shawanese. While sugaring, raiders had come upon them, kilt their daughter Rhoda as she had tried to escape, and made off with their son, John. They'd since kept an ear to the ground for news of captives.

"Sometimes when a trapper or trader passes through, they claim they seen some young'uns in the company of the Shawnese, but none match the description of my John. Or your little gal, there," Vanbibber said.

The little gal there was part of a strange coincidence. Chloes all around!! Captain Vanbibber's wife was named Chloe, and so was one of the daughters. They took such a shine to that third young Chloe that they begged to keep her, promising to look out for her relations.

Daniel and Rebecca would sorely miss that little mite. Sweet thing, tow-headed, hair nearly white and full of curls, but no delicate rose. That gal was a caution.

Vanbibbers were eager to have a playmate for young Hannah, so sad after the loss of her own sister and brother.

At first Rebecca did not want to let go of young Chloe, but finally gave in. They both realized that if they wanted to get the load on to Philadelphia in one piece, it might be helpful to have both Rebecca and Nathan's eye on the river, now that Nathan wouldn't be entertaining young Cory, as he called her. No shenanigans on this trip. And afterwards, why Vanbibber convinced Boone and the wife to leave Limestone and relocate down by them. Boone could not help but notice that his son Jesse had an eye for Chloe Vanbibber, so Jesse was especially keen on that scheme.

The little one's eyes filled with tears as they said their goodbyes.

"It's not for long, Cory," Boone said, ruffling her hair before they boarded their craft. "We'll be back for you before you know it."

Then they were off to Philadelphia and back—with one last visit to Boone's

Tavern in Limestone—before they started with a new life down the river.

# CHAPTER 28

## Priscilla

*Talitha Cuny*

**Polly**
**February 1788**

Sometimes it did not seem real, that in less than two years she could have all these changes in her life. She was now a wife and mother with two children to raise. The lying-in was a hazy memory. Once her labor began, she had floated above the pain, watched as her sister-in-law Mary and mother-in-law Barbary hovered about her. Little things bothered her, every smell and sound. Polly remembered at one point asking Mary to take the wedding ring off her finger—it pinched her so.

"No!" Barbary shouted. "The witches will gain power over her!"

The witches had not gained power. She'd given birth to a healthy baby, just like so many other women. She thanked God that her baby had lived and thrived, not like poor Charlotte's. And she thanked Him again for her own survival. She would be here for her children and husband, unlike the unfortunate Mary Maddy.

She mended as Adam sat by her side and smoked his evening pipe. The babe slept in his cradle while Elsie sprawled on a bearskin, playing a string game before the bright fire.

Adam interrupted her thoughts. "*Meine Eltern*—the parents—would like for us to come for dinner on Sunday. It is a celebration for my cousin Jacob Miller's wedding."

Polly looked up, a hint of alarm in her eyes. "He married her?"

"*Ja.* At *Weihnachten.*"

Polly glanced down, tried to concentrate on her stitches.

Elsie popped up, interested. "Who is married?"

"My cousin Jacob married Priscilla. The one your cousin George calls Lilly. Remember, you met her this fall when *Großmutti* made *Saumagen*?"

"Oh! The Indian one."

Polly fixed her gaze on Elsie, and spoke firmly. "No, she is not Indian. She just lived with the Indians for a long time."

"She looks like an Indian and she talks funny."

"No, you speak *Deutsch*, so to some people your talking may sound strange, too. You just need to get used to her way."

Elsie, losing interest, turned back to her string and nodded, serious now. "I will."

"She seems a good woman. A healer, some say," added Adam.

Polly, too, had heard this. Priscilla knew plenty of the medicine cures of the Shawnee, those she had lived among for so many years. Polly wondered, might Priscilla have any ideas about where the Shawnee raiders had taken the Flynns?

"And she has birthed many babies. All lived. All the mothers lived, too." Adam voice teased. "Maybe you have one for her?"

Polly made a face. "*Nein*. I have nothing for her."

"I know how we can fix that." Adam rose, removed the sewing basket from her lap, and placed it on the floor. He knelt before Polly and reached for a curl, loosed from the ribbon that held back the rest of her hair. He brought the lock to his mouth and kissed it, then leaned in and kissed her neck.

Polly grinned and pointed at Elsie, looking up from her rug with curiosity.

"*Aus mit du*! To bed!" Adam said. Then he crawled towards her like a bear, grabbed the shrieking child up in his arms and carried her to her room.

In a few minutes he was back, and bent down towards Polly to finish what he had started.

At the dinner at Barbary and Johann's, Jake Miller was attentive to his quiet bride. But when they had finished eating, he left to join the men outdoors for a drink of rye and a pipeful of tobacco. Polly found herself sitting next to Priscilla, searching for the right words to say. Polly held six-month-old Adam on her lap. Taking Jake Miller's place on the other side of Priscilla whom he called "Lilly," was cousin George Miller. Polly had noticed before that George seemed expecially attracted to Lilly's "Indian-ness." He stroked her braid as he eyed the baby.

"Will you go back to the Indians?" he asked.

Lilly was speechless a moment, taken aback. "Why no, George. I am married to your cousin. I am here to stay."

Was the look on George's face one of satisfaction or disappointment?

"Only I heard some folks run away. Back to the Indians," George mumbled, dropping his eyes.

Priscilla put an arm around him. "No, I reckon you all will have to put up with me till the end of my days."

George's face lit up with a smile. He rose and trotted off to a group of children playing nearby. Lilly gazed longingly at the baby.

"May I hold him? He is so lovely."

As Polly handed over the sleeping child, she tried not to stare too hard at Priscilla, now transfixed by little Adam. Her light brown hair hung in a long plait down her back. Her pale blue eyes, fringed with dark lashes, seemed full of secrets. Though Lilly was thin and frail, Polly could not help but feel a quiet strength radiate from her. In the midst of winter, she gave off a spicy scent of something sweet and green. They sat in silence a few moments, and then Polly trusted her voice to speak.

"I heard you did live among the Shawnee."

Priscilla's eyes brightened for a brief moment, then took on a faraway look.

"Yes. Many years. Since I was a young child. I was adopted into the Mekoche clan."

Polly swallowed. It was still hard to talk about that dark autumn day, now over a year past. "Did you know my family was taken?"

Priscilla nodded.

"Do you know Simon Girty?" Polly's heart pounded as she said these simple words.

"I have seen him at council fires. I have never spoken to him. But I have met his wife, Catherine. Do you know Katepacomen?" She caught herself. "I mean, Simon Girty?"

Polly frowned. "He was the leader, they say. Of the ones who took my family. The ones who killed my Pa."

The pale eyes grew thoughtful. "There were three children taken?"

"That's right. Nancy, and my small sister, Chloe, and John, my brother. This one looks just like Chloe," she gestured at the sleeping infant.

"It is likely the Shawanese still have them."

Polly stiffened, and Priscilla reached for her hand. "I was treated kindly, always, as were the other children I knew: the McKenzie sisters, and Stephen Ruddell."

The pounding of Polly's heart calmed, but then she seized on the unspoken. *What of Mother?*

Once more, this soft-spoken woman read her mind. "It is hard to say if they would still have your mother or not. It is often difficult for grown women who are separated from their children to become used to life in the tribes."

Tears pooled up in Polly's eyes, but she turned, mercifully distracted by the noise of the menfolk returning. She dabbed her eyes and retrieved the baby, rising from her seat so that Priscilla's groom could reclaim her. Lilly reached for her as she turned away.

"Polly. It was so good to meet you."

"I saw her scar!" said Lizzy Stigard.

"What?" The three sisters-in-law turned in unison.

"*Ja*. I helped her *mit* her hair, and there was the scar. The combs got caught on it."

They waited.

"On her scalp! When the army got her back they thought she was a squaw! Und whack!" she made a chopping motion with her arm. "Right in *die Kopf*. Then they saw the blue eyes."

All were silent. Lizzy spoke more quietly. "*Sie* says it is fine now. But *miene Gott*. It is a *big* scar."

As they worked in the kitchen, cleaning up the aftermath of the dinner, Lizzy regaled them in a mixture of Deutsch and English, with a gruesome tale of Captain Logan's men entering an Indian village, killing people and carrying off folks as captives. Polly remembered, hazily, that it was while Logan's campaign was taking place many miles to the north, that her own family had been taken in the Indian raid.

Priscilla had nearly been killed in the attack, and would have been, had it not been for one of Logan's soldiers who realized she was white. She had been captured—or rescued—it was hard to tell which. While being nursed back to health, she had later been recognized by her brother, a part of the very company that had attacked the village where she lived, and brought back to the white world.

Lizzy turned to Polly, eyes wide. "You see, you might get your own family back some day.

# CHAPTER 29

**Chloe**

**Fall 1788**

Those Vanbibbers were sad folk. Indians stole upon their brother and sister at sugaring time and killed Rhoda, and lit off with the brother, Jacob. The Captain and his black man, Davy, went after them and killed a lot of them Indians, but they never could get Jacob. And them Vanbibbers missed their Rhoda and Jake so much that they didn't mind having another gal in the house.

Best of all, though, was the Vanbibbers had themselves a baby bear. Someone had hunted its ma and kilt her, and they found that young'un and he was just a part of the family after that. He even let Chloe love on him. He sometimes came in the house but slept out in a shed at night.

Another surprise was that there was three Chloes here, when she herself was hardly used to being Chloe again. There was Old Missus, who was still real pretty and her real name was Chlorinda, but sometimes the Captain called her Chloe. And Young Miss, who got sweet on Jesse Boone when Boones was there was also called Chloe. And then she her own self was Little Chloe, but sometimes she got them to call her Cory, like Nate Boone and Old Dan'l did.

She might have had some fun with the youngest gal, Hannah Vanbibber and the bear cub, but Hannah missed her brother and dead sister so much that she wasn't much fun to be around. She was bigger than Chloe, but not so grownup as Young Miss Chloe. And when she did talk to Chloe she asked about what it was like to live with the Shawanese, but Chloe didn't remember any of that.

Sometimes at night, though, in the strange bed, the one that had belonged to the killed girl, Chloe heard Hannah crying, missing her lost ones. It made Chloe think back on all the others who had come and gone. Though Young Miss was always asking her about Jesse, who she took such a shine to; it was Nathan's face that was clearest in Cory's mind. They had such sport playing on the boat before the 'sang went overboard and she ended up here.

But when she pictured Nate, sometimes other shady faces crowded in.

Boones told her that she'd lived with the Shawanese for a spell. Sometimes Chloe missed a big Indian feller who always made her laugh and had a name like "Mouse." Mouse brought her to a place where there was a big swap, and for some reason the Shawanese weren't going to trade her over to the white folks. But Boone sneaked off and fetched her away anyway, and another lady who'd been captive told Boone that her name was Chloe. It was important to know the young ones' names in case their folks could get them back some day. No one knew her family name.

At least Jacob Vanbibber was old enough to remember his family name when he got took. Someday they might get him back.

Sometimes girls' faces showed up in her mind. One about eight years old, like Nathan. And there'd been a boy with brown eyes. She wished Boones would come back. She loved Young Miss, but in spite of all the people at the Vanbibbers, it could be lonesome. Maybe she could again be Boone's "little yeller haired gal," as Dan'l called her—when they came back to Crooked Creek.

But one day, late in the afternoon, Captain gave a shout from outside and they all rushed to the door to see a strange sight.

A fine horse trotted up. On its back was a woman, but she looked like a man. Had on buckskins like a lot of the soldiers wore, and she held a gun.

"Anne Bailey, hooray! And Liverpool," shouted Hannah, running down from the porch to greet them. The bear cub ambled after them, and Chloe ran along behind, curious to see who could make Hannah forget her troubles, even for a little while.

When she saw the woman up close she felt a jolt. Did she know this one?

The one called Anne Bailey let go the reins, handed her rifle off to Davy, then jumped right down from her horse like a feller, and clapped the captain on the shoulder. "John, you are a sight for sore eyes. But I sure am sorry to hear about your recent troubles."

The captain nodded. "Yes. We haven't had any word on John. Boone is headed east, though, and he will keep a sharp eye out—as only he can."

"Well, you're in good hands there." Anne looked at Chloe and Hannah. "Who do we have here? She clapped a hand on Hannah's head. "Surely this can't be Miss Hannah?"

Hannah looked down, shy all of a sudden.

"You are growing like a weed." Anne fixed her eyes on Chloe, squinted. "Who is this'un ye got here?"

"That's another Chloe," Hannah answered for her.

"Cory." Chloe/Cory corrected.

Anne raised her eyebrows.

"Yes," the Captain said, "Boone brought her. He got her when they did the captive trade—the treaty—up at Limestone. No folks claimed our Cory."

"What?" That big Anne kneeled down in front of her and cupped her chin in her hand.

"Well, I do declare. I knew this'uns folks. I know this here gal. You've got yourselves a Chloe Flynn."

# CHAPTER 30

## Five for Laughing

*One crow for sorrow*
*Two for mirth*
*Three for a wedding*
*Four for a birth*
*Five for laughing...*

**Polly**
**Winter 1788**

Besides the somewhat useless lessons in *Deutsch*—Polly just never could seem to form her mouth around those strange words—there were cooking lessons from Barbary, who wanted to be sure her son and grand-daughter would continue to get their favorite foods under Polly's care.

One winter evening as they had a supper of stewed chicken and *Klöße*, a new dish she'd learned to make from her mother-in-law, Adam made an announcement.

"I saw Isaac Estill today. He was at the mill, meeting with Jacob about a gunpowder order. He's married Betsy."

"Betsy Frogg?"

"*Ja.*"

Polly was silent, thinking. "She lost her pa at Point Pleasant?" Anne Bailey's face flashed in her mind. Point Pleasant was where Anne lost her first husband, her son William Trotter's father.

"*Ja*, they lost him. She was just a girl, but she dreamed it. The death. She woke from a nap and screamed to her mother that her father was *tot*—dead. No one believed her at first. But he had been killed at Point Pleasant, right at the time of her dream."

Polly recollected Nancy's dream. So long ago it seemed, but also like only yesterday. No one had taken that prediction seriously, either.

Or had they? Had Mam sensed what was about to happen?

Elsie, now finished with supper, took her *Puppe*, a lovely doll crafted by *Großmutter* Barbara, to the small cradle built by *Großpapa* Johann. Baby Adam lay sleeping in the larger cradle nearby.

Polly wondered about the newlyweds. "Will they live in the stone house?" The Estills were among the earliest settlers in these parts. The stone house was built by Isaac's father, Wallace, around the same time Cook's Fort was built. Adam and Jacob had helped build the massive Estill place back when Isaac—who was much closer to Polly's age than Adam's—was only seven. Later on they also helped build the Cook's Mill, where folks along Indian Creek ground their corn and rye.

The Estill house was even bigger than the Big House on the Mays' plantation. It was three stories tall, with walls eighteen inches thick. With the Great Road going in all the way to Lexington and newly married young couples all along Indian Creek, their community would soon be lively. The last few months had seen Priscilla marry Adam's cousin, Jacob, and now the Estills were newlywed. And within the year, Lizzy Stigard was sure to marry the Frenchman, Joshua Louis Michel—now calling himself Mitchell, who had fought with Rochambeau alongside Washington in the Battle of York.

Lizzy *knew* they would marry. After all, this New Year's Eve, her *Bleigeßen*—in the shape of a *fleur de lis*—had clearly predicted that blessed event.

Daniel Jarrell with his brood lived on a bordering property, but their marriageable sons were working away from Indian Creek at present. Polly did not mind that these neighbors were not frequent visitors, what with the rascal Simeon and his tricks.

At the rate of weddings hereabouts, not to mention all the Mann and Miller cousins, baby Adam and Elsie would have plenty of playmates as the years went by.

There was a fine kitchen in the house Polly shared with Adam and the children. Barbary had made sure her daughter-in-law was provided with spiders, trivets, and all manner of weights and pulleys crafted by Old Johann. There was even a spitjack for turning the meat that roasted in the hearth oven. Cooking now was far less a chore. Polly suspected even the cooks at Mays' plantation would even admire such a kitchen.

She reflected on her peaceful day she as she prepared  Barbary's receipt for sauerbraten. The children and their cousins had spent the day with *Großmutter* Barbary at Mann's Station. Polly was grateful they would be tuckered out when they returned, and she herself would have a chance for a restful evening, too.

She hummed as she stuffed bits of bacon and onions into holes pierced into a tender hunk of beef. Later, she would place the meat in a crock and soak it for three days in vinegar water with pieces of onion and spices. Learning to cook food the Prussian way was far easier than learning their language.

The flock of crows—there were at least five who made up the family that nested in one of the tall pine trees near the house—raised a ruckus. Then there was a dance of horses' hooves and a shout.

"Halloo!"

Polly wiped her hands on her apron and opened the front door to the wintry world without. She was shocked to see Anne Bailey there, on Liverpool. A little one was bundled up in front of her on the saddle, blankets tucked all round.

"Miss Polly." With a flourish, Anne swept off her broad-brimmed hat, the same as the men wore.

Anne's tiny companion also wore an oversized hat—perhaps one of Anne's extras. Anne pulled the hat off the child.

Polly's hand flew to her mouth and her heart stopped as the blonde curls tumbled out.

"I've brought ye your sister. Young Chloe."

# CHAPTER 31

## Midnight Ride

*...And bravely rode the woman there,*
*Where few would venture,*
*Few would dare...*

"*Anne Bailey's Ride,*" by Charles Robb

**Anne**
**Clendenin's Station**
**December 1789**

Anne could not shake off her dark mood. Oh, some folks might say things were getting better here, more civilized. Washington was president, and Kanawha was a county. Anne and her husband John made themselves useful at the fort built by Colonel Clendenin of the Kanawha Militia, situated where the Kanawha met the Elk River, not too far from the Battle of Point Pleasant—what some called the Battle of the Kanawha—where she had lost her first husband.

A settlement had sprung up, seven cabins with nigh on thirty settlers, as well as soldiers at the fort, of course. John served the Colonel as a ranger, and Anne still did her own bit of scouting and delivering news.

The Clendenins lived in the fort, which also served as courthouse and public house. At the first court meeting, Anne ran into old friends: Boone, Leonard Morris—the Flynns' neighbor back on Cabin Creek—and James Vanbibber, son of Boone's old friend Captain John Vanbibber. They'd all been made "gentlemen justices," as if one could imagine Boone with such a title.

Boone made good on his promise to come back and settle near John Vanbibber, and it was clear to all that Jesse Boone would soon be married to pretty young Chloe Vanbibber.

Now Boone had gone missing.

The Colonel reckoned he was dead.

The *United States Gazette* declared him dead.

He had gone out on business with his young son, Daniel, and never returned. Rumor had it Boone was kilt, and young Daniel taken. Or sometimes it was thought to be the other way around.

But she just couldn't feature it. True, the Shawnee were riled up as ever. In the last few years, fifteen hundred settlers had been killed or carried off, but Anne just couldn't picture Old Sheltowee as one of them, even though he had been captured and adopted by the Shawnee before.

Peevish, she sat on a stump outside the fort palisades, filled her pipe with tobacco and watched the smoke fade into the wintry air. Her husband, John, was at Fort Washington. Other scouts were off warning folks of impending attacks, or trying to pull in some volunteers for the militia. The job of recruiting men was now like pulling teeth.

The army wanted foot soldiers. And these boys from Kaintucke and Virginia sure could shoot; they'd learned from their paps or from men like James Halstead, Kenton, Boone, Logan, or even George Rogers Clark. But they fought best from the back of a horse, could shoot and reload their long rifles at a run. The sight of them boys scared the bejesus out of British spies if'n they stumbled upon their shooting contests—or worse—had to face off with them in battle. In the late war, Anne knew British soldiers gave buckskin-wearing backwoods militiamen a wide berth on the fields.

With so few volunteers, there was even talk of a draft. Anne snorted in disgust and took a long pull on her flask. Those with enough money could hire an immigrant to take their place, and that lot could not shoot a musket, let alone a long rifle. She shuddered at the thought of such "soldiers" facing off against the Shawnee.

She set aside her flask, heard a whistlin' and saw Andrew Wallace headed her way with one of the scouts and a young'un in tow. Wallace was an old highlander, rumored to be a rare survivor of Culloden. He'd been at Abercrombie's failed assault on the Ticonderoga where the Black Watch was butchered during the Old French War, had fought at Point Pleasant, *and* at Yorktown. The scarred old soldier was First Lieutenant of this Kanawha militia.

"The Colonel told me to bring ye this one," said Wallace. "Thought ye might know him." Wallace held the lad by the arm.

Anne looked into gray eyes that peered out under a mop of sandy hair, set in a pale face full of freckles. The *wamus*, leggings, and moccasins the boy wore were Shawnee made. He looked to be around twelve years of age.

"Well, it ain't John Flynn," she said, sour as a polecat. "And it ain't Jacob Vanbibber, nor his cousin Isaac, and it sure as hell ain't young Daniel Boone nor George Washington, neither."

She turned to the lad. "Speak up, young'un. What's yer name?"

The boy only stared at her.

The scout spoke up. "We cut him off from his raiding party. He doesn't have much English. But I got enough Shawnee to know he's a-scared of you, Anne."

Anne wished she could wipe the smirk off his face.

"On account of you bein' the Great White Squaw, magical and all." The young pup winked at her.

Anne was in no mood for teasing and ignored him.

"How long you been with the Shawnee, son?" she asked the young'un in a softer tone.

The boy remained silent, eyes wide.

"He cain't say," the scout broke in again. "I done asked him that. So I reckon he's been with them a long time. Since a baby."

Anne sighed, let out a quiet curse. Lord only knew who this one had belonged to. "We'll keep him at the fort, spread the word around Kaintucke and up and down the Ohio that we've got him here." She spat, then rose from the stump. She laid her hand on the boy's shoulder and noticed him flinch.

"No need to be afeared of me, son."

She turned to Wallace, "I'm headed off to home."

That evening the fort bell clanged, and Anne rousted herself from her pallet on the porch. She never could stand to sleep indoors if she could help it, especially if her husband John was away. She made her way to the meetinghouse where men thronged around three scouts who had recently returned with news.

"The Shawnee are up to more mischief. We got us'ns a new prisoner here who told us that in a few days' time they will attack the forts, including this one."

Faces were grim. No one made a peep. Anne knew they were low on gunpowder. In their present state they would not be able to defend themselves.

Colonel Clendenin spoke up. "I need someone to ride for powder. Tonight."

It was a hundred miles to Indian Creek, where they could get gunpowder from the Manns or from Cook's Fort.

Once more no one volunteered. The mounts of the newly returned scouts were worn out. The scouts, too, were exhausted. Clendenin's eyes darted around. He cleared his throat, waited. Anne reckoned Boone would have offered to go if he was here, but he wasn't. And she was restless.

"Colonel, I'll go," she called out.

No one else made any offers.

Clendenin glanced around again. Some refused to meet his eyes when he said, "I'll not send you alone."

Anne gave a snort. "I ain't never needed no escort. Ask that young'un that's locked up here. The Shawnee are a-scared of me. I trust in the Almighty and can only be killed once, and it ain't happened yet. But I ain't taking Liverpool on this journey." Liverpool was growing old; she dare not ride him hard. Clendenin had a few horses, among them a fine black one she guessed would do.

Clendenin paused, waiting for other offers. "You can take my Blackie," he said when none came.

A couple of scouts clapped her on the back and there was quite a commotion. Then she was off with Andrew Wallace to load up supplies for her trip.

"Lord willing I'll be back before too long, Andrew."

And she spurred Blackie off into the cold star-spangled night.

# CHAPTER 32

## The Cold Comfort

**John/Quetaske**
**Summer 1790**

The English words were mostly gone, except for trade words, and he didn't really need that language in this village along the Ohio. He knew the signs that would work just as good. He could talk some French, and because he'd been traded so many times he knew all the tongues of the Western Nations.

His foot had never healed up, so he was still lame. For that, his Shawanese captors called him, Quetaske, "One Who Limps."

That had only urged him on to better his considerable hunting skills. Otherwise, he'd have long ago been burnt, or worse yet, left a slave to work in the fields with the women.

He swallowed hard. He couldn't remember her face. The mother.

He knew there had been three sisters. Sometimes he dreamed of them, but their faces were smudged. One wore Shawanese dress. But whenever he came close to them, they went up in smoke. Gone.

In another dream of the one dressed like an Indian, she had a dog with her. But they disappeared into a woods that quickly sprouted a thicket, blocking the way for him to follow after her.

He rubbed a finger against his gun. He was the youngest boy in the tribe to have one, but they needed him to hunt, especially with most of the men off warring for the tribes that were banding together into a group that some called the Miami Confederacy, or Western Confederacy. He sat down to polish his musket, his main companion. Its cold comfort was better than none.

Hunger and circumstances had forced him to change his loyalties so many times. Now he had learned to be loyal to just one thing: Himself.

# CHAPTER 33

## The Great Serpent at Work

**Talitha/Nancy**
**September and October 1790**

Time in the village along the banks of the Maumee flowed smooth as the river. One day, memories of those days would carry a sweet scent of green corn and river grass.

Like stitches on a quilt, festivals joined the seasons of the year into a bright patchwork.

At Christmas, rendezvous, and festivals Nancy and Tepeke—Becky—often visited Kekionga. There had been changes in the villages since she first visited at that Christmas so long ago.

Shawneeawkee, the Silver Man, wasn't happy like before. If they got him to play his fiddle, it was mostly sad songs. Yes, he got the wife he thought he'd wanted—Kisathoi who used to live in Becky's village and was friends with Tecumseh and Sinnamatha, and the first Talitha Cuny. But now that Kisathoi was married to a white man, she wanted to be called Margaret, and she didn't cotton to having Shawanese custom in the store when she was there. She even pretended she did not know Becky. She'd turned ornery, didn't mix with the others in Kekionga but for her sister, Tebethto, now called Elizabeth.

Elizabeth, who lived right next door to Kisathoi—Margaret—and Shawneeawkee, wasn't nearly so angry all the time. But old Margaret pestered Silver Man night and day to go find her old white pa so she could have her old white family again.

Dove Trees was Nancy's near constant companion. And she'd been right about at least one thing. Since his vision quest, White

Buffalo was with the men most of the time, and Johnny Logan only occasionally returned to the northern villages.

So now it was just Nancy and Dove Trees who practiced reading together under the oak. But even with those reading lessons, Nancy—Talitha—had lost a lot of English. Yes, she could still read some, but she surely had no knack for writing. At least she was better than poor Dove Trees who could only read the simplest English words and couldn't write at all.

White Buffalo told her the whole thing was a waste. "The way things are going, Talitha, the Long Knives will soon leave and stay on their own side of the mountains, just like they promised earlier. Then we Shawanese need not worry about reading and writing English." He smiled. "Except when we trade with our British fathers. We know even they will cheat us if they can."

Tecumseh and Sinnamatha were still down south with the Chickamauga Cherokee but rumored to return soon. Young warriors spent hours, sometimes days, in the council house, meeting with chiefs and elder women of the tribe, and the talk was all of war. Nancy was sorry that in this matter, Dove Trees held a wrong opinion. Battles did *not* seem as if they were coming to an end soon.

Nancy was lonesome for White Buffalo. He and his family stayed in the Kispoko village south of the Ohio River most of the time, but one day, late in the month the whites call September, he and Standing Elk came to the village along with some warrior chiefs—Kispokos, mostly.

They met in council with elders and peace chiefs. White Buffalo was not allowed in, so while the council met, he visited with Nancy and Dove Trees. All three suffered Becky's complaints as they sat together outside the *wegiwa*.

"Witches have been set loose on us. Motshee Monitoo makes his mischief on us. The war chiefs speak before the civil chiefs. The young chiefs do what they will while the world of the old chiefs is shattered. The wise women are disregarded. Disrespected. No one listens to the peace chiefs."

She let out a long disgusted breath. "And I think some of the sacred bundles must be lost. Evil spirits are around us, those pieces of the Great Serpent."

Talitha had been interested to find that just as a serpent had tricked old Eve in a story she remembered from the Bible of the whites, a serpent had caused all sorts of trouble for The People, the Shawanese, as well.

A funny look danced across White Buffalo's face as Tepeke continued her lament He never could stand to be among unhappy folks. Then he spoke up.

"I should be there, Aunt, in the council with the men. I am young, but I am ready to fight for The People." "So many are gone," she replied. "You are not so old. There will still be plenty of time left for you to fight."

"I am sixteen winters." His eyes were filled with longing as he looked past them towards the *msikamekwi*—council house. "I will go soon." He disagreed with Becky, but his tone held respect.

Nancy knew he did not wish to argue with Becky. She watched, amused as he turned the conversation away from dark things by reaching into a pack.

He pulled some bundles from it and flourished them before Tepeke. "Aunt, my mother sends you gifts!"

After the gifts—cloth and some new pots and pans—had been properly admired, there was a clamor. The council ended, warriors went their separate ways.

Standing Elk gestured to White Buffalo.

"Father calls and we must go. I will see you soon." White Buffalo hurried away to join his father and some Kispoko warriors. That evening they left for Kekionga.

A week later, as she and Dove Trees worked in the cornfields picking the ripe squash and beans that grew among the stalks, they were distracted by Scout's excited bark. White Buffalo was back. Scout ran to him, jumping and yipping.

He had only been gone a few days but seemed different. Older. More serious. "Come," he said, reaching for Talitha's hand. "You both have to leave. Right away."

Dove Trees dropped her basket in surprise, and vegetables scattered everywhere.

"Why?" they asked together.

"Just come." He bent to help gather up the spill. "You need to go to the Elkhart River. I'll tell you on the way." He lifted the basket. "But you may need all of this."

As they hurried back to the *wegiwa*, he gave them details of the meeting in Kekionga, held next to Shawneeawkee's store. More than fifty warriors had been there. Michiniqua—Little Turtle—the great Miami chief was among them, as was Blue Jacket of the Shawnees. There were also warriors of the Potawatamie, Sacs, and Foxes.

"While we were there, some of our scouts arrived. They warned us of a Long Knife called Harmar. He leads his men north along The Great Miami, and they will destroy every village in their path. Now my father and I must ride out to warn the other Mekoche and Wapatomica villages. After that we will return to Kekionga to wait for Harmar there, with Chief Little Turtle and our brothers."

Dove Trees turned around to face the fields where they had lately worked. "But what of the corn? And the rest of the harvest?"

"You will take what you can. Some of the old ones will not leave. They say they will hide and save what they are able."

"I don't want to go, either," Talitha said. How many homes would she lose? She, too stopped to gaze at the fields of crops. At her heels, Scout whined.

"You need to come." White Buffalo's voice had a commanding tone Talitha had not heard before.

Dove Trees moaned softly and tugged on her. "We do have to go. You weren't here when Logan's army came last time. Becky will never let you stay."

The other Talitha, she whom Johnny Logan called Priscilla, flitted across Talitha's mind, a fleeting shadow.

"Yes, you *will* go," added White Buffalo. "Already Aunt is packing."

Talitha's every step was filled with dread as they made their way to their lodges. "Surely they do not think they can destroy Kekionga?" She could not bear to think of Little Henri and Bright Star—and all her other friends there—under attack.

White Buffalo's face was grim. "My father says it is their main goal. It is our most important trade town, the richest of all, and our tribes will be crippled if it is taken."

They reached the village to find it in disarray. Women gathered packs and loaded horses. Children wailed. Animals made a ruckus, barking, and neighing. Squawking chickens were forced into baskets, and horses were herded together to be driven to the village to the west along the Elkhart River.

Though it was no job for men or boys, White Buffalo helped them bundle up blankets and clothing. Once more, Talitha gathered the bark box that held her treasures. Inside was the tiny doll she still had from when she was white, though now it looked very Shawanese, moccasins and all. But the little figure retained the dress made of a scrap of blue fabric, the same shade as her white pa's eyes.

Standing Elk trotted up, an urgent expression on his face. He drew White Buffalo aside, and soon their heads were together in deep conversation.

Talitha and Dove Trees were nearly finished with their packing when he returned astride his horse a short while later, war paint on his face, and his hair loose and shimmering around his shoulders, like Tecumseh's. He was sixteen summers now, and looked every bit a warrior of the united tribes, The Western Confederacy.

"Talitha, I have to go now with my father. But I will come back to find you on the Elkhart." Then he pressed his heels into his mount and wheeled away.

Talitha's heart sank as he grew smaller in the distance.

Dove Trees gaped after him, then grabbed her hand. "Little Sister, you know I have often wished for a husband. But that one acts like he is *already* your husband."

*After 20th October 1790*

The new village was a mishmash of many tribes. Several villages from the Wabash also had taken refuge along the Elkhart, and many found it hard to get used to their new surroundings. Or in the case of their hosts, to get used to the newly arrived. After working in the nearby fields, Talitha often escaped with Scout to the banks of the river, where she wove grass mats for the new lodge and watched the clouds, wondering about the fate of White Buffalo, Standing Elk, and the others she knew. She prayed to both Moneto and Jesus.

And after several days, her prayers were answered.

Dove Trees raced towards her, flushed and brimming with joy. She stopped near them in the shade of a willow and panted, "The warriors are back. I saw White Buffalo."

Talitha's face broke into smiles, and she began to gather her things.

Dove Trees reached out a hand to stop her. "The ceremonial fires are being built. They are meeting in the council house with the chiefs. But you will see them tonight."

There were victory dances that evening. Songs were sung, and heroic feats were praised, but the celebration was subdued. Though many Long Knives had been killed in the recent battles, the Shawanese also suffered huge losses. By now, some of the old ones, those they'd left behind to hide in caves or woods near the abandoned villages, had arrived. These brought with them tales of destruction, of the burning and plunder of their homes by drunken Shemanese in the company of an even drunker General Harmar. From now on, the clans must make every effort to put by enough food to make it through the winter, though surely the English Fathers would help them.

When Nancy awoke early the next day, she was not surprised to find that the men already had left on hunting forays. And still she had not yet spoken to White Buffalo.

She longed to be with him, to talk to him. As the days shortened into late autumn, she glimpsed him from time to time about the village, but always from a distance. Just when she'd manage to catch his eye, he'd quickly turn away. Or maybe he had never seen her at all? Her heart was sore.

It was a few days later, as she and Scout made their way to her spot on the riverbank, that she came upon him, fishing in the shallows. Scout gave a short yip and leapt to greet him. White Buffalo slowly turned to her.

"Hello," he said. His eyes met hers and then seemed to look beyond her.

"I'm glad you are back." She felt silly, strange, torn between anger that he had not looked for her earlier, and relief, to finally have him here before her, unharmed, glowing in the glittery reflections off the water.

"Yes." He lay down his spear. "We have been busy hunting, trying to get enough food stores before winter."

She ignored this. In spite of all the work, there was always a chance for a visit in the villages, especially this crowded one.

"I thought I'd see you in the evening, at the fires." Her tone accused him.

He avoided her eyes. "We had to help those in the village who have lost their men."

"We have no men."

"Yes. But." His eyes held hurt. "I knew *you* were fine. My father told me he had spoken with the female chiefs. They said you would be provided for by your many sisters and brothers. And I know you have been."

He reached into a basket beside him, and unwrapped a fish that lay covered in river grass. He carefully placed it in her own basket, under her newly woven mats.

He reached out and touched her cheek. "And you are like my sister. While I am around you will never go without."

The angry and confused band around her heart loosened. Though a little voice inside her reminded her she would rather be *more* than a sister.

White Buffalo lowered himself to sit on the bank, and Scout snuggled in beside him, licking his hand. Talitha sat beside them.

"You were at the battle."

His face clouded. "Yes. Eel River, with my father. Besides the Shawanese from the Glaize and here, there were other warriors from Kekionga and Le Gris' village. About a hundred of us."

"We attacked the Long Knives from three sides. Killed forty or so. I took scalps." He glanced up quickly, saw her eyes widen. "But we took them that we might receive bounty for them, from the British in Detroit."

Talitha realized that with the need for food, trading the scalps for supplies was a better idea than keeping them for trophies.

He laughed, but it wasn't a happy laugh. "We hunted a buffalo, and some even took the hump from him and stretched it just to look like a white man—or black man's—hair, and sent that in, too. They said the English Fathers would never know."

They sat quietly a moment.

"Then we waited above Kekionga and ambushed some more soldiers. We killed around twenty before they fled, but two days later they were back with reinforcements. Not enough, though. We outnumbered them three to one."

There was great pride in his voice as he continued. "Little Turtle was brilliant. Once more he led us to attack them from three sides. We killed so many. Around one hundred thirty. And nearly as many lay wounded."

His face grew somber again. "Little Turtle calls it 'The Battle of the Pumpkin Fields.'"

Her eyes questioned him again.

His voice grew soft as he stared into the gray river. "There were so many of them lying dead in the field, scalped. Mist rose from their bloody heads where their hair had been, and Little Turtle said it reminded him of how we steam squash in the autumn haze."

A jolt ran through her. Her mind fled back to another October, a hank of bloody red hair hanging from a club. For one brief moment she was Nancy Flynn again.

White Buffalo seemed to read her mind. "Then I thought about you. Your white father. And what Johnny Logan said about Captain

Logan, his white adopted father and how he'd never fight against him. I fought beside one named Apekonit, from Eel River. He has red hair. Like some of the colors in your hair."

He leaned forward and held one of her braids toward the dim sunlight. Glints of red danced off the auburn plaits. The oils she rubbed in her hair never could dim the bright strands, try as she might.

"He's a white Indian, like you. Apekonit is son of Chief Gaviahate, known as Porcupine. He had a wife and daughter of the Wea. But a white war chief called Wilkinson took them in a raid, and he believes they are no more. Apekonit told me his white brothers found him a year or two ago. His white name is William Wells. He said he would never want to come up against his white brothers in battle, though he is one of the bravest warriors I saw."

In spite of these tales of victory, White Buffalo's face was troubled.

"We had losses, too. At the Pumpkin Field alone we lost around one hundred twenty men. Blue Jacket's niece, Bluebird, was mistakenly left behind in her village on the Maumee, and the Long Knives took her. Some say she is held by one named John Hardin, a brave heart who fought us off for more than three hours while we had him surrounded. He did escape, though he lost many men."

White Buffalo's face darkened as he continued. "Becky was right about one thing, though I did not want to tell her. Tecumseh told me the sacred war bundles, *meesawmi, were* lost at the Battle at Point Pleasant. That knowledge has been kept from the people, to save their hearts from breaking. Perhaps the bundles will turn up yet. But for now we have nothing but troubles."

He stared into the river. "He seemed torn between the two worlds, that Apekonit." The eyes that lifted were filled with concern. "Are you? If you return to the whites will you marry a white man and act like Kisathoi, who now will only answer to the name 'Margaret'?"

White Buffalo hated Shawneeawkee's angry wife, Margaret Kinzie, and had to be coaxed into John Kinzie's post.

Talitha reached for his hand. Though she had held it a hundred times, she felt a pleasant shock as he wrapped his around hers, though his brown eyes still troubled.

"No," she replied, "I am not in two worlds. I am Shawanese. Like you. My heart is your heart."

A fish jumped.

White Buffalo smiled into her eyes, and this time she did not know if it was a fish in the water, or a fish in her veins that leaped.

"Dinner," he said, and reached for his spear.

# CHAPTER 34

## Return to the War Path

**Polly**
**October 1790**

She couldn't lift the water pail; it was wedged against a rock or some such. Polly swatted a gnat from her eyes and bent down to release the bucket. Fear gripped her as she glimpsed a dusty boot perched on the rim, holding it down.

There were workers nearby, neighbors and some hired men laboring on the road. Rough characters, some of them. Her heart pounded as her eyes followed the boot leather up a pair of fringed leggings topped by a soldier's jacket. Above the collar was the face of her Uncle, James Halstead.

She jumped, yelped. Water splashed everywhere.

They gave each other wet hugs before they stopped to take stock of one another. James's hair was nearly white now, but his eyes were yet a startling blue against his tanned face. The crow's feet surrounding them deepened as he gazed on her, smiling.

"Would you look at you, now, " he said. "All growed up."

"I must look a sorry sight," was all she could say. She patted her hair back in place and smoothed out her skirts, felt all of fourteen again.

"Well, to me you're a sight for sore eyes." He glanced up the slope at the house. "I stopped up home already and saw the young'uns. Fine children. They wanted to come down here with me, but I told them I aimed to surprise you."

He chuckled. "Still, it was hard to stop that Cory. She said Old Boone learnt her how to sneak up on folks, so I should let her come, too. Tried to stare me down." He laughed again. "She's a mind of her own. Reminds me of Nancy."

"She's more wild than Nancy ever was, if you can imagine." Polly looked up towards the cabin. The children had stayed where James told them, but they raced around now, excited over this stranger. Polly shook her head, exasperated, as Chloe chased after Elsie with a stick, the fringe on her buckskin shirt flying.

"I can't get her to take off those buckskins. Apparently, that's all she wore when she was with the Boones. Young Miss—Chloe Vanbibber—made a couple of dresses for her to match her own, and Cory looks pretty in those when I can get them on her. She's almost like a doll with all those blonde curls. But she's like to tear or dirty the frocks if she wears them more than one minute."

As they watched her run towards them, Polly noted with satisfaction that Cory had almost outgrown her leggings. "But that *wamus*—the shirt—may take a while for her to wear out." She frowned as she thought on some of Chloe's other troubling habits. "I'm not sure what I'll do with her. She hates her lessons. I can't hardly school her at all. And she won't mind Barbary. Claims she can't understand her, when I know full well she can."

James grinned. "So she's full of the dickens."

"You could say that."

Yet there were some bright spots she should mention. "At least she has taken to Adam. She'd rather be with him in the fields or at the mill than here helping me. And she actually looks more like him than his own daughter Elsie does, which pleases her and causes much grief for poor Elsie."

While they watched the children rough house, Polly pondered all the lost fathers and mothers. The sad events of the past crowded in, but the pull of the present won out as the young'uns raced over to join them, whooping and hollering. As Chloe ran on the attack towards

James, he reached down and then tossed her up in the air, laughing at her shrieks.

Polly wondered just who this happy Uncle James was, this one who was suddenly treating her like a grownup. Well, she was now, wasn't she? Four short years and so many things changed.

He set Chloe down and the children ran off again, hollering and screaming.

"She's got the gray eyes." He looked after her wistfully. "Like your ma, Elizabeth." So he missed Mam, too, Polly realized. She *was* his younger sister, after all.

"Cory doesn't remember what happened to any of them."

"Poor little mite. Not remembering might be a blessing. From what I've heard and seen," James said.

"You're not here because you've learned something about the others, are you?" A glimmer of hope struck her. First Priscilla, and now Chloe. Folks *did* return to their families, sometimes.

"Ah, no," he let out a long, tired breath. "I've been at Vincennes, with Hamtramck. We went down the Wabash. Tried to draw the Shawnee off Harmar—the General— who is right now striking there. But the Kickapoo were on to us, warned the Shawnee so's that all the villages we came across were abandoned. We burned whatever they left behind. A scout we ran into later on told us our presence drew off six hundred or so of the Indians who were set to strike Harmar's forces."

There were troubling reports of General Josiah Harmar. Harmar was important and had once been a brilliant soldier. Back in 1783 he was riding high on a wave of success, even chosen to carry the signed Treaty of Paris to Ben Franklin. But rumor had it he had since taken to drink and become an unreliable commander.

"They took off and were just a-waiting there for us while we never showed. Best fight I never was in." James flashed a wry smile. "We only had half their strength. Good thing we turned around."

He looked around in wonderment. "It's been so long since I've seen you, and to know you have Chloe back, or Cory, as I guess she's fixed on being called." He paused for a moment, swallowed hard.

"I asked leave from Hamtramck to stop here before I went back. Said I'd check at the mill about the possibility of munitions. That went down easy with him. A lot are deserting. The colonel seemed almost grateful that I at least asked before I took off. Though, of course, I'll go back. Unlike many others. I'll meet back up with them at Vincennes."

A horse whinnied.

"That'd be old Apollo, asking for dinner. He's lucky to make it through this last campaign without being 'et himself like some of his friends. I better get up to see to him."

Polly reached for him, caught his sleeve. "But you'll stay the night?"

"Surely."

She called up to the young'uns to help her with the pails.

Adam always asked strangers who came into the mills or the smithy if they'd seen any folks like the missing Flynns.

Once in awhile some soldier or trader claimed to have seen a boy like John—a dark one with a pronounced limp—in the company of Indians or traders, but the stories never matched up. One person told how he'd come across him with Ottawas up near Detroit while another said he had spied him at some post up the Mississippi. But no one ever seemed to have noticed anyone who matched the description of Nancy or Mam.

They asked James if he had heard anything on his travels.

"I did hear tell of a captive boy who'd be near his age. But he was blonde. Told a trapper his name was 'Van' something or other. Dutch, I guess. I wish I had more to tell."

The children cut up at the supper table, putting on a show for Uncle James, even Elsie. But now they slept like a pile of puppies on a bearskin rug by the fire while the men lit up pipes and sipped on rye. Polly knitted.

The call of an owl softly echoed in the dark October night.

Polly asked James, "What do you hear of Marie?"

"What?" He looked as if he had been slapped.

"Marie DeForest." Polly set down her handwork. " How is she?"

"Ah, yes. You two were close. Well, I saw her when I was down at Post Vincennes, before, when I was getting ready for this march. Her pa is a part of that Beaver Club up in Montreal now, so he has her doing some trading down at Vincennes."

He took a long draught on his spirits, and his face reddened.

Was it the rye or something else?

"She speaks French, which comes in handy down there, you know. Since her mother was Delaware she knows how to talk with a lot of the tribes."

He pulled on his drink again. "Seems she's turned into a bit of a nurse, too—been helping folks around the fort." He cleared his throat and studied the amber liquid in his mug.

"Still no beau for her?"

Adam raised his brows at Polly, curious, but she ignored him and fixed her eyes on James.

"No." He gulped his rye. "Not that there ain't plenty who'd like to court her."

Polly waited for more details, but James gave none. Instead, he wiped his mouth.

"I'll be sure to give her your regards." He aimed himself towards the fire, took an interest in the sleeping children.

"Seeing Chloe with you again sure brings back memories. Gives me encouragement. There's bound to be more exchanges after these wars up on the Maumee. I heard Hardin had one of Blue Jacket's nieces. Bluebird, I think she's called. She'll be sure to fetch a fair trade. The kin of those chiefs always do bring a good price."

Seeing James brought back so many recollections of the fort and Marie. As she readied herself for bed, Polly brushed her hair and reminisced on the times they'd spent together. She chuckled when she thought about Marie's attempts to school her.

Adam sat in bed reading by the soft candle-light.

"What amuses you, *Liebchen*?"

"Did you see James's face when I brought up Marie's name?"

Adam glanced up from his book. "*Ja*. I thought he would swallow his tongue."

"Those two started out likely to kill each other. He's surely taken a shine to her now." Polly settled into bed beside her husband. "What are you reading?"

Adam held up the leather bound volume. The gilt script was in Deutsch. "*Ach*," he said, seeing her puzzlement. "*The Sorrows of Young Werther*." Too sorrowful for me tonight, I think. Why don't you tell me a story, *Liebchen*?"

"Oh, I am just thinking back to before I met you. Before I lived with the Mays. Marie had plenty of advice for me then. And now here we are; so much has changed." She paused, pondering. "Do you think he is sweet on her? Isn't he too old for her?"

"Pshaw. No he is not too old." He pinched her cheek. "There are a few years between us, after all, *Liebchen*. *Und ja*. It is all over for him. He is—what do you say? Smitten. Life is over for him now she has him by the neck."

Polly thumped him playfully. "Oh, you tease me."

"*Nein.* I can see he cares for her."

"Hmmm." Polly ran her fingers through her hair, thoughtfully. "She never cared one whit for any of the men at the fort. Thought they were no account. None wore the fine cockades she had seen elsewheres. In fact, you know our militia don't even *have* uniforms."

"And you, *meine Liebchen*, did you give a whit for the men at the fort?" He pulled her more tightly against him."

"No! And stop it! He'll hear!" she hissed.

"Well, just think. If they ever were married, Marie would be your aunt. Dear old *Tante* Marie."

He kissed her mouth before she could respond. "As for the rest of your family, James seems to think—I think—You may get them back yet."

"I have my family." Polly burrowed into him, inhaled the vanilla smell she loved so well. "But maybe. Yes."

# CHAPTER 35

## "Expence without Honor or Profit"
### George Washington on Harmar's Defeat

**Polly**
**Early November 1790**

Supper simmered on the hearth while Polly went to the porch to watch out for Adam. He should have been home by now. She heard horses and muffled voices, and then through the trees skirting the road she spied them, Adam trotting on Schultzie, and beside him a thin pale shadow on a gaunt black horse. Pitiful. As they drew closer, she recognized the horse before she did the rider.

So did Dolly, who whinnied to him from the field.

Polly stared in shock at Sabre, the once magnificent stallion, now a frail skeleton. Mounted on his wretched back was Moses Mays in a similar condition. Polly held back from greeting him. *This* Moses Mays did not match the proud man of her memory. Thankfully, the children still played at the creek, and there would be peace until she rang the supper bell.

She watched the men dismount and head off to the barn to put the horses away. Then she slipped into the kitchen and evesdropped when they returned and stopped on the porch to smoke.

"It is the worse loss yet of American soldiers at the hands of the Indians," Moses said. He let out a ragged breath. "General Harmar's brilliant campaign now is known as Harmar's Defeat." His voice was tired, hardly more than a whisper. "Caesar, my good man, was with me throughout. And Sabre, too, of course. I will not ride that one farther, but give my loyal companion the rest he deserves on the journey home."

The conversation died away.

"Supper's on," Polly announced.

"Miss Polly," was all Moses said as he sat down at the table. He ate hungrily and silently. The children, in from the creek, caught the melancholy mood and ate quietly for once.

"We have been at Jacob's," Adam explained. "Moses is buying some horses from him, and Caesar is at the smithy fitting them."

Moses nodded, fixed on his food. Yes, this frail gray creature was a far cry from the well-fed tomcat of a man that Polly remembered from her long-ago stay in Augusta at the Mays' plantation. Half-starved, he'd glance up only briefly to respond to Adam's questions. Mercifully those did not concern the recent battle, but Moses' plans for the plantation.

At a pause in the conversation, they invited Moses to bring his bedroll in and sleep before the fire, and he gratefully accepted.

He dipped his head in thanks. "Caesar will sleep in Jacob's stable, and we will make an early start for home tomorrow." His eyes met Polly's for a brief moment, and she caught a glimpse of the old tomcat. "I appreciate your kindness, Miss Polly, Adam." He ducked his head again, eating ravenously, then raised it to ask, "May I have some more sausage?"

Elsie passed him the plate, and he attacked his supper anew.

Afterwards, he quietly excused himself to the porch to smoke. Adam pulled out a jug of rye and two glasses, and left to join him. Uneasy and unsettled by the changes in their guest, Polly put the young ones down for the night.

She drowsed off before Adam came to bed, but when she rose early to wait on their company, she discovered Moses was already gone. Adam heard her moving about and soon came to her, wrapping his arms around her as she readied corn cakes and rashers for breakfast.

"What happened to him?" She gently removed his arms so she could return to her task. She understood from listening the night before that the Americans had suffered a horrible loss. Surely that alone could not explain the drastic difference in Moses Mays?

Adam poured himself a mug of hot coffee and sat on a kitchen stool. "He has found out what it is to be a month in hell."

"But he is seasoned. He distinguished himself in the War for Independence. Decorated, even. Charlotte told me. *Many* times."

"Fighting the Shawnee is a far different thing. The British may pay for scalps, but they don't like to be seen taking them themselves. Nor do they occasionally eat a foe's heart, or burn him to death." He took a sip of coffee, gazed thoughtfully into the cup. "On the other hand, the Shawnee do not rape enemy women, as many British did in the last war."

She shuddered, smelled a corncake about to burn.

"I'm glad James was with Hamtramck."

"*Ja*. That was *güt*. While James headed north from Vincennes, Moses traveled along the Miami with General Harmar's force. Most of the villages they set out to destroy were already deserted. Moses said Harmar and half the men were drunk most of the time. Wasted their time looting. Pillaging." His open face grew somber. "I imagine, they did some of the sins they accuse the British of."

"When they got up to Le Gris' Village, Moses went out with Hardin's cavalry. They set out after a lone Shawnee—turned out to be a decoy—into a swamp where Little Turtle ambushed them on three sides. Fontaine's horsemen had followed as backup, but Hardin sent them out after stragglers, which left him with no reserves. They were greatly outnumbered. Moses was in a group of men who finally escaped with Hardin."

Adam took another drink of coffee. "They warned off Fontaine and his men. Out of thirty regulars, only eight lived. Nearly a quarter of the militia was killed. Hardin is taking some of the blame."

This was bad news, but Polly had heard much worse over the years. She raised her eyebrows in question.

"It wasn't over. The next day the General—Harmar—sent out three hundred more men, back to the site of the ambush, and *they* were attacked. So he retreats in a panic, then later on refuses to let his men go back for the dead. Almost a mutiny then. Hardin finally got permission to take a company out to the battlefield and bury the fallen."

"And Moses worked on that unpleasant detail." Adam shook his head as if he were trying to shake off the image.

Polly poked the bacon frying on the cast iron griddle, then raised her head. "And?"

"When they started on their way again, they found a thousand warriors waiting for them at Kekionga."

"Ah, no." A shiver took her, and she left the hearth and sank to her knees near Adam, clung to his free hand with her own. The old panic seized her again, that fear that had never really left since that day she lost her family so long ago.

Yes, Harmar's battles were far from home at present, but if the Shawnee and their friends continued to devastate the American army, could they take back this valley? The whole territory? She could not let herself think on that.

"*Ja.* A mess. Hardin had only four hundred—counting Moses. He sent for reinforcements, but his messenger found General Harmar drunk. Instead of coming to their aid, the General moved his men into a defensive position. Wouldn't budge."

Polly squeezed her eyes shut tight, tried to block the hopeless image.

"Hardin's men fought well, but they lost many. Fontaine was killed. Three hours they fought, before they fell back and rejoined the General's company."

He paused and stared into his mug of coffee. "There's rumor General Harmar is asking for his own court martial—but that's mainly so's he can clear himself. Thinks if he requests it, it'll just be a case of clearing his own name. St. Clair's taking over."

He took another sip and and gazed into the fire. With the near-constant activity at the gunpowder mill and smithy, weaponry and war were a daily part of the Mann family's lives. They were safer than most. But that did not make it easy for the wives, perhaps not so easy for some of the husbands, either.

Yes, Adam had seen his own share of fighting, both in the War for Independence, and against the Indians in the forts out here in the Territory. Yet he was a tender man. This time it was she who rose and slipped behind him to wrap him in her arms.

"And now he is on his way back to Charlotte," she said.

"*Ja.* It is so late in the season. There is not enough forage for the horses. They starve, and the men are deserting. Moses easily received permission for leave." He gave her a wry grin. "I am a little surprised to see he is already gone. This is one of the first times I have known him in a hurry to get back to Charlotte."

# CHAPTER 36

## The Battle of a Thousand Slain

### St Clair's Defeat

**Anne**
**Boone's Tavern at Limestone**
**November 1791**

Anne and Boone had gone downriver in Dan'l's flat bottom boat to await news of the Battle on the Wabash. She watched as ragged scouts and soldiers straggled in stopping for rest on their way to Fort Washington.

Yes! Boone lived!

Two years ago he had been declared dead, but had merely been extending a successful hunting trip, so prosperous he'd hated to quit. He and his son, young Daniel, surprised the folks back at Fort Clendenin when they showed up in January, alive and kicking, and laden with furs and tales of several other caches left hanging in the woods.

Boone liked to tease her now. Some folks called her a hero and treated her special on account of what they called her "Wild Ride." She never had to buy her own drinks anymore, that was sure and certain. After returning to the fort with the much needed gunpowder a year ago, folks took to calling her the" Squaw of the Kanawha." Embarrassed her half to death.

But today she sat in the tavern on her own, smoked and fretted. Boone's daughter was running the Limestone Tavern with her husband Philip Goe, now that Boone had moved over by the Vanbibbers at Clendenin's Station. Boone was with young Rebecca now, having a look at the wares over in the storehouse.

In spite of the good fortune of finding Boone among the living, Anne had a bad feeling.

Earlier that year she helped recruit militia for St Clair. He was to lead them down the Wabash and build a fort at Kekionga—once they had driven out all the redskins along the way, of course. St Clair wanted a thousand foot soldiers from Kentucky, but the Kaintuckes wanted to fight on horseback, as was their custom. So many, like Moses Mays, who had weathered Harmar's catastrophe, refused to go, and untrained immigrants took the places of seasoned men.

She couldn't blame Moses. After Harmar's Defeat, he'd had a bellyful of war for a while, had earned a break from battle.

To make matters even worse, in the midst of recruitment, the rains started and ague raged throughout the territory. Despite widespread reluctance and illness, some of the best soldiers she'd ever known had answered the call.

But many more joined up that had never even fired a rifle.

The tavern door swung open and brought in a gust of cold autumn wind, a splash of dead leaves. Two weary soldiers limped in. Anne's heart leapt. One was Captain Edward Butler, the youngest of the famous brothers, "The Fighting Butlers," heroes of the late war. If she and Boone had a modicum of fame, the Butlers surpassed them tenfold. After Cornwallis' surrender, Washington had tried to bestow the vanquished general's sword on Richard Butler, the eldest of the five, who shared the command of this latest campaign with St. Clair.

Butler had declined, and offered it to his second, Ebenezer Denny. This nearly set off a duel with Baron Van Steuben, who would have liked it for himself. There was no shortage of legends about the Butlers.

Richard Butler was especially well known in these parts. After the war with the British, he had been an Indian agent hereabouts, even had a son with Cornstalk's sister, Nonhelema, the Grenadier Squaw. Yes, the Butlers were five of a kind. No less than Lafayette had said, "If you want a job done well, give it to a Butler."

*Why was Edward Butler in such a sorry state?*

Anne caught his eye and waved the two men over. As Butler made his way, she noticed he limped and bore a purpling gash on his pale face.

"Anne Bailey. It is good to see your face."

She stood to greet him, clapped his hand in hers. Edward's companion, arm in a sling, nodded hello.

The tavern wench brought them food: roasted venison, squash and cornbread, a pitcher of ale. Anne watched as the men attacked the victuals as if they hadn't eaten for days. Finally Edward leaned back, pushed his trencher away.

He did not meet her eyes. "My brother Richard is dead," he mumbled.

Anne cupped her ear. Surely she had misheard. "Beg your pardon?"

"Richard is dead."

Richard the Invincible, dead?

Something had gone horribly wrong.

Edward's pale blue eyes stared into the distance and he spoke as if in a trance. "He forced me to leave him. Told me I had to get Thomas—our brother Thomas, both his legs were broken—out of there. Richard was hurt too bad." Edward faltered, fumbled with his fork. After a moment he continued. "He had me prop him up in his tent, held a pistol in each hand...and ordered us to ride. That's the last I saw of him."

He gulped his ale. "He gave his sword to one of his men. Told them to never wipe the blood off." He locked his eyes on hers. "I know you lost your first husband at Point Pleasant, Anne. But you never saw anything like this in your life."

"We lost our cannon. Some white Indian—Apekonit, they called him—led the Miami. Destroyed the artillery." He shook his head. "Now the redskins have even more of our weapons. But the worst was yet to come."

What followed was a most gruesome tale of more than six hundred men lost and a third more wounded. Half the officers were wounded or killed. The US army was decimated.

"One of my men, his son hid in a downed tree. St Clair's call to retreat had been given almost immediately, you see. The Indians gave chase to those on the run—which was everyone who still had legs to do so—so the boy came out of hiding and searched the field for his father. The wounded, most of them already scalped, begged for him to finish them off. But he could hear Little Turtle's men returning, and hid again in the branches and brush."

Edward's silent companion rose and made for the door.

"His wife and child were killed there. Camp followers. He has no stomach for listening to this again." Edward pulled out his pipe. His hand trembled as he filled it with tobacco, took a long draw.

"The lad was trapped there. Could do nothing but watch and listen as those still living were tied to trees, their heads used as targets for tomahawks. Nigh two hundred camp followers, —wives and children, not just whores and washerwomen—were put to death. St Clair had hoped to set up a town after winning the battle. Well, it is a town, all right. A town of bones." Edward's bitterness stung the smoky air.

Gorge welled up from Anne's guts. She had recruited men for the militia, helped send them to their deaths. Hot tears blinded her as she rose and grasped Butler's shoulder.

"Butler, you must pardon me, I am unwell," she stammered and stumbled away.

# CHAPTER 37

## A Hazardous Business

**John/Quetaske**
**Spring 1792**

Long Knives—soldiers—spied him out hunting. Caught him. They were stunned that he was a crack shot at the tender age of thirteen or so—he never was sure of his age—summers. They also were astonished he had so little English. But one of them spoke French, so he was able to tell them at least some of his history. And each day in their company he was able to recall a few more words of English. He could not speak it too well, but was steadily gaining clearer understanding.

The soldiers ended up passing him on to a company of scouts led by a white named Hardin, Colonel John Hardin. Hardin was on a mission commanded by the President George Washington himself. The War Secretary Henry Knox, told Hardin's commander, a General Wilkinson, to get together some men together to carry a peace message to the Shawanese, Miami, and Delaware. After the heavy American losses in the last few fights, especially Harmar's Defeat, the Long Knives were ready to make peace. Now he himself, John Who Limps, was part of this mission.

One of the soldiers who handed him on to the scouts with Hardin had once lived with the Indians. William Smalley assured Hardin that John could talk in at least seven Indian tongues, and French, too. Smalley had been a white Indian adopted into the Delaware. He still wore the ear decorations to prove it. He knew most of the Indian languages John did, and French, too, but also could talk English better than John. Sometimes he called John "Quetaske," his old Indian name, and John did not care for that. Now that he was among the whites, he liked the way the name "John" fell upon his ears. Plus it was Hardin's given name.

There had been some arguments among Hardin's men over taking on a young'un. Then they had a shooting contest and let him take a turn. That's when old Hardin took notice of him. A keen marksman, the Colonel always won the contests and let out a holler and a whoop of laughter when John came close to besting him.

Plucked out of his leadership of the Kentucky Militia, the Colonel with this group traveled from Fort Washington, through the ruined villages—some now rebuilt—along the route of Harmar and St. Clair.

There were other messengers besides Hardin. Major Alexander Trueman came out of the Regular Army. A third man, Dr. Isaac Freeman, had two assistants: Thomas Lynch and William Smalley.

Dr. Freeman had Joseph Gerrard to help him, because Gerrard, too, knew some Indian tongues and French. And John himself had been paired up with Colonel Hardin.

John took a liking to the man. The Colonel had lots of stories, and John could make out the gist of most of them, even if his own English still wasn't so good.

Hardin had soldiered in Lord Dunmore's War, then the War Against the British Fathers where he was a sharpshooter in Morgan's Rifles, and most recently at a battle called Heller's Corners where he said the Americans took a lickin.'

And now, he was to beg for peace.

"Yes, John," the Colonel said, " I have fought the Shawnee alongside some of our best. Sheltowee—that's Daniel Boone—as well as Kenton, and Logan. I have had many successes, but I also have made my share of mistakes. That attack upon the Piankeshaw at Vincennes, I sorely regret that." He sat quiet awhile. "Perhaps this is my penance."

John had heard versions of what had transpired at Post Vincennes and the attack on the Piankeshaws many times, from French traders, different tribes, and a British soldier here or there. The Piankeshaw

Hardin regretted killing were friends with the Americans, and George Washington had commanded that no Piankeshaws be harmed in the Indian wars.

Hardin had attacked them by mistake, and this error led to many more battles and raids along the Wabash and the Buffalo Trace. Upon hearing this, John reckoned those skirmishes happened right along the time his own family was attacked and carried off to the tribes.

One day while out hunting their supper, Hardin asked him, "What of your own family, John? Your white family?"

John managed to come up with enough English to say his mother and father were dead, and he did not know what had become of his three sisters. He did not tell Hardin he could hardly remember their faces, and did not even rightly know his surname.

"Someday you will find them, or they will find you. Perhaps our work of peace will lead to the trading of many more captives, and you will see your lost sisters once more. I will help you to find them after our mission is over."

Problem was, John had no inkling of where to tell him to look.

"I have children who I bet would be your own age. They are home safe in their beds. And here you are with me, facing certain dangers along our way. I know your life has not been easy, lad."

Hardin then confided to John that he was not keen on the task laid before him. "I have had dreams that trouble me. This time, lad, I fear I will not make it back to my loved ones. Perhaps that is why I am all the more grateful for your kind company."

John remained silent, thinking on Hardin's words. Dreams and visions were Big Medicine. One of his sisters had even dreamed up their own capture.

Hardin interrupted his thoughts. "I got an Indian gal, a pretty little thing called Bluebird, in one of the raids. Says she's going to marry Tecumseh's cousin, a boy called High Horn, though I think some of my own sons would like to stand in the way of that. We've all have grown quite attached to her, though we'll have to give her back, of course, once all this peacemaking is over and done with. She has been teaching me some Shawnee. Reckon you could teach me more, John?"

Hardin and Smalley made him learn Washington's peace speech by heart. He recited it to them throughout the day so that he could say it to the different Indian tribes they came across. He had to be able to say it in the Indian tongues, which of course was easy, but also in English. That was much harder since he couldn't read a word of it. The big words felt strange on his tongue and he stumbled over them when Hardin had him repeat them after him. This was it:

Brothers:

The President of the United States entertains the opinion that the war which exists is founded in error and mistake on your part. That you believe that the United States wants to deprive you of your lands and drive you out of the country. Be assured that this is not so; on the contrary, that we should be greatly gratified with the opportunity of imparting to you all the blessings of civilized life, of teaching you to cultivate corn, to raise oxen, sheep and other domestic animal; to build comfortable houses; so as ever to dwell upon the land.

Oh, but it was hard not to laugh at some of it, and even the Colonel knew it was comical to pretend a feller could teach the Shawanese anything about growing corn.

The three groups of emissaries had clear instructions to travel together till they arrived at a certain junction where they would separate and head off in three different directions to the various villages. They came to the parting of their ways on the eighth day.

Hardin and John bid farewell to their companions and headed for the Shawnee villages. They were well received at the towns, but on Turtle Creek they met up with a small party of Shawanese warriors. Though they had spied a village earlier and planned to visit there now with their message, their visitors swayed them, urged them to wait until morning.

In spite of John's misgivings—he still really trusted no one—Hardin agreed to make camp and pass the evening with the men on the shores of the creek as a sign of goodwill.

Then they slaughtered him at dawn.

They kept John alive, he reckoned, on account of his skill as a hunter. He'd be useful.

Well. He'd wait and watch. He'd gotten free before and he'd do it again.

# CHAPTER 38

## Most Cheerful and Merry

**"They are the most cheerful and merry
people that I ever saw..."**
David Jones, unsuccessful missionary to the Shawnee

**Talitha**
**Late July 1794**

Kekionga, arisen from the ashes, thrived again. Many from their clan had returned to the rebuilt towns. The sun shone, and the corn grew tall in the fields near the river that bordered their homes.

Becky's heated complaints of witches and evil spirits had simmered down. Shawanese and their friends were still on the warpath, but this time they were winning. The previous month, a raid on Fort Recovery yielded nearly three hundred packhorses and cavalry mounts. Though many of the pack animals had been eaten, others had been sold or traded. The trade goods and supplies found their way to villages in distress.

Tecumseh, Sinnamatha, White Buffalo, and other young warriors were among those who'd handed out prizes to the needy. Becky now had a new brass pot and several woolen blankets along with plenty of food.

With the fields green and a brief respite from want, the female chiefs of the village met and decided that the celebration for this bounty would be combined with this year's Green Corn Festival.

And since Moneto now smiled upon The People, they would hold the Courting Dance as part of the gathering. Now was a good time, when so many different clans and tribes inhabited the village together due to the destruction of their own towns.

As she prepared food for the feast to come, Talitha smiled a secret smile. She already was courted, desired. She shook the sleeve of her blouse upwards and basked in the soft glow of the silver circle that glinted on her finger. It felt warm, warm as the touch of White Buffalo.

Earlier in the day, she had escaped to her spot by the river. Dove Trees worked on festivities in the village, and even Scout had stayed behind. Today he'd keep eager eyes on Becky and Dove Trees as they roasted meats for the feast, tossing him a juicy morsel from time to time.

She basked at the riverside, lost in her reverie when she felt a presence—a shadow danced across her. She turned at a rustling in the tall grasses and knew it was White Buffalo before she glimpsed the strong dark legs, the long black hair, and the startling white teeth in his easy smile.

He looked happier, less anxious than he had in ages.

Without a word, he came and sat beside her on the rocks. They dipped their toes in the stream and watched dappled schools of fish glide beneath the leafy canopies.

While they sat, entwined in repose, a cloud passed over his face. He had not only helped to distribute the goods won at Fort Recovery but had been involved in the raid itself. He told her the mission was not the complete success that many of the Shawanese believed.

"You know I scouted—but did not fight—alongside Tecumseh at the Battle of the Wabash, where we defeated St. Clair?"

She nodded.

"Once again I saw Apekonit—William Wells—there. He is the one who led three hundred Miami against the St Clair's artillery soldiers and wiped them out with no mercy. After the battle, he buried their cannon, with plans that later we could go back and use them against the Long Knives. The British would give us balls and shot."

She remembered. There was much feasting and rejoicing after the defeats of Harmar and St Clair.

"Well, when we got to Fort Recovery the cannon were gone. Apekonit had told the Long Knives where the weapons were buried." His frowned. "He spies for them now. When our British fathers came with ammunition, there was nothing to shoot it from. And the Long Knives no longer fight like children. Black Snake has trained them well."

In spite of the tribal victories over Harmar's and St. Clair, Shawanese scouts bore troubling reports of the white warrior chief who never slept: General Wayne, whom they called Black Snake. Right now he was headed their way, wriggling down the river, building forts as he went.

White Buffalo wiped the serious expression from his face. "Still. We did come back with supplies for the people." He grabbed her braid. "And I saw two of your old friends. Guess who!" He put his arms around her and began to tickle her.

"I can't when you do this!" she spurted.

He wouldn't stop, and all Talitha could do was laugh and beg him to cease.

"All right. You give up. I will tell you, and then you will pay your forfeit. I saw your old friend Katepacoman—Simon Girty."

That stopped her laughter. How long it had been since she had taken her journey with Simon Girty and made her passage to this new world.

"I also saw Silver Man."

He and some others had made their way to Shawneeawkee's post to trade some of the goods from Fort Recovery. He had ventured into their friend's shop—in spite of his dislike of Margaret Kinzie, the former Kisathoi—to ask him to make a special gift from British silver. And Silver Man had crafted it for him.

He reached out playfully and again tugged the plait that had fallen over her shoulder. "I bet you thought I forgot to bring something back for you." He tried to conceal a small doeskin pouch in his left hand, partly hidden behind his back.

"Ah!" She grabbed for it, and they wrestled briefly until the struggle became an embrace. White Buffalo held her tightly to him, his arms strong around her. She felt his warm breath in her ear, his lips on her hair. The balance had shifted. He was now definitely the stronger, and she the weaker. In the summer heat, she felt as if she was melting in his arms.

"I missed you," he whispered in her ear.

Her heart sang.

Her mouth pressed against his shoulder, and she had an urge to lick him, knew he would taste of the summer sun.

She did not.

Instead she pulled away to gaze into his eyes and say, " I missed you, too."

There was his wide smile again, his heart shone in the dark eyes that were both kind and powerful, full of promises. Time slowed to a stop. The bright sun, and the buzz of bees dazzled them. They stared at one another silently, smiling as if they would burst.

He took her hand and placed the pouch in it.

She carefully pulled out the shiny silver circle.

"This is what I had Shawneeawkee make. For you."

It was beautiful, etched with twining vines and flowers and curled words.

She puzzled over them. White Buffalo could hardly read, and could not write at all. And though Shawanese women wore rings, they were not necessarily *wedding* bands. A ring might signify so many different things. If a man wanted a bride, he might present his loved one with a deer hoof. If she desired him, she would give him an ear of corn. These symbols told of how they would provide for one another.

"Shawneeawkee said your people often write words on their silver. Then he said that ever since he first met us, when we were children," and here he reached for her hand again, "he thought of us as one heart. One soul."

He laughed and added, "I am not so sure what this 'soul,' is, no matter how many times Johnny Logan tries to explain it to me, but I realize Shawneaeawkee is right about the heart—how I feel about you. You are much more than a sister."

He slipped the ring onto her finger, and she traced the inscription, "One Heart." She felt the letters, engraved in an embroidered heart, with the letters "TC and WB" beautifully wrought. There was also the Kinzie mark on the inside.

"It's beautiful," she said, holding her hand up to see it sparkle in the sun. Her eyes flitted over the faded scar, then lit upon the glittering ring. Her heart swelled.

He put his hand under her chin and she met his eyes.

"Are you my heart?" he asked in a whisper.

"Yes. Yes." This time she pulled him to her, overcome once more by these strange urges, the desire to feel his lips, touch his face, lose herself in him.

The Green Corn Festival was much like her first one of many years ago, but this time the words of the ancient ceremony rang out in the many different tongues of the Confederated Tribes who took part. Most had some form of this ritual, and though Dove Trees no longer needed to explain the happenings to her, Talitha saw children asking for understanding as she once had.

The hot day melted into a cool and pleasant evening. Sweet breezes floated up from the river. As the women sang, and gourds rattled music to the Choosing Dance, the evening passed too soon, fading away like smoke from the fires.

Many young people rose then to join in The Bringing Dance. In the old days, it was always the women who engaged the men in the dance. But now, the men chose their partners by giving a tug on the tunic of the woman they wanted. She saw a handsome Seneca pull Dove Trees up to dance. She noted the surprise and delight on Dove Trees' face, then chuckled as she saw her immediately give her new—and surprised—partner an earful.

She felt a tug on her own shift and turned to see White Buffalo at her side, his face beaming. An Ottawa girl looked after him with disappointment, while a Fox who had been strolling her way turned away with a frown when she joined the circle with White Buffalo.

It did not matter. When they moved round and round, hand in hand, palm touching palm, her heart's blood sang. When the dance ended far too early, the dancers returned to their families and clans. Becky was silent as Talitha sat beside her and reached for her hand. Nancy held her other hand aloft to show her treasure. Her eyes once more briefly lit on the ragged scar that was fading away on the back of her hand. She looked into Becky's eyes and saw they were filled with tears.

"I am glad for you, *netanetha*, my daughter," she said.

Yes, Talitha thought, these were hard times. There was war, but soon there would also be a wedding.

Moneto indeed smiled on them again.

# CHAPTER 39

## The Legion of the United States

### "Prepared to Meet Every Species of War that May Present Itself"
Frederick Wilhelm von Steuben,
*A Letter on an Established Militia...*1784

**Polly**
**July 1794**

The Great Road slowly took form, and the saltpeter mine, mills, and shops along Indian Creek hummed in the late July heat. Adam visited the mill nearly every day and brought back news: President Washington still smarted over the staggering defeats of Harmar, and St. Clair. He set into motion a series of new strategies, among them, the recruitment and training of a new army, The Legion of the United States. If the Indians refused to parlay, the next time they spoiled for a fight they would face a much stronger foe.

There was so much to do at this early harvest time, crops to preserve and children to mind, whether war was headed their way or not. And now Polly and Adam had one more. Baby Sarah, whom they called Sally, had joined them in the spring.

How she would have loved to christen her Elizabeth, after Mother. But there were far too many Elizabeths around here as it was. Her new daughter was not dark like her half-sister, Elsie, but blonde and blue-eyed like her brother Adam and the Manns. Adam Jr, seven years older than she, proudly carted his little *Schwester* all around, a big help on a day like today. With Sally just old enough to toddle into trouble, Polly was glad to have her under little Adam's wing.

Barbary doted on her. She claimed Sal's good nature and popularity were due to the umbilical cord tied around her neck before she was birthed, and the fact that Barbary had the chance to feed her a few spoonfuls of the baptismal water Pastor Miller had christened her with. This last ritual, Barbary claimed, would not only make Sal, "bright" but also a great singer. Well, she hadn't done any singing yet. They would have to wait and see about that.

On a warm summer evening after a supper of fresh trout caught by young Adam and Cory, summer greens picked by Elsie, and berry tarts with thick cream, Polly and Adam lingered beside the creek. They talked while the children played in the shallows.

"There is a new army headed by General Wayne, the one they call Mad Anthony," Adam said. "This new Legion of the United States is all anyone can talk about up at the mill. Last year Wayne drilled his men below Pittsburgh at a place called Mingo Bottom. But this spot was too close to town—and drink— so now he has moved them to Fort Washington, the post General Harmar built before his disgrace."

He grinned. "I guess there is less whiskey below Cincinnati—or Losantiville—as Filson named it." On the wall of their cabin hung a framed copy of Filson's *Map of Kentucke*. The sight of the tiny wiggle that was "Cabbin Creek," brought back mixed memories of joy and sorrow, thoughts of her old home place.

They also had Filson's book, *The Discovery, Settlement and Present State of Kentucke*. This was Cory's favorite, as the back contained "The Adventures of Boone." But there were some dreadful barbarous accounts among those pages, and Polly was careful of what she read to the children. She kept the book out of Cory's hands. Yes, Chloe could finally read some, and Polly suspected it was the Boone stories—not the Bible—that provided the motive for her hankering to read in the first place.

Poor Filson. He had stopped off at the old fort from time to time when making drawings for his famous map. Now, he too was gone, killed just a year after Pa. Anne Bailey brought the sad news to Polly and Adam in the fall of '88. Shawnee attacked Filson's surveying party as they worked near the Big Miami. His body was never found.

Adam's voice brought her back to the present. "Now the news is—secret of course—but you are not a spy, or how do they say—intelligencer—are you *Liebchen*?"

He chucked her under the chin. "Wayne brings his troops north to set up forts all along the Maumee, where Shawnee villages once sat."

Her heart sank. "So, this is where Uncle James will go."

Would she lose yet another?

According to his last letter, James now served as an artificer under General Wayne. Years before he started soldiering, he had been trained as a surveyor—back when Mam and the Halstead family lived in Pennsylvania. Back before the English war broke out. Wayne's artificers would oversee the building of the bridges, roads and forts the General required.

"Thanks be to *Gott* that James is south of most of the fighting," Adam said, taking Polly's hand. "Still, the settlers are afraid. Jacob just returned from making some deliveries to the forts up north and tells me they are a mess." He frowned. "Folk are living in tiny *Hütte*, what do you say—"hovels"?—inside the palisades and it is hot *und* filthy."

"That's a shame." She sighed wistfully. "I loved it when we stayed at the fort. Always something happening. Friends to talk to." An image of Marie flitted through her mind and the old lonesome pang bit at her. Surely there were few, if any, that she still would know if she returned to the old fort, the place where her family once lived. Their dear neighbor, Peggy Morris, had passed on, and Leonard had already married again. He and his new wife moved away, now lived near Point Pleasant. Time did not wait for any of them.

The Mann women, Barbary and her daughters and daughters-in-law as well as any friends or neighbors who wanted to join in, used Fridays as a day to bake or put food by. Polly gathered with them in the summer kitchen and pickled cow cumbers and other vegetables. Some dried meat and strung leather stockings.

The soft murmurs and spicy tasks lulled Polly away from thoughts of danger that might come to James and his company. She glanced out the kitchen's half-door. In the small apple orchard, green fruit peeked out through the leaves on the trees. Children shouted as they shimmied up the trunks.

Mary Jarrell worked with them today. She was regaling Lizzy Stigard—now Mitchell—with a story when suddenly she threw down her work and rushed outdoors to grab son Simeon, poised with a young apple in his fist, aiming to pelt Chloe.

Even from a distance, Polly read defiance in young Simeon's fiery blue eyes. At the sound of a quick swat to his hind-end, ten-year-old tomboy Chloe silently dropped the fruit she'd hidden behind her back and gawked with pleasure.

"If this doesn't come to a stop, you'll not have a swim with the others down at the creek when the day's work is done," his mother warned.

Simeon paid her no mind and stalked off. He broke off a low-hanging switch and swiped it at stones in the dust as he swaggered away from the orchard.

Polly fixed an eye Chloe, likely to follow him, but was distracted by a question from Lizzy about one of the receipts.

They conferred over the directions in Hannah Glasse's popular receipt book, *The Art of Cookery Made Plain and Easy*, which sister-in-law Mary Mann had brought over when Polly flinched at the sound of a loud clomping on the stairs that led into the kitchen.

"Now they're riding the pig," announced Elsie. Older than Chloe by two years, poor Elsie was often made her reluctant overseer. Elsie's *Deutsch* accent was almost gone, but Mother Barbary had no trouble understanding her.

Barbary's normally placid blue eyes lit up, and her linsey woolsy skirts swooshed down the porch steps as she set out to stop the abuse of her precious pig. Ties on her lawn cap fluttered in the hot summer breeze.

"Mother, I'll go," Polly called after her.

Barbary whirled around. "*Nein*. I vill go. That *Schwein* might teach them a ting or two, but I don't want them to hurt *meine* sow. *Und*," she said, eyes twinkling, " I think *mehr* beans are ripe." She grabbed two baskets that sat empty nearby. "Now I go to get my pickers. *Und* snippers."

Mary Jarrell looked up from her pickling crocks, choked back a chuckle. Son Simeon was here so she could keep an eye on him while her older boys helped in the mills and shops. The younger two were allowed the pleasures of fishing in the creek. Three-year-old Mary Polly, youngest of the Jarrell children and the only girl, dozed with the other babies and toddlers on quilts laid in the shade of the porch. Her mother's belly swelled against the table where she worked. Mary Jarrell was with child again. Her eyes danced in amusement as she said, "We'll see how long this lasts."

"I don't know," said Polly. "Barbary has a way of getting what she wants. Even out of Chloe—or Cory—as she likes to be called, and that's not an easy chore."

She motioned to Elsie, lingering at her side, clearly longing to help. "Elsie, why don't you fill that crock?"

In the early evening, the men returned from their labors, and the women and children spread more blankets along the shores of Indian Creek. Neighbors and kinfolk relaxed and supped along its leafy banks. There was roast chicken, baked summer squashes, cow cumbers in cream, biscuits, and fresh berry cobblers with more sweet cream.

When dinner was over, many of the men rose to smoke while the women reclined, full and content. Some cooled their feet in the current and watched the children splash below. Simeon Jarrell must have redeemed himself as he was among those cavorting in the shallows.

He reached out to dunk Chloe when Daniel Jarrell, his father, shouted, "Simeon!"

The red-haired boy's ears turned nearly as bright as his hair. He gazed downward. "Yessir," he mumbled.

"Out!"

The boy clambered out, trousers, sopping and clinging to his skinny legs, causing him to resemble a penitent half-drowned, red rat.

Daniel, chatting with Lizzy's husband, Joshua Mitchell, simply pointed to a spot on the grass beside them, and Simeon, eyes downcast, joined them, shivering. His father whispered to him, and Simeon nodded, respectful for a change. Daniel then resumed his conversation with the Frenchman.

Not only had Lizzy found a husband—*finally!*—but was pregnant with her first baby. The *Bleigießen* had indeed predicted correctly this past Silvestri. What Lizzy had not realized that long ago New Year's Eve when Polly first knew she herself was with child, was that Joshua came with a passel of his own children. Turned out he was a widower, and the children had been staying with an aunt in Virginia. Now they were back with their father, and Lizzy, like so many other women along Indian Creek, had her hands full.

Lizzy sat near Mary Jarrell, comparing the size of their bellies. Polly heard them debate as to whether they were carrying boys or girls while Priscilla Estes Miller looked on contentedly, holding her own sleeping son on her lap. Her three-year-old daughter dozed beside her. Polly's Sally cuddled next to this cousin, playmate, and neighbor.

Polly tried to count all the babies Priscilla had safely delivered since she came to live on Indian Creek when Adam stooped down beside her and joined her on the grass. "A beautiful evening, *ja?*" He plucked a piece of grass and tapped her lip with it.

"*Ja.*" That much *Deutsch* she could speak.

He sighed as he wearily stretched out his legs. The long days split between farm, smithy and the gunpowder mill took a toll.

"Did all go well at the mill today?"

"Some of the Army was down again. Artificers, mostly." Adam picked up a small pebble that lay beside them and skimmed it into the creek. "Wayne has *Haussnitz*—Howitzers—now. Until they get more of our powder, they are practicing with these stones." He skimmed another one across the water. "But the magazine was nearly full. We got them loaded up with all the powder they need."

"I'll be happy when it's empty," Polly murmured. In spite of her worries for her own children and husband—well, the entire Mann/Miller brood—the return of Priscilla and Chloe continually reminded her of the others still out there. Her brother John would be fourteen now, and quite possibly fighting on the side of Indians. Would the gunpowder from their mill be used against him?

Her thoughts flew to another family member.

"Did they have news of James?"

"*Ja.*" He smiled. "He is *güt*. Good. He is an old friend of the wagoner who came today. He told me old James grows tired of this army life, moving from fort to fort, even though surveying beats soldiering." He raised his eyebrows. "Sounds like he'd rather settle down with your friend, Marie."

Polly's eyes widened. Could Adam be right about James's feelings for Marie?

"I am only the messenger. But his friend dropped many hints of a coming *Hochsheitstag*—wedding. Said Marie left Kaintucke the same time as James. She is in Philadelphia now with her aunt, but has an eye on trading in Detroit, or thereabouts—somewhere with easy access to the French-Canadian fur trade, when this fighting is over."

"So it's true that they care for one another." It was hard to keep the wonder from her voice.

Adam noted her surprise and nodded. "*Ja.*" He held Polly's hand to his hear. "They say there is no accounting for taste."

Polly flicked water on him with her foot, and he squeezed her hand in return.

"I heard news of the new army, too. The Legion is a horse of another color, the driver says. General Wayne seems to never sleep. Recently two soldiers were court-martialed simply for laying down their muskets and sitting while on guard duty. They each got a hundred lashes. *Und* he will not tolerate drunkenness."

Yes, it was surely the dawning of a new day. Polly thought back to her old life at the fort. The hijinks of old, Marie's, fooling around with soldiers' arms while the men passed the time with shooting matches and ball games, would no longer be tolerated. How strange it was that Marie's misbehavior lead to this connection with James.

While musing on the peculiar nature of love, she felt a pair of wet hands brush against her from behind, coming to rest over her eyes as a small wet body pressed up against her.

"Guess who, Mama!"

She smiled. "Cory."

There was a squeal. "No!"

"Then Elsie."

"No!"

"Could it be...?" She reached around and grabbed a wet leg, "Ah—it's me own wee Adam."

There was another yelp from the wee Mann, this time as his father reached down and hoisted him up onto his shoulders and twirled him through the sheltering trees toward the slow peeping stars as the twilight melted into evening.

# CHAPTER 40

## The Intrigues of Camps

*"It matters little whether the disasters*
*Which have arisen are to be ascribed to*
*The weaknesses of Generals, the intrigues of camps,*
*Or the jealousies of Cabinets…"*

William Pitt, 1795

**James**
**August 1794**

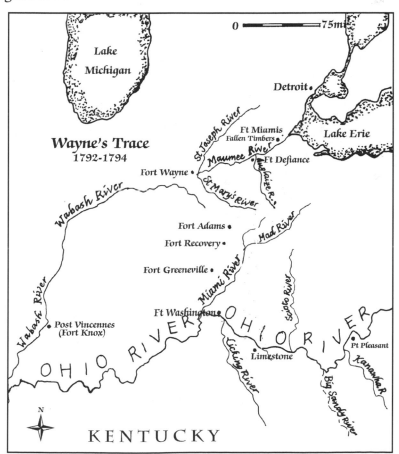

He heard the trudging of tired boots even in his sleep.

Two years ago, after the disaster of Harmar and St. Clair, Colonel John Hardin of the Kaintuckes had traveled to Indian villages with a message of peace. The Shawnee had murdered him for his troubles.

In response, a new delegation now traveled through the villages: Wayne's Legion of the United States. The General had kept the exact nature of their mission private, but seasoned soldiers among them reckoned there would be a battle at the end of the trail. For now, they were occupied putting up a string of forts.

James felt his years, all forty-eight of them. The marching, and the backbreaking road and bridge building took a toll on men half his age among.

As an artificer, he had the luxury of focusing on things besides mere soldiering. He was lucky to be spared the heaviest fatigues. And it was hard to complain when there were many older than here. One old Dutchman named John Lusk had started out in the French and Indian War, fought on the Plains of Abraham, as well as the Conquest of Acadia and the Battle of Saratoga in the English war. There was also a highlander here, ancient enough to have fought at Culloden. Old Andrew Wallace had been at Yorktown, too, and then in St Clair's failed campaign, where he'd taken a musket-ball in the left arm. Now he was one of Mad Anthony Wayne's sergeants, and wandered the wilds of yet another new land.

He heard him now, loudly singing an out-of-tune version of "Green Grow the Rushes" by his favorite poet Robbie Burns.

*The warly race may riches chase*
*And riches still may fly them, O*
*And though at last*
*They catch them fast*
*Their hearts can ne'er deny them, O!*

Well, Wallace surely could not get accused of chasing riches—being a part of this campaign.

He noted others too who had served in the Continental Army *and* in the Harmar and St Clair campaigns. James's former commander, the French Canadian from Quebec—Lieutenant Colonel Jean-Francois Hamtramck was one. Camp gossip held that he wasn't entirely happy—smarted under Wayne's failure to promote him to a higher rank.

General Wilkinson also stung under Wayne's leadership, and had schemed against Mad Anthony ever since they left Hobson's Choice in Cincinnati. Old women might hold the reputation as gossips, but plenty of tales were told in camp. One of the silliest—but most likely true—was that Wilkinson bore a grudge against Wayne on account of Wayne refusing to an invitation to share in a bottle of Lachryma Christi at Wilkinson's Christmas gathering.

Wayne was mystified by the acrimony, claimed he had meant no slight, was simply moving headquarters to Fort Greenville and could not spare the time. At least that was the word James had from Edward Butler, Wayne's former adjutant general. Still, paltroons and rancorous character assassins penned dreadful accusations against Wayne which found their way into "Dunlap and Claypoole's Daily American Advertiser," and soon the camp appeared to be split into two: those for Wayne and those against him, who supported Wilkinson.

Many of James's fellow Kaintuckes sided with Wilkinson. General Charles Scott and James were among the exceptions. But James reckoned all must admit Wayne could inspire men in ways few others could. When one saw Old Tony riding about camp urging his men on with praise, a fellow just wanted to make him proud, no matter if he was a young pup or a seasoned veteran like Old Wallace.

Even outside the factions, the Legion was not without its worries. James occasionally spied the shadows of Indian scouts shifting through the forests along the trail. They might make an ambush, capture a soldier here and there, or steal some horses, but once in a while the company snagged one of them. The army was shocked to find that more often than not, the captive's chief desire would be to meet "General Black Snake," the one the Shawnee also called, "He Who Never Sleeps."

He may not have slept, but his exhausted men needed rest. They stopped a moment for respite as they made their way along the newly cut trail that some already called Wayne's Trace. A veteran who had previously served under Wayne revealed that the General's fear of treachery and spies within the camp had led to secrecy as to the nature of their mission. They were headed due north, that much was sure.

As James reached for his canteen, his fingers brushed against a leather-bound book, the journal from Marie. He smiled wryly. Only she could imagine an old warhorse like him would ever put down his thoughts in a diary. He pondered her inscription, which he now knew by heart:

*"To he alone who knows the depths of my heart and my tenderness.*
*Ever thine own dearest One,*
*Marie"*

Well, he couldn't write words like that to her, wouldn't even know how. But as this trail led his old bones into uncharted territory, Maria was leading his heart into a new country. No, he had not the skill to pen a real love letter, but he could put down his thoughts in this diary, and know, too, how she had once touched the same with her own delicate hands.

He wrote a little as he took his lunch of corn and beans gathered from the old Indian fields around their camp:

*4 August*

*We are not far North of the site of St Clair's Defeat, where Wayne has built Fort Recovery, named for the recovery Last Christmas of nigh 1000 Boddies that was left here by St Clair. It is dreadful hot and to escape the heat we have pitched our tents among the trees. Which led to the Near Death of our leader General Wayne as a large Beech has toppled over onto the tent where he and his aid Henry de Butts slept. Many thot the general kilt but tho De Butts cot was smashed and the tree came but 6 inches of crushing the general both survive. Wayne did appear dead at First but revived having much damage to leg and foot. Those who were present say a old stump what caught most of the force of the falling Beech and is all that saved the general from death. Wilkinson calls it a miracle. Some whisper tho what if it is an attempt to murder the General who is not without Enemys?*

That evening he smoked his pipe, and despite the noise of the camp, felt calmed by the chirp of crickets in the late summer night. By the light of his cook fire added:

*There are more problems as we make our Way in that Our main Surveyor Newman has been gone now since the 1ˢᵗ. Some now believe he may NOT be taken by Indians as supposed but is Spy and Deserter. The General calls him Villain. Now that Newman is gone, a fellow named Cooper was to replace him. I will assist Edward Butler, One of the Five Fighting Butlers, who is a Captain and lately was the Generals assistant to survey the way before us.*

James laid down his pen. The scent of his supper, a rabbit roasting on a spit and some fresh corn baking in the coals, drew him away from his writing. He carefully set aside the journal and poked at the rabbit, turned the corn. When he looked up he saw that Captain Butler had joined him by the fire.

"Set a spell," said James.

Butler rolled up a log and laid it on end, sat. He had a piece of wood with him, a sort of picket. Had been whittling on it, from the looks it.

"Rabbit smells good," said Edward Butler. Butler was a bit of a puzzle. He and his four brothers, "The Fighting Butlers," had served in the Continental army and were renowned for their bravery. Yet Edward Butler had recently left the General's side, the side of glory, James reckoned, to serve with the artificers. He was still a young man, early thirties or so.

"You're welcome to it." James sliced off a juicy hunk and offered it to him.

"I thank you kindly." Butler held the meat aloft to cool it, then gingerly took a few bites. "Good."

The strains of a fiddle drifted over the camp. James knew it as "Hold on Until Tomorrow." The sweet notes were a backdrop to the soft laughter and mild cursing of men winning and losing at cards. The evening air had cooled, and the first faint stars appeared.

"Wilkinson has it out for me," Butler muttered.

"So I've heard." According to camp lore, the trouble had started with an argument over an ax. Hamtramck of the Kaintuckes had ordered one for a detail, and Butler wouldn't provide him one. Major Cushing, who was mentored by Wilkinson, got in the middle of it and Butler ended up arresting him.

"Of course that earlier trouble with Cushing irks him yet, but he also cannot understand why one of my rank would choose to work with the engineers. I tell you, I have no desire to be in the way of Wilkinson's feud with Wayne." Butler pulled his mess kit from his necessary pouch, took out his trencher, and pulled off another piece of rabbit. His dark blonde hair fell into his eyes, yet did not hide the frown on his face, the tense posture.

"Help yourself to corn, too."

"Don't mind if I do."

They ate awhile in companionable silence. Then Butler pulled out his pipe and tobacco. He held the pouch out to James. "Have some. This is from Virginia. No sumac mixed in." He stretched his legs out in front of him and let out a tired breath, then relaxed as he loaded his pipe.

James filled his own, and they sat contentedly smoking. After awhile, Butler pulled out his knife and began to carve again on the stick of wood he had brought.

"What have you there?"

Edward turned it towards him. The words, "General Richard" were etched into it, but there was space left for more writing.

"Oh, aye, for your brother." Butler's picket would make part of a cross, a marker for where brother had died.

Butler nodded. James watched as he continued to whittle. The sound of his knife scraping at the wood played a counterpart to the tones of the tune wafting over the camp.

"I found his bones, last year, near the spot where his tent sat. Knew him by the marks on his broken thigh bone—horse jumping accident when he was young. The Indians didn't lose many of theirs, but we knew our men. Their skulls were all broken by tomahawks and marked up by the scalp knife." Butler glanced up from his work. "I feel his spirit here."

The Butlers were from Ireland, and Irish and Scotchmen felt haints more than most folk. James remembered some of the gruesome tales Old Patrick Flynn—his dead brother-in-law John's father—used to tell to frighten his grandchildren. Yet though this journey had not been without omens, too many and too troubling for James to dwell on, Butlers did not seem a superstitious lot. But strange things had been seen and felt—and by plenty of men, not just the Celts—at the sites of bloody battles.

Butler paused a moment, and James wondered if they pondered the same mysteries. Everyone knew that the slain Richard Butler had a son with Nonhelema, the "Grenadier Squaw," a peacemaker among the Shawnees in spite of her name. What they may not have known was that this son, Tamanatha, was yet another "fighting Butler," –except he had fought on the side of the Shawnee, against his own father, in the battle where Richard Butler lost his life.

It was a riddle. How could you love someone so much, have children with them even, and then end up in a place where father butchered child and brother slew brother? Yet here James was himself, sweet on a woman who was half Delaware, a tribe in cahoots with the Shawnee. It did not matter to James one whit. Yes, it was a puzzle, one that would not be solved anytime soon.

Butler interrupted his thoughts. "We learned later, from reports after my brother was killed, that the turncoat Simon Girty arrived shortly after the scalp-taking, while the savages were feasting on Richard's heart." The voice faltered. Frontier folk had come to learn—the tragic way—that his gruesome practice was but a grisly compliment, inflicted only upon the bravest. A bite of a heart full of courage would give each who partook of it his own "brave heart."

Butler worked at the wood some more, while James observed him, silent.

"Yes, I was here a year ago Christmas. Two years the bones been lying out till we came and laid folks to rest on Christmas Eve and Christmas Day."

At this pronouncement, the fiddle launched into a haunting air, and from a nearby campfire, a sweet tenor voice sang out "The Chevalier's Lament."

Edward held up the picket, the name "Butler" now completed. Light had faded from the twilit summer sky, and early stars looked down on them. Edward stood and laid a hand on James's shoulder. "I am sorry to eat your food and prove such sorry company. I thank you for the fine dinner, James."

James tipped his hat in salute. Not necessary, but a habit, and watched as Butler returned his courtesy and walked to his own tent, as one who carried a heavy burden on his shoulders.

The following day, as they made ready to march on, James stole a moment to write more:

*We now leave this fort to be known as Ft Randolph behind us only halfdone and filled with invalids and cripples. Some are Kaintuckes I have known since Fort Knox and I pray they will live to see our return again this way. There are twenty Able bodied Men left there but in charge of them is Lt Underhill who is downcast and believes those who are Fit will soon be digging graves for the Sick rather than finishing the Garrison. Those in charge of the Livestock already let them run off and all is in a Sorry State as we leave them behind. We move North.*

He swatted at the cloud of mosquitoes that surrounded him, then tested the nib of his quill. Oddly, he felt like adding more, talking to Marie about things closer to his heart. The stars overhead reminded him of the stars in her eyes, but that seemed a foolish thing to say, so he just thought of her as those lights winked out one by one, and sleep overtook him.

The next two days they were on the march again.

*7 August*

*We made twelve slow Miles today as the road cutters have a hard time working in this Thicke brush and Swampy ground. We stop often, so the road is not Hard for us, but for those Misfortunates who must hack the Way clear the before us. Price's scouts ride out first then follow the Volunteers of Kaintucke and finally our legion where I ride. I believe this Price is a relation to Margaret, who was married to Leonard Morris, once neighbors to my sister Elizabeth. Now Margaret, kind Peggy who was so good to my niece Polly after the Raid, is passed on, and Leonard married to another. Somehow I fear Elizabeth my Dear Sister is long dead. It is rare for Women who would be the age she Now is to ever return from Captivity. I mourn her loss and wonder if Peggy and Elizabeth visit again in the Great Beyond. Or do they Each watch over there Brothers here below? Butler and I often are called upon to consult about the way so I have come to know many of the men on Fatigue and feel there Plight.*

As he tucked away his journal, his thoughts remained with his lost sister, and the two children, Nancy and John. When it was time for dinner, he foraged corn from the fields that bordered their trail. Butler strode up and joined him. So far, they'd come across three different kinds of corn, all cultivated by the Shawnee. Edward and James often fished or foraged together now, and shared supper.

They turned at a commotion on the road behind them.

"It's Wells and his boys—those Miller brothers," Butler noted.

Wells was hard to miss. His curly red hair flamed in the noonday sun, and even from a distance one could see the freckles on his face. He wore the outfit of an Indian: leggings and moccasins worked in designs of both the Wea and the Miami. A former captive, he grew up the adopted son of Chief Porcupine of the Eel River Wea, married a woman of the tribe, and had a child with her. The Miller brothers had also been taken as young'uns and come up as white Indians, though James had heard far less about them.

Butler dropped his voice. "Some here say Wells is as much a spy as Newman. He actually fought on the side of Little Turtle at the Wabash—St Clair's defeat. Didn't know it, but he was going against his own white brother." He stopped a moment. "Of course you know Captain Sam Wells, Kentucky militia? William is his long lost brother."

James nodded. Sam Wells had once lived close to Boone's Station, was a hero in the War with the British and had survived St. Clair's Defeat. Considering the odds of surviving that last battle, Sam was lucky to be alive at all, let alone to have survived a death, that might even have been at the hands of this younger brother, equally skilled in warfare, but equipped also with the wiles of the red savages.

"Wells was after revenge on Wilkinson. Thought he'd killed his Wea wife and baby in a raid back in '91. So as payback, he led in three hundred men and took out St Clair's whole artillery squadron. Caught the eye of Little Turtle and later married his daughter, Waganapeth. They call her 'Sweet Breeze.'"

James fixed a curious eye on Wells, now engaged in an animated conversation with one of Price's scouts. For all his bravery and leadership, Wells was not a large man—rather on the small side, though not frail. He had a liveliness, an intensity perhaps, that lit him up as brightly as his hair.

"I heard this morning they spied an Indian village about six miles yonder. Wayne sent them back with some of our scouts, and when they returned they said the place was deserted. Fresh tracks, though. An Indian party has been there lately, and Wayne thinks it might be that scoundrel, Newman."

James was not surprised Butler had this information. As former Adjutant General to Wayne in the War of Independence, Butler remained privy to all sorts of news not available to the average legionnaire or artificer.

James left off gathering corn for a moment and asked, "So why does Wells spy for us now? Can he be trusted?"

"Ah, who knows? Newman was no redskin's adopted son, but look how he's turned on us. I reckon now that he's met his brother, William feels the pull back to the Americans. He even got permission"—Butler raised his eyebrows and paused—"from Little Turtle to scout and translate for Wayne."

James chuckled. The Indians never failed to surprise him. This one, Apekonit or Wells or whatever one wanted to call him, had ingratiated himself with Wayne by returning to the site of the infamous defeat of St Clair and turning the buried cannon over to the Legion.

James looked more closely. This time thought he saw something of Wells' brother Sam in his carriage. Then Wells caught Butler's eye, and Butler left to confer with him.

The artificers moved on. By afternoon they reached a stream they followed to the 'Glaize, and the village Wells had spoken of earlier.

That evening, all feasted on the corn, beans, and potatoes that grew in the fields around the deserted village.

*8 August*

    *Rains came heavy Today. We made our Way down to the Maumee and came upon what looked like Paradise to the Eyes of many. Where the Maumee and Auglaize meet is a land of plenty. We passed four or five miles of well cared for Cornfields on our Way In and everywhere saw an abundance of other cultivated Vegetables. Here there are Several Towns close together that have been left in a Hurry. Brass Kettles and Tools are hid in the weeds. Many barrels and Kegs Lay about and give evidence White traders dwelled Here. Someone found Blue Jackets Rich Home and burned it. One of the artificers James Morrow found a trunk Full of Money. All were able to gather enough vegetables and Melons to have a Feast tonight and some even caught fish.*

    *I found myself in Wonderment over who had planted such Bounty. Tho I fear my Sister Elizabeth is dead, when I see those like Wells and The Millers I hope for the eventual Reunion with her dear Lost children. Could any of this be the Work of those Hands? I think of That Hand with The Map of Ireland burnt on it as My Dead brother in Law Liked to Call it—That Hand of my long lost niece Nancy. May be it has sown some of the Seeds that bore these Crops? Has my Nephew John been one that traded goods to Obtain these Kettles? I wondered if we ever Come upon White Captives would they come with us or would they Shun Us for their darker Kin.*

    *Now again I think upon William Wells and the Miller Brothers who even Now are not Fully Trusted tho It Is Pretended they are worthy of Trust. But they were Indian So Long.*

At last James had a chance encounter with William Wells. While foraging vegetables one evening, he came upon Wells and some scouts, hurling tomahawks. He paused to watch.

"Don't go up against that'un," one of the contestants warned him, gesturing at Wells.

"I didn't plan to." James watched as Wells threw his hatchet, then whooped as he hit the target—a slab of tree stump painted with the British flag.

The young scout clapped and hollered along with Wells. "I've known that one to try to school bears in the art of courage." The fellow then told James about the time Wells had wounded a large bear while on a hunting trip.

"That animal let out some yelps and started up a-wailing and Wells went right up to him and gave him a talking to. Told him that the bear knew better, knew the fortunes of war, that one or the other of them must fall. He stroked that bear on the snout and told him it was his fate to be conquered, and he ought to die like a man, like a hero, and not like an old woman. Said that if the case had been reversed, and he had fallen into the power of my enemy, he would not have disgraced his nation as he did, but would have died with firmness and courage, as becomes a true warrior."

James tried to hide his amusement at the young man's pride in his leader.

"He's still got the skin," the fellow added. "The bearskin."

Wells came back to stand beside them and watch some of the others throw.

James took the opportunity to ask about his niece and nephew, whether Wells had come across captives matching their description.

Wells looked at him with something like pity. "I am sorry. There are just so many white captives. Who turn Indian, like I did. Like I was," he corrected himself. "I was with both the Wea and Miami, and I have not seen the children you describe. From what you say—the information Boone gave you about your niece, Chloe, who was returned— well, the Shawanese may have the rest of them." Wells must have read the disappointment on James's face. His hand brushed James's shoulder lightly. "Don't give up, though. Look at me." He smiled his lively smile.

"Miracles happen."

When they stopped that evening James added one more line to his journal:

*Wayne will have us build a fort here.*

*9 August*

*Kentucky volunteers Laid up all day or Scoured the abandoned villages. One got several bushels of shelled Corn he sold to the Quartermaster. We are eating Better than we have since Hobsons Choice. I am busy as the legion has its Commands to Cut Logs for the blockhouses and pickets and Butler and I must make Sure All is in readiness for construction. Patience wears thin again and tho no one Threatens to Duel as they did in Hobsons Choice many Bicker. Today officers bitterly argued over the Position of the Fort but Waynes Decision remained.*

Mad Anthony as many call him not for Insanity but Brilliance still Suffers from when the tree fell upon his tent at Ft Randolph and this makes his Temper Short at times as does the gout he suffers So Severe.

That day James ran into Butler as he oversaw a crew working on the road. Butler stopped to share more news of the wider world.

"Wayne tells me there is a Whiskey Rebellion in Pennsylvania, and Washington wants thirteen thousand militia. Those distilling spirits see no reason to pay taxes on them. Highlanders, half of them. Worried they'll be taxed as much under Washington as they were under King George. That's what this belligerence is all about." Butler let out a sigh of discouragement. "This country's downfall will be the refusal of folks to pay their taxes. And Wayne cannot look up from his targets here to recruit men for that campaign."

So much already rested on Wayne's shoulders, and now there was more bickering here, as well.

"I heard some of the arguing over where to set the fort," James said.

Though they had not yet decided upon its exact location, there was no doubt that wherever the fort sat, it would defy invasion. Plans called for pickets fifteen feet tall and one foot across at the top, but

244

much thicker at the bottom where they met the ground. A blockhouse would stand on each corner, and a ditch eight feet deep and fifteen feet wide would surround the fort. Beyond that would rise a wall of earth eight feet high.

"Wayne wants to call this one Fort Defiance for all its defences," Butler explained. "Though the moat will wait 'till we return from battle." He winked. "If'n there is a battle."

Towards evening, Edward and James cooled off in the shade along the banks of the Maumee and watched as Kaintucke volunteers roughhoused, sported, and splashed in the shallows across the stream from camp. Though the Kaintuckes were carefree at the moment, worry followed others in the Legion. As they got closer and closer to the spot where they reckoned Wayne would pitch battle, thoughts turned to the defeats of St Clair and Harmer. Men spent hours cleaning their guns, sharpening knives, axes, and sabers.

After supper, Butler and James inspected one another's weapons. They both had long rifles, the gun Edward's family manufactured, and which Johann Mann, Polly's father-in-law, also produced at Mann's Station. James realized with a shock that when he thought of Kaintucke his heart ached. He missed his family. But most of all he missed Marie.

The next day, he noted things indeed were changing for those Kaintuckes who had frolicked in the water such a short time earlier.

*10 August*

*The Kaintucke Volunteers who have Camped across the River from the Legion are now coming under Waynes command tho there General is Scott. Today they have 140 axes and are to build a Breastwork as Wayne wants every man Safe. He has forbidden them from swimming in the River and Gathering Corn unless at least 10 go out together with arms. Also they are Not to burn more Indian Cabbins. Some will be surprised to get Court Marshal after they Refuse orders. Butler tells me Wells and his Fellows spy out Roche de Boo and see how the British work there Mischief which Wayne is sure they Do.*

*11 August*

 *I have met with old Comrades in Hamtramcks Kentuckes as they construct there Defense. Among them is one who also Writes a Journal and is a Surveyor tho he does not work with us in the Legions Artificers. He is Lt William Clark Brother to George Rogers Clark the Famous Indian fighter and Hero of Old Vincennes. George Rogers is now Disgraced but as Wilkinson is one of his accusers that testified he was drunk on Duty some Wonder as to its verity. Most kno Wilkinson to be full of Envy and a Schemer.*

 *Clark draws many Maps but what he writes in his Book I do not kno. I am sorry to say that Some Times I do Wonder if our words will end up in some Indian Hut or molder with our Bodies. Or will they make there Way back to our Loved Ones?*

*12 August*

 *I have more intelligence from Butler. Wayne today sent 200 to go down the Maumee and lay a Camp at Snakes Town. Wells and his Spies have come in with 2 Prisoners a Male and Female. Wells will not be winning anymore Tommyhawk contests as he is shot thru the Wrist and another scout took a Ball thru the Shoulder. The Captive redskins we got tell that Newman was No Prisoner when they saw him in Company with there Brethren rather he loved the Savages and was One with them and warned them of Waynes Strength and told them to clear out there Towns. These Shawnee prisoners said there was two Hundred British soldiers at Ft Miamis and 700 Warriors Camped nearby and 500 more coming from the united tribes. They do tell that Newman is on his way to Detroit with British Captains and plans to bring more British soldiers to Defend The Glaize. These Shawnees said some of there chiefs are not happy with the British Fathers who tell them to fight but will not Take the Field. They said May be the Indians would let the Long Knives go all the way to the British. And if The English will not help the Shawnees now those Indians will fight against there former English fathers on the side of the Long Knives. But This Cannot be True.*

Tensions rose higher still. Butler carried troubling news of more intelligencers as they ate a dinner of biscuits and salt pork.

"Captain Richard Taylor—one of your Kaintuckes—has found a letter lying in the road, our proposed movements left for Indians to find, Wayne supposes."

James choked on his bite of food.

"It is written in Cooper's hand." Daniel Cooper, their fellow surveyor, was the missing Newman's former companion. "Wayne has had him arrested. Tomorrow he will send out Chris Miller to spy, and to ask one last time: 'Will the Indians parlay or not?'"

*13 August*

> *The General has been abed from Gout since 10 August but did Question these Indians caught by Wells and sent one with C Miller who knows there Language and Ways from being a captive so long, to Roche de Boo with a last attempt to make peace. But Wilkinson does not trust Miller and fears we will be Betrayed. Butler tells me Chris Miller Did Conspire in the Capture of William Fuller while living in the Shawnee Nation in '91. But This Same Miller now tells us secrets of the British, how they discourage all Talks of Peace and promise the Shawnee every Comfort on Condition they will continue there Warring Which seems True. We see They send Warriors out to Ambush this Military Road we are on and to Steal Our Horses and it is while Acting in these pursuits the Tables were Turned and Christopher Miller himself was made our Captive and now is turned Our own intelligencer.*

The female Shawnee stays Behind with us As Ransom. The Shawnee always pay More for a female.

Then finally the General made his decision.

# CHAPTER 41

## The Grand Emporium of the
## Hostile Indians of the West

**White Buffalo**
**August 1794**

It was the eighteenth of the month the whites called August. The Shawanese knew it as The Green Corn Moon, though some called it *Miini kiishthwa*, Blackberry Moon. The air was oddly quiet as White Buffalo and Tecumseh's small band waited on the bluffs for Black Snake's army.

Surely it would not be long before they would celebrate another victory. Spies had kept them well informed as to the army's movements. A friend to the Indians known as New Man had deserted General Black Snake's legion, and riding in the company of some Delaware and Shawnee, warned the villages along the river of Wayne's coming attack. War chiefs sent women and children north, while the various tribes gathered to fight.

Standing Elk and other emissaries left for the northeast in a last effort to draw in the Chippewas, Ottawas, Potawatomis, and Lake Indians, rumored to be angry yet at the outcome of the recent raid and attack on Fort Recovery. Angry they had no fair share of spoils. The Indian confederacy did not need every man, but once the Shemanese Long Knives were defeated, it would be important to have a semblance of unity in the new world that would open up to them. They had suffered many losses. Now, as one, they should share the glory of victory.

From their high perch, White Buffalo and his companions kept a hawk's eye out for Chickesaw and Choctaw scouts who traveled in the vanguard of Wayne's scouts. *These* would not share in the glory.

"They are the ones who caused the rift between the Lake Indians and ourselves," said Tecumseh, " with their spying for the Long Knives since before the raid on Fort Recovery."

The first day of the raid, the traitors had hidden in the trees around the fort and then slipped out from behind the raiding party and slain warriors from the Lake tribes, who were in the rear. And now they were at their treachery again. Confederacy scouts had seen them advising the Americans as far north as the newly built Fort Defiance.

"We will know them by the yellow ribbons they wear in their hair, so the Shemanese will not mistake them for the enemy—us. Well, their red brothers can spot a yellow ribbon, too. They will pay for this."

Tecumseh's companions nodded in agreement. Besides White Buffalo and Tecumseh, the little troop included Big Fish, some Kispoko cousins, and Tecumseh's two living brothers, Sauwauseekau, and Lalawitheka. They were part of a set of triplets, though their third brother had died as an infant.

White Buffalo was uneasy with the presence of Lalawthika, who was known more as a drunkard than a warrior. He was a noisemaker, and even his name meant "rattler." He had not taken part in the campaigns against Harmar and St. Clair but fled to the Elkhart with the women and children. To even have him in their party was bad medicine. He had lost an eye in a hunting accident, and the corrupt orb gave him a look of evil. Though he was good at hiding the rum—the "English Milk" —he tippled as they traveled, his one good eye was already bloodshot.

Earlier that day their party rode easterly along the Maumee, riding at times through meadows of prairie grass that rose above their heads, the scarlet and white flowers flashing in the summer sun. They also passed through patches of nettles. One of the Kispokos stopped to harvest some. "We will want to make tea. If Black Snake makes us wait for him, this will help purify us and keep us awake."

White Buffalo thought of the compresses Talitha, Tepeke, and other Mekoche healers made of this herb. Dried, it could be ground into a fine powdered that soothed cuts, burns and stings.

Was Talitha making her medicines now? Who would use them?

As they left the meadows and trotted towards the wooded bluffs, a breathless Shawanese messenger greeted them. "Blue Jacket and the chiefs have decided we will meet near Roche de Bout."

The rocky island jutting up out of the Maumee River was a familiar landmark. Their British fathers looked down on it from Fort Miami to the east. Soon White Buffalo and his companions  spied the island, too, as they made their way along the cliff just west of it. They slowed as they approached a place of fallen timbers, just above stony Roche de Bout.

Tecumseh spotted the fallen trees and twisted branches, the roots in hopeless tangles, and his face broke into a huge grin. "Cylone Woman was here. Her braids have flown about and caused destruction, but in her anger she has provided this cover for us. There are perfect hiding places for when we will ambush."

The wind spirit, Cyclone Woman, was a Grandmother Spirit and friend to the Shawnee. Surely the sign of her presence here was good medicine. They settled in among the downed trees to watch and wait. They could see the island and the river and as far as the bank on the south side of the Maumee. But there was little activity to observe.

"I wonder if New Man has led us astray," murmured a Kispoko cousin.

"No," said Big Fish. "Our Delaware grandfathers trust him. He would not lie."

They passed time talking and joking, and for a moment, White Buffalo's thoughts turned away from the battle to come.

"I hear you will be taking a wife, joining the real men of the tribe." The words of Big Fish were directed to White Buffalo, but Sinnamatha cast Tecumseh a teasing look as he said it.

A Kispoko cousin joked, "All the women want Tecumseh. He can't decide on just one."

White Buffalo was thankful the topic no longer centered on Talitha and himself. As for Techumseh's power over women, Talitha shared some gossip on that matter.

"Dove Trees says Tecumseh already *has* a wife. But he will not live with her and never will speak of her. It is a poor wife who cannot even keep colors in Tecumseh's paint pouch."

Would Tecumseh tell them of his mystery wife now?

But Tecumseh said nothing, only continued cleaning his musket. Then he spoke.

"It is good, little brother, that you have Talitha. She is a good Shawanese. A good sister."

"And not so bad to look at," said one of the cousins.

White Buffalo's face grew warm under the praise. After this battle, sure to be as successful as St Clair's defeat, they would be rich again, and he and Talitha would start a strong life together.

He heard a commotion and glanced down at the river. Canoes. Some warriors had arrived with their families, planning to share in the plunder that after victory would soon be theirs, the treasures of the slain Long Knives.

Yet though scores of warriors drifted in along with troops the British brought in from Canady, they did not see any of Black Snake's men. The white chief was living up to his name, waiting patiently before he struck.

"Perhaps he intends to strike by night," said Big Fish.

It was a possibility. Black Snake was so wily that even the Shawanese respected him.

Towards evening, in readiness they purified themselves for battle, made a tobacco offering to Moneto, and then drank the black liquid that would purge their bellies. The Kispokos sang as they painted one another, using themselves as mirrors.

White Buffalo painted himself like Tecumseh. When Tecumseh drew vermilion paint from his pouch, so did he. Like Tecumseh, he wiped a clean stripe down the middle of his face, from his forehead to the tip of his nose. Then they both drew stripes from their nostrils to their earlobes. Finally, Tecumseh took black and painted a line around his left eye. White Buffalo finished with a line from the sides of his mouth to his earlobes. Both men's hair hung long, not shaved with the scalp lock some of the cousins wore.

They sang again.

They fasted.

Black Snake didn't come.

But another messenger did, on a froth-covered horse. "Black Snake continues at his camp about ten miles upriver. He is not coming tonight."

They slept fitfully, taking turns at watch, sipping the nettle tea the Kispoko brewed, but the night was uneventful.

By morning, the woods and banks filled with more brothers of the Western Confederacy: the Delaware grandfathers, and the younger brothers, the tribes of the Ottawa, Chippewa, Potawatomi, and even a few Miamis and Mohawks.

But still Black Snake did not come, and the humid day passed. They were all hungry and tired. When evening fell, and there still was no sign of Wayne, they broke their fasts with small meals. Some foraged in the woods or ate from the small stores in their pouches.

Then a spatter of raindrops fell. Dark clouds tumbled towards them, and a loud rumbling surrounded them. Lightning flickered in the sky, and they were soon soaked to the bone.

Tecumseh was cheered by the deluge. "The Great Spirit is angry with our enemies; the Thunderbirds speak. May they swallow up our enemies."

The Kispokos smiled. As the warrior clan, in their ceremonial dance they honored the Thunderbirds as the patrons of war. The birds guarded the path to heaven, and all Shawanese knew thunderstorms came about when the Thunderbirds fought with the Great Horned Serpent and other evil creatures. Lightning flashed from their blinking eyes.

First, Cyclone Woman had blessed them with this vantage spot, and now the Thunderbirds showed their favor.

In spite of their hunger, their spirits soared. The storm ceased, and the sky felt fresh and new. Once again some attempted sleep. Others stood watch, hoping to meet messengers who could alert them to more of the Long Knives' plans.

# CHAPTER 42

## Mad Anthony Makes His Move

**James**
**15 August 1794**

They were on the move again. Before they moved camp, James whittled a quill, dipped his pen, and made his entry:

*15 August*

> *Wayne does not wish to Expose his Men to danger and will not wait Longer on an Answer from Miller Who Has not Returned. We leave this morning down The Maumee and will pitch battle with the united tribes. We know not Yet the Day nor the Hour. The Chickesaws and Choctaws Scouts who have been with us now will go no Further tho they Earlier Swore they would be Faithfull. The sight of them abandoning us has filled some of the Young Ones with Fear. Old Major Hunts who served under St Clair stays behind in Command of Ft Defiance with All of the Sick and Lame and most Wagons and heavy baggage as Wayne would have the Army travel Light. I write these words as we Depart and as the Foe is so close I do not kno if I will ever write More.*

He heard men the drummer thump the cadence of "Katie Cruel" and heard the men sing as they marched:

> *"Oh that I was where I would be*
> *Then I would be where I am not*
> *Here I am where I must be*
> *Where I would go I cannot*
> *Die dum diddle die dum dee day."*

The going was slow, and James idly mused upon the real Katie, the "Roving Jewel" camp follower fallen on hard times. But it seemed to him as if every camp follower had a hard life. He was distracted by a group of scouts up ahead, riding as if they were on the chase. They continued to protect the road builders as the Legion made its way to Snakes Town. Wayne's gout had worsened, and he suffered yet from the injuries of the falling beech tree. Even so, James could see him up ahead, pressing his men onward.

As evening fell, they stopped to make camp and fortified it as always. The next day, the 16th of August, they crossed over to the north bank of the Maumee and proceeded downriver. James rode away reluctantly, hating to leave the lush fields surrounding Fort Defiance behind.

Edward Butler soon trotted up beside him. "Miller's back with an answer to Wayne's truce letter. The tribes want more time—ten days—to think on Wayne's requests. Most—but not all—want war. They feel feisty and strong after the whuppings they gave Harmar and St. Clair."

James's stomach churned uneasily as he watched Butler ride away.

The following day, the legion traveled along the pleasant banks of the Maumee while Hamtramck and Lt Clark, in the left wing of the Kentucky Militia, had a hard time when they became lost while attempting to make their way through a thick wood. There was a fight that day, too, between a legion captain and an artificer. Wayne, believing the captain at fault, released the engineer, causing further bickering among the ranks.

The air buzzed—was it anticipation or fear?—when they finally stopped for the night at the Head of the Rapids. Many of the men reckoned that Roche de Bout and the coming battle was close, a mere seventeen miles away. A thrill, a fever, spread throughout the camp, gripped the men as they imagined a huge Indian host awaiting them.

After a restless night, the march began again. They passed small villages, all abandoned. James found the strange stillness unsettling. The hairs stood up on the back of his neck at the sight of the silent storehouses and trading posts. In the storehouse of one deserted town, account books were uncovered along with silversmithing tools rumored to bear the marks of John Kinzie, known to the Shawnee as Shawneeawkee, or Silver Man.

When they stopped among lovely abundant orchards to allow the hungry horses to graze, the anxious mood of the men seemed out of place. After the respite, they pressed on and finally came within the impressive sight of Roche de Bout, a small island of rocky crags covered with cedar trees.

Then scouts up ahead galloped towards them in a flurry of dust. Mounted warriors had ambushed them and they had barely escaped. As they fled, one of their number, that fearless scoundrel, William May, was taken by Indians as his horse slipped in the river. There was no point going after him. The possibility of losing more scouts was far too dire.

The afternoon passed in a blur, a flurry of activity in a sultry shimmering summer haze. Wayne decided to build a fort right there, where the men would deposit all provisions and extra supplies. Wilkinson ordered the soldiers to sleep with their weapons. More scouts returned, having spied a large Indian army. The enemy truly awaited them.

In spite of the fevered atmosphere, before the sun rose on the nineteenth, construction of the new fort, which would be called, "Deposit," began. While some set about building the breastwork, others continued scouting. One battalion drove back a group of Indians on horseback in the direction of Fort Miamis. They then returned to report that the Indian camps south of the British Post appeared to be deserted, and the trading post of McKee and his fellows also seemed abandoned. But they could not see round the bend to the fort itself.

Later that day, the men were given their orders. With an odd mixture of relief and regret, James discovered that he would be among those left behind to defend Fort Deposit with nigh a hundred other men. Yet Wayne gave no marching orders to the rest.

As evening fell, the men gambled. What would happen next? Some believed the order to advance in a surprise attack would come by midnight, but midnight came and went.

At five o'clock in the morning they were finally called up. Then another eerie portent: lightning struck. There was a violent thunderstorm and the camp was drenched. Nevertheless, Wayne readied his troops.

It was a stirring sight, the Legion in full form and regalia. Though the drums were wet and could not be played, the fifes and bugles rang out loudly as the men assembled. The spies led the way, followed by sixty-five scouts, and Major Price's hundred and fifty horsemen of the Kaintucke Militia. The infantry who came next made a vivid contrast to the scouts in their tanned buckskins.

James smiled at the thought that even Marie would have approved the outfits of the foot soldiers: blue jackets with red facings, white lining, buttons, vests and trousers. Bandoleers crossed their chest, and they carried the improved musket with Wayne's favorite weapon, the bayonet. Their cocked hats bore crests of bearskin and leather cockades. Bright plumes, a different color for each sub-legion, fluttered in the drizzly breeze. The thunderstorm had scrubbed the air, but already it was humid again. Dazzling as the soldiers were, James felt no envy for them. In spite of the August heat, Wayne ordered that not one coat—or any other article of uniform—be removed either on the march or in battle.

Edward Butler lead one of the two companies of the 4th Sublegion Rifle Battalion. Behind him followed a stunning array of horse troops and the dashing dragoons, swords and pistols flashing at their sides. A group of brilliant dragoons preceded General Anthony Wayne—Black Snake—on his black stallion, at the head of the artillery column. He was every inch their leader—hair was dressed and powdered, arrayed in impeccable blue coat and black hat, tan breeches, and gleaming boots. His pistols were tucked into his belt, and his saber hung at his side. Next to him, both eager and anxious, rode those trusted officers who would deliver his orders on the field.

James was not envious of them, either. Their most important task was that of keeping Wayne himself out of the fight. His fervor during battle was legendary. It would be hard to restrain him, even though it had taken three of them to hoist Wayne onto his horse. No doubt the General's gout was worse than ever.

A train of horses transported sixteen howitzers and ammunition. Then followed more riflemen, more infantry and cavalry. More than three thousand soldiers slogged their way into the distance as they headed the short—around four miles, James reckoned—yet dangerous way towards Fort Miamis.

The fifes and bugles faded.

And James realized he was praying, making pleas to God for the safety of Butler, Wayne, Clark, Hamtramk and the Kaintuckes.

All was in God's hands.

James's stomach churned as he faced camp and interminable waiting. Would the Indians prevail as they did with Harmar and St Clair? Would they destroy these very forts so recently erected? Or could this be the end of the wars with the Indians? Might he hope to see his lost loved ones again?

*He hardly dared pray for this last wish. Could he finally have a life with Marie? A family of his own?*

# CHAPTER 43

## The Battle of Fallen Timbers

**White Buffalo**
**20 August 1794**

As morning dawned on the third day on the bluffs, hunger arrived with it. Many had exhausted their food supplies and the supply of any game nearby in the woods.

"We are going to Fort Miamis to get food," White Buffalo heard again and again.

Anxiety pricked at him. "How many of us are left here?" he asked. Their numbers were dwindling.

It was then that British traders from Fort Miamis arrived, bearing refreshment. Warriors crowded around them.

"This will make you strong for the battle ahead." The British smiled as they offered their jugs of rum, their splendid "English Milk."

Tecumseh pushed their prize away. But Lalawethika followed them, only to stumble back much later, his good eye red, and his speech slurred. No one bothered to speak with that rattler, and White Buffalo surely did not care to hear his garbled talk. It was bad enough when he was sober.

Big Fish climbed a tree, then ran to Tecumseh. "There's four hundred warriors and a few British. Mostly traders. I cannot tell if the English come prepared to fight."

They returned to their hiding places among the downed trees. Finally they heard the high whistling of the pipes and flutes the Long Knives played. There air pulsed with the hoof-beats of warhorses and the steps of marching men. Black Snake's army approached.

Several of the warriors stripped down to their breechclouts, and the Kispokos painted their bodies with bear grease. "We face off with Black Snake and his snake men, but we have a few tricks of the serpent, too."

The grease allowed them to slither up on their enemies or to slip away from them if the need arose. White Buffalo saw little need for it here in the forest. But in tall meadow grass, it was a helpful strategy. For Kispoko warriors, it was a necessary ritual.

Sinnamatha's voice rose in excitement. "We're in the vanguard!"

Blue Jacket called out orders and the Indian army scrambled into the shape of a half-moon. A band of older brothers, Wyandottes under Chief Tarhe, was in the right horn as were Mingos with Katepakomen—Simon Girty—as their leader. The uniforms of the militiamen the British brought down from Canady stood out—among the warriors, but soon their bright colors mingled and blended into those of the Indian forces on the right flank. The Shawanese, Miami, and Delaware made up the base of the half moon.

"This is the formation we used to outsmart St. Clair," a Kispoko noted with satisfaction.

Blue Jacket urged his warriors into place, and Tecumseh's small band positioned themselves in front of them, wriggling into the underbrush to ambush the enemy. The air stung with the scents of wind and fire, the scent of a mighty battle. Did the Thunderbirds fly above?

White Buffalo's heart raced as through the shouts came the huffing and straining of thundering horses as they broke through the trees. Trumpets burst and flutes shrieked. The enemy horsemen were here.

His chest thumped furiously as he held his musket steady. First they surprised a group of Wayne's scouts. Their horses reared in panic, and the scouts, fighting for control, retreated.

"Ah, this is almost too easy." Big Fish grinned and aimed his musket at a fallen scout, scrambling to catch his horse's reins.

Incredibly, his shot missed. And though the scouts retreated, it was not by much. Instead of fleeing in confusion and cowardice as they had during the losses of the drunken one called Harmar, and the other one called St Clair, this new army of General Black Snake regrouped and pressed onward unharmed. Relentless.

White Buffalo's group continued to fire at them from behind the leafy screens of fallen leaves and branches. Tecumseh directed him to stay close, and both fired off several more rounds. Then there was a break in the shots, and White Buffalo spun around to see Tecumseh fling away his musket in disgust. Jammed. They fell back, bleeding and burning as hot bits rained—*what was it?*—down on them.

"Stand strong," Tecumseh urged. "If someone will give me his gun, I will show you how to fight."

A Kispoko quickly tossed him a fowling piece, and Tecumseh led them all forward again only for them to fall back once more.

The Americans were strong. They now used their bayonets in a way White Buffalo—indeed the entire Indian nation—had never seen. One of the Kispoko cousins fought in close combat with a Long Knife scout on horseback. White Buffalo took aim, only to see his comrade fall dead before he could shoot. The American wheeled away onto his next target.

Through the smoke, flying cinders, broken tree limbs and debris, White Buffalo scanned the scene farther off. Horsemen, dragoons, he'd heard them called, whipped forward. With sabers and pistols they successfully beat back the points of the Indian crescent—the flanks. He tried to spot his friends. Lalawethika was nowhere to be found, but it appeared as if most of their party was still intact.

The groans of wounded men and the neighs of panicked horses echoed in his ears when through the din he heard Tecumseh shout. "Where is Sauwaseekau?"

Soldiers thundered toward their hiding place.

The scouts were nearly upon them now, followed by leaping foot soldiers. With a discipline not seen in the battles of two years past, the Long Knives ran forward, stopping briefly to shoot, stab with their bayonets, then reload and race away, scrambling quickly over the downed logs in their path.

They easily climbed over the barricades; like swarming ants, they were everywhere. Then White Buffalo spied the origin of the fiery hail. The Long Knives had a new weapon, a cannon with a shorter barrel which shot ammunition much higher than the cannons of the past. Molten shards of hell showered down upon them. The Great Serpent was truly at work.

Several of his group were cut and bleeding; some were seriously wounded. Slick pools of red dotted the ground surrounding the areas of brush and fallen limbs. Severed heads and limbs littered the battlefield. The new cavalry was obviously skilled in the use of their long knives.

The air was a bitter, burning haze, and sweat trickled into White Buffalo's eyes. He could barely make out his next target—a horseman attacking a Wyandotte brother—when through the clouds of smoke and thundering of weapons, he heard Tecumseh's command, coming as if from miles away.

"Retreat!"

Scores of warriors fled towards the water. Tecumseh blocked off their little group and flailed his arms at them to stop. "Do not go down to the river! Get horses!"

They managed to capture some riderless mounts, and together they galloped for the slightly higher ground skirting the bluffs of fallen timbers. They raced north for Fort Miamis.

From this position, they once more had sight of the river, and a sorry sight it was. Wounded warriors strove to escape the Long Knives' murderous reach, but slipped on river rocks and found themselves stuck to the ends of bayonets. The Maumee flowed red. Tecumseh's brother, Lalawethika, The Rattler, suddenly reappeared and traveled alongside them, quiet for once. No one had seen Tecumseh's older brother, Seewasekau, since the battle had started.

Tecumseh rode in angry silence.

Then they caught sight of the British traders.

From a safe distance near a curtain of forest, Alexander McKee and Matthew Elliott watched what was left of the battle.

"They persuade others to fight, but keep themselves safe," Tecumseh muttered angrily.

"They dare not come closer," said Big Fish. "I heard that if any white Indians were caught by the Americans it would be worse for us than you." Indeed, they had passed an acquaintance who had warned them of the torture of Charles Smith, a white Shawanese. Shot through the knees by a Long Knife during combat, once discovered to be white, his captors had stopped and taken the time to quarter him alive.

They finally arrived at Fort Miamis, only to find the gates barred to them. Soldiers, too, from the Canady forces that had fought beside them were also locked out and told to go home by the British Major William Campbell.

At this betrayal, the broken forces fled in every direction. White Bufffalo watched in dismay and confusion. Many of the conquered said they would go down the Maumee and on to Lake Erie, and through the smoky air they faded into the forest along the riverbanks that led north.

A warrior who had fought alongside Blue Jacket approached their group as they waited in shock amidst the chaos by the fort. Blood streamed from a right arm dangling useless.

"McKee urges us to fight again," he said.

Tecumseh scowled. "Three times we tried and were driven back. Our medicine here is bad. I will search for my brother. Then we go to our families and gather on Swan Creek."

# CHAPTER 44

## Red River

**John/Quetaske**
**Fallen Timbers**
**20 August 1794**

Adopted—well, at least taken in— by the Shawnee once more.

Now that he was a valuable hunter, Quetaske was never in danger of being put to work with the women and slaves. And they didn't bother to change his name this time, either. "He Who Limps" just fit him too well, he reckoned.

Well, his new Indian father had hauled him down by canoe to a branch of the Maumee where they could look on the battle that was soon to happen on the bluffs above. Like many others, they would wait nearby so that when the Long Knives fell, as would surely be their fate, they would be among the first to share in the spoils.

But there was no rushing forward to plunder white corpses. Quetaske knew he would not do this anyway, not since his friendship with Colonel Hardin. He had gotten good at disappearing, and he might get a chance to do it again, in the ruckus and melee. There were Indians and whites—and white Indians—of every possible loyalty scattered through these parts, awaiting battle and its aftermath. It would be easy for him to slip in with a group of his choosing.

But even his new father had no chance to plunder. Before they even pulled their bark to the bank, wounded Indians rushed towards them, slipping and stumbling on the rocks.

The river ran red.

He and his new father paddled away from the carnage and death along the shore and returned to their camp to the south. Not full of riches but woe.

# CHAPTER 45

## Scraps of Eternity

**Talitha**
**Swan Creek**
**August 1794**

While they'd waited for the battle to end and their loved ones to return, Talitha and Tepeke continued to gather more herbs—and willow bark to treat pain—from the banks of the Swan Creek. Tepeke would not speak, and to Talitha's shock, her hair, once black and glossy as a crow's wing, turned white overnight.

There was no time to worry about their missing. They must use their gifts as Mekoche healers to soothe the suffering wounded who had fled there after the battle on the bluffs.

Together they bound an injured man's arm, when Tecumseh appeared before them, gaunt and gray. He waited quietly for them to finish, then led them to a the shelter of a twisted tree almost bare of leaves.

"Sit and rest a moment," he said.

They wearily sat upon a pile of dry leaves. But this was no resting time.

"Auntie, Little Sister, there is bad news. My brother Seewauseekau is killed in the battle. And the father of White Buffalo, Standing Elk, lives no more."

That familiar claw of fear clutched at Talitha's heart.

He squatted beside them. "White Buffalo is with Prairie Deer and his family. The men of Prairie Deer's clan, your Mekoche, will

ready the body of Standing Elk for burial, and the Turtle clan will prepare my brother."

He rose, pulling them up with him, and clasped them to him in
turn. "I am sorry."

Then he left.

Through tears, they watched him slip away into the smoky haze of
burning fields. This should have been a time of happiness, the Festival
of Green Corn. Instead, their world blazed around them. All was death,
destruction, and pain. The ashes hung in the air, mere fragments of lost
lives, scraps of eternity floating in the breeze.

Tepeke was right about the path they were on. Not only were
sacred bundles lost, but also—as she had warned—the war charms.
Surely the Great Horned Serpent slithered freely in their midst and
tormented them.

In the days to come, they laid the men of their clans to rest in the
way of the Shawanese, and many came to honor them. Kekewepellethe,
now acting as chief at Swan Creek came, as did Blue Jacket and other
important leaders.

One last comfort was old Scout, who hobbled after them, legs
stiff and muzzle as white as Tepeke's hair. In the cold evenings 'Talitha
sat beside him where he lay on a pallet near their fire. She scratched
him behind his ears, and praised him for his years of loyalty. Tepeke
told him the dog story.

"Sometime after creation, there was a great rumbling, and a big
canyon opened up, splitting the earth in two. The first man and first
woman were on one side of the chasm, while all the animals were on the
other. As the canyon opened wider and wider, the animals grew fearful,
and ran to hide in the forests. All except the dog."

Talitha rubbed Scout's head and his eyes blinked open. His ears
twitched.

Tepeke continued. "This one stayed behind, looking over at the people. He wanted to join them. His love for The People was greater than his ties to all the other animals."

Scout gave Talitha a lick as she, too, stroked him.

"So the brave dog took a leap across the dangerous abyss. Yet he could not make it all the way. Only his front paws clung to the far cliff. And then the people came to the dog, and pulled him up, hugging him to themselves."

Scout let out a long groan.

"Now," they said, "you will be our companion forever."

One cold morning they woke to find him lying stiff beside their pallets. They buried him at Swan Creek, near their other lost ones.

Talitha missed him so. Strange, though. Afterwards a crow followed her from time to time throughout the camp, peeping at her with bright eyes. She remembered when Scout first appeared, there had been a crow following then, too. Among her people, the bird meant good luck or 'good medicine.' But in a place like this, after all the bloodshed, burning, and pain, it was hard to imagine good fortune.

Dove Trees married her Seneca, and was often busy with new wifely duties. Talitha grew even more lonesome when she did not see much of White Buffalo. After the twelve days of mourning ended, he joined Tecumseh's hunting party. Not only were Tepeke and Talitha supplied with fresh meat, the venison the hunters brought was shared with other hungry folks who had no one left to hunt for them. The game was a welcome addition to the salt pork and meager vegetables and rice that the British from Fort Miamis shared.

One day, as a Scotch redcoat distributed rations to them, he took notice of Talitha.

"It's my own sister back in Aberdeen you remind me of. Your eyes, of that same blue, and ye've got that russet in your hair, though ye've tried to hide it." It was true; she had tried to darken it with bear's grease.

He touched her hair, lightly, and in the late summer light, red glints danced off the strands. "Ye needn't fear," he said as she recoiled from his touch. "I'll not interfere with ye. I'd say ye've all been interfered with enough."

He limped away. Even though he was one of the redcoats, her heart softened towards him. Had they not lied and urged them into this predicament, only to fail to come to their aid in battle?

Her anger did not burn long. The soldier could not have been that much older than she was, and was far from his own family. She reminded him of his sister, and she realized his limping reminded her of her long lost brother, Johnny.

Out of the thousand or so Indians at Swan Creek, few felt pity for the British, once their "fathers," but now their betrayers. Oh, they had thrown up a blockhouse for their defense here at the creek. That much was true. But the clanging shut of the gates of Fort Miamis—in their desperate faces—still rang in their ears. The shame clung to them and little trust was left.

The chiefs bitterly repeated the words of Campbell, the British chief who had betrayed them—shut the fort gates on them. "I cannot let you in! You are painted too much, my children!"

Many came to believe the British had only used the Shawnee and their allies, the whole Western Confederacy, for their own purposes in acquiring more land and trade for themselves. Stranger still was talk that Blue Jacket might soon take part in a peace party that would approach Black Snake—General Wayne—in the new year.

Talitha, however, had other things on her mind.

In the dismal autumn, brightness fell. After a particularly successful hunting trip, White Buffalo approached Tepeke as she and Talitha sat tying herbs ouside the entrance to their *wegiwa*. He carried a bale of furs. "Auntie, I know it is not much. But the time has come. I will wed Talitha, and these are the gifts I bring. I ask your blessing."

Tepeke rose and accepted the bundle, tears in her eyes.

"My son," she said. "You have always had my blessing. May Moneto bring you his favor now, and many children. May we have peace and a return to our old ways." She embraced each of them, then slowly turned back to her work.

Talitha and White Buffalo exchanged a worried glance. Tepeke had not recovered from the losses to the tribe. Would the loss of Talitha be too great?

White Buffalo wrapped his arms around her. "She has always wanted this, Talitha," he whispered. " My mother told me. She will be happy one day again."

He reached into his bag and pulled out a deer hoof, and Talitha realized he was carrying out the old custom. The deer's foot was a symbol that he would always provide her with meat and furs, food and clothing. She, in return, was to present him with an ear of corn, to show him that she would be a good wife, one who would provide bounty for the family from the fields and gardens.

As he handed her the gift, he said, "I know you cannot give me corn as it has all been destroyed."

She reached to accept his token, then held on to his free hand. "Surely, you do not think I am the sort of wife who would let a small thing like that stop me." She put down her treasure and pulled him onto a pallet beside her, then picked up a woven basket from one end of the bed. She took off the lid, and showed him the contents.

"I gathered some before the fields started to burn." Her hand burrowed beneath some moss and she pulled out a perfect ear. "For my husband." She proudly placed it in his hand.

He put down the corn and clasped both of her hands in his, and filled her eyes with his smile.

"I do not want to leave you. But I must go with Tecumseh to hunt again, to make sure you have food for the winter. But soon, before the new year, I will be your husband, and you will be my wife."

And now it was her turn for tears, but happy ones.

# CHAPTER 46

## Mad Anthony's Revenge

*"The Black Snake, the great General Wayne...*
*was a true warrior and a brave man;*
*he was equal to any of our chiefs that we have,*
*equal to any that we have ever had..."*

Reverend John Heckewelder, quoting the Shawnee

**James**
**Fort Defiance**
**September 1794**

James enjoyed his extra gill of whiskey after a messenger brought news of the Legion's victory to Fort Defiance. Mad Anthony had done it, run them Indians off the bluffs and chased them out of the Glaize. Some headed for Detroit, while others went down below the Ohio, though it was true a good many were still camped on Swan Creek licking their wounds and waiting for the British to come to their aid with food and shelter.

The battle had been short lived. Less than an hour, most said. Afterwards, Wayne himself traveled the two miles up to the British fort to participate in the teasing and taunting. Told General Campbell to get out of American territory. Tried to goad them into engaging.

They wouldn't, of course. So right under their noses he set their crops and gardens afire and they couldn't do a blessed thing about it, not since the Indians had hightailed it. The Americans finally feasted on the taste of victory.

Old Tony fired up a swathe nigh fifty miles long and ten miles wide of Indian corn fields and villages, mostly abandoned before the battle. A smoky veil hung over the whole area, all the way back to Fort

Defiance. Now Wayne was back at what had been called Fort Deposit, and James and the artificers kept busy strengthening the place in case the British decided to make a fight of it after all. He took up his journal, and once again, recorded the happenings.

*1 September 1794*

*Three Hundred of us now Labor under Major Burbeck. Our task to build up this Fort to Defy any attacks as its name suggests. The Howitzers that confounded the Indians on the Bluffs will now go one to Each Blockhouse. I have again met up with Lt William Clark brother of Famed Indian Fighter who complains the Work goes on too Slowly.*

Clark joined him one afternoon as he took a meager dinner of biscuit and dried fish beneath a tree on the riverbank. "The Kaintucke's are weary of their orders now that the battle is won," he said. "They won't come out, even when the trumpets call. Some of them are sleeping on guard duty or leaving their posts."

"You forgot to mention the prank they pulled yesterday," James added.

Clark leaned back against the tree. "Ah yes. That was a proud moment."

The Kaintuckes had been fooling and sporting and fired their muskets in camp. The Legionnaires, thinking it was Indian insurgents—some were skulking about again—formed into lines to repel the enemy only to find it was the Volunteers at play. James could not help thinking of Marie's trick of so long ago, back at the Kaintucke fort where his heart was first stirred by her, and he could not be angry at their antics. He smiled, wryly. "I did hear that commotion."

"Now they have been sent out to forage—you know our stores have not yet arrived from Fort Greeneville?"

"Yes." The lack of food was a constant worry. "But I have not noticed that the gleaners ever bring back much."

"No, there is not much to be had." With the burnings of the surrounding cornfields and deserted villages, food was indeed scarce.

"The chore is merely a ruse to keep them out of trouble. And," he said, lowering his voice, "many pass their time at the sales of the property of the dead. They spend their pay either there or in gambling over the belongings afterwards."

They sat silently a moment, mulling over the losses of the recent battle. James held out a scrap of fish to Clark.

"Thank ye." Clark chewed awhile and swallowed the morsel. James knew that as fellow Kaintuckes, both he and Clark were partial to the volunteers. Clark struggled now, seemed to be of two minds: torn between anger at the men and thinking up excuses for them.

"They're young lads," Clark mused. "Homesick, a lot of them. And now the fever and ague is back. There is no bark. They are eating unripe vegetables because they can find little else, and with these great fatigues they must do…" His voice trailed off.

Clark shivered then, and James remembered William himself suffered mightily from the ague.

The lieutenant's face was peaked and pale. At least his welts were gone. Many men had been stung by nettles that grew in waist-high patches on their way to the recent battle. Most quickly recovered from the pesky stings. But it had taken days for Clark to recover from the painful rash the nettles left on his freckled skin. In spite of his troubles, Clark was no shirker but a favorite of the men.

As if reading James's thoughts, Clark gathered himself together and stood. "But then we all have our work set before us, isn't that right?" He wiped his hands on his breeches. "I'd best be off."

He began to walk away then slowly turned about to face James. "You are still keeping that journal, aren't you?"

"Yes sir."

"I am happy to hear it. I have been writing in mine for five years now. My sister is the one who first encouraged me in the practice, back when I was in the Kaintucke militia—the volunteers—under John Hardin. I believe it is a habit that may serve one well. Who knows who may read our words one day?" As he turned away, the lips on his long, white face curved into a faint smile.

James wrote in the firelight while crickets sang.

*3 September*

> *So many sickly that Wilkinson does say his Right Wing will not have 120 left to Defend there position should an Enemy Come. There is also other Discontent among the Ranks. One of the Artificers is confined for Insolent Behavior by Capt Tilton but Wayne himself has rode into his tent in a Rage to abuse Tilton in Grossest Terms and now our man is Back with us. Captain Butler continues to labor Mightily showing Great Skill be it Ax, Spade or Pick.*

Butler was more at peace now that the battle was over. Perhaps, like James, he was happier to be build than to destroy. They still shared supper of an evening, and afterwards Butler pulled out his jaw's harp. In spite of his brighter mood, he had taken to playing a tune called "Sinclair's Defeat," a song about the battle where his brother lost his life.

It was a mournful melody, and Butler stopped abruptly to reflect on the recent battle.

"While we were on the bluffs our company lost its way. I was not sure we would make it. We got all caught up in the woods. Redskins popping up from the tall grasses and fallen trees, the whole forest was tumult of flying branches. Hot metal rained down on us—from the Howitzers. The sound of the horns deafened us." He raised his eyebrows. "I guess we didn't know if we were headed for heaven or hell, at the sound of all those trumpets. All we could do was run forward. So we did. Regained our position. Then we could back up Gibson and save our left flank."

The Indian forces' strategy to surround the US army was a dismal failure. Instead, the Legion had trapped them. But all was not well in the victorious Army of the United States.

*Waynes Great Industry stays with him But the Dragoons feel their Losses with Major Winston now sick and all four of There Commanders Dead or Wounded. Clark tells me all they talk of is the glory to come, the longed for return to the Doings, Courtings, Gallanting, Balls and Assemblies of Lexington.*

James put down his quill and smiled. No belle of Lexington could match the beauty of his Marie. Where was she now? He was almost used to the dull pang in his heart, the ache that thrummed in him when he thought of her and wondered how she fared.

The following day the cattle arrived along with the packhorses and sheep, but sadly, no whiskey. The work of the poor fatigues would be doubly hard, and in their wretched state some preferred spirits to food. But there was no time for much worrying over them with so much to be done.

Clark, who was quartermaster as well as lieutenant, continued to fret over worried about supplies, even after the arrival of additional stores. That evening he announced a reward to a gathering of Kaintucke Volunteers.

"The food shipment is not enough. Wayne will pay three dollars to any of you who will use his horse to transport one hundred pounds of flour from Greenville. That pay will be taken back from the contractors who were to do it in the first place."

Grumbling arose. Greenville was near the southernmost end of Wayne's Trace. Back where they had started. They were expected to go all that way and come *back?*

"Listen!" He held out his arms to shush them. "He promises an early discharge to those who carry these burdens."

During the more hopeful murmurings that followed this offer, William turned to James who stood near him. "We are most desperate for supplies," he said quietly. "Worst of all, the lack of provenance is not accidental. There is intelligence that some of our suppliers may be intentionally holding back stores."

*11 September*

> *There are more Deserters now. They go to the British at Fort Miamis and Do Tell of our position putting us in Grave Danger Wayne believes. We are Left with Few Men to defend us With so many sick or leaving for Greeneville for supplies. Most of the horses in Camp have been given Over to escort the Food Convoys. This makes Further Dissension.*

*14 September*

> *We now leave behind the Sick and Wounded with many officers in Charge of them, We go to Build Waynes Fort South West of Here.*

James came upon Edward Butler as he felled timber with some of his men. He stopped to hail James. Worry lines etched his face.

"Halstead, our situation is dire. We are so short of horses we will need to use soldiers for the wagon teams—to haul the logs to build the fort."

"There's a recipe for a mutiny."

"Pray to God that more rations arrive soon."

Along the way, many of the packhorses gave out. Wagons broke. After countless missteps and miseries, late on the fifteenth of September they found the place for the fort, on the site of old Kekionga where the St Joseph and St Mary's Rivers met and formed the Miami.

Among the scattered relics in the ruins of the town lay children's playthings and the cooking tools of women. Once more, James could not help wondering about the fate of his sister Elizabeth and the children who had not returned—his niece, Nancy and nephew, John.

Were they dead? Would this victory lead to another prisoner exchange?

Eight long years they had been gone now. Could he dare to hope they were alive, that he might see them again?

The following day, four deserters from the British army arrived. They said 1600 warriors were at Swan Creek. The soldiers also told of twenty-five American deserters who were seen at Fort Miami. Indians had another six American deserters as captives.

"The Indians are not interested in trading them to the English. Or back to you," one of them reported. "One they have already scalped, and they make ready to burn the rest."

Well, James thought, that would save the Legion from having to shoot them. But James hoped this last news might help stem the rash of desertions, especially among the Kaintuckes.

*24 September*

The work of the artificers seems to grow daily. Each Company has give us two more Ax men to Cut and Trim timber and they will get a extra half Ration for this but it is all very Poor beef and Musty Flour. Horses give out so that now Officers drive teams of 15 to nigh 30 soldiers in Place of Horses to haul the Heavy Logs.

Then, at last a good word.

*30 September*

*Finally we have Flour, Cattle, Salt, and Whiskey.*

But it was not long before that, too, turned sour:

*Already some Soldiers stole a large quantity of Liquor from the Quartermaster and are drunk. Also the food will Not Last Long.*

*1 October*

*There is much fighting and Mutiny in the Kaintucke Camp. General Barbees Kaintucke Volunteers were to go once more South to Greenville to bring Supplies but as they were to be discharged in 10 days they refuse. Now Wayne visits their Camp and promises immediate Discharge upon Their Return and Four Days Whiskey Rations if they will go. And if they go Not they will loose all Pay and be made known to The War Office as Revolters. Barbee left at 5 this evening with only a few following orders while the rest are drunk and refuse to Obey.*

*2 October*

*At Daylight the Rest of Barbees left to join him. All but the sick.*

*7 October*

*Our Head Artificer Dodson Tharp has built a flatbottom boat that will carry 25 Barrells of Flour. It will go up the River towards Greenville and Wayne now will have a Supplie Route that no longer is upwards of 300 Mile as it is Overland but 20 Overland in times of High Water.*

In another week, the roads were much safer. Sutlers with trade goods started arriving from Detroit and even from Post Vincennes in the south at Fort Knox. In spite of all the labors of the last few months, to James it seemed like a dream when finally on the seventeenth of the month, the fort was complete.

*22 October*

*The fort is Dedicated today on this 4th Anniv of Harmars Defeat. It is Called Fort Wayne after our General and My Old Comrade Hamtramck is made First Commander. This Fort will hold 100 men and their families and many Traders as well.*

Two days later he sat alone under a full moon, and near the warmth of his campfire wrote his final entry.

*24 October*

*My old fingers Tremble as I write that My Marie has arrived with Some Sutlers she has known in Detroit and Her Own Stores to Trade. The sight of her again Fills Me with Joy and now this War is Past I will not wait to ask her To Wed. Mayhaps we can make a Farm nearby as Many Others even Hamtramck and Wells plan to do Who are no longer Needed to Defend the Fort.*

# CHAPTER 47

## Swan Creek

**Talitha**
**November 1794**

As the winter grew deep, dark news came their way.

White Buffalo returned from the hunt and spoke with Kekewepellethe and some of the young chiefs. He had aged since the battle of the fallen trees, when even Cyclone Woman had betrayed them. The bones of his face were chiseled, that of a man, not of the boy Talitha once knew.

"Blue Jacket is meeting with General Black Snake. To ask for peace."

Tepeke sat listening as she sewed moccasins in the last of the day's light, a small lantern with a dull flame at her side. Talitha and Tepeke had tried to make their *wegiwa* cozy in spite of the cold and their strange surroundings, far from their old villages.

"Blue Jacket brings with him our grandfathers, the Delaware, our younger brothers the Miamis and Ottawas, and our older brothers, the Wyandottes of Detroit River. They speak for peace with one voice. The Wyandottes on the Sandusky have already asked for a truce." White Buffalo frowned.

"Our people our divided. Some who do not wish to make peace will go to Loramie's across the Mississippi." Loramie's Store stood at the fork of the Great Miami. It was at the point of portage between the Miami and St. Mary's rivers where the French Canadian trader, Peter Loramie's had once had his popular trading post.

His eyes met Tepeke's. "Auntie, I know you and my mother will to go there with some of the uncles."

She nodded. This was the very best plan for her, to be with Prairie Deer and cousins who would hunt for her.

He held Talitha's hand. "At the new moon, Talitha and I will marry. She will come with me on the hunt at Deer Creek with Tecumseh and Sinnamatha, and Lalawethika and some others."

The frown flitted across his face again. The tribe bore witness to the shame of Lalawethika, the coward. The Rattler was drinking more and more of the white men's whiskey and the English Milk, and becoming more troublesome by the day.

On a gray morning towards the end of the month of *Kini kiishthwa*— November to the whites—Talitha and White Buffalo exchanged gifts and became husband and wife.

White Buffalo brought her a lovely doeskin robe made by Prairie Deer. Buttery soft, it was sun-bleached nearly white. Its hem twinkled with tiny silver bells. He also gave her sparkling brooches made by Shawneeawkee, shaped like suns with small flames surrounding them and designs cut into the middle.

Talitha dressed in the gifts that made her a wife. She wore new leggings she had made herself of soft buckskin decorated on the edges with more silvery bells. Under the robe she wore a gift from Tepeke: a long, light-blue calico shirt held closed by smaller silver disks similar to the ones on the robe. Beads and ribbons bordered the hem.

After they traded gifts, White Buffalo left to put on his new clothes. He had never looked more handsome. His glossy hair hung down, and round his neck a silver medallion—that matched the brooches Talitha wore—hung from a leather thong.

Talitha had made him a long shirt a shade darker than her own. One of the sleeves was adorned with a large silver circlet, a gift from Tepeke. Two bright feathers hung from it. Below the shirt were soft leather leggings and new moccasins Talitha made, decorated with colored porcupine quills and beads. There was more silver; Shawneeawkee had done well. Draped over one shoulder and fastened with another silver brooch at the side was a light colored trading blanket with a blue stripe around the edge, a gift from his mother.

Tepeke wept as she embraced them both.

In this camp filled with people of so many different tribes and customs, there was little ceremony, no days-long feast or dancing. But they did have a small dinner and celebration that evening: a delicious roasted beaver feast with corn pudding made from some of the ears Talitha had hidden away.

The Shawanese women taught girls how to be good wives. Talitha did not know, however, exactly what would happen when she went to share a *wegiwa* with White Buffalo. Yes, women spoke of their husbands in the moon huts, but the grandmothers who took care of the young-est women would give married women a warning just when the tales became most interesting.

Yet it was a wonder to be with White Buffalo, alone, grown up, wrapped in warm robes before a hot fire while a cold wind blew outside.

How could things be so bad yet so good at the same time?

In the cold days that followed their union, they snuggled in soft furs and fed one another, licked luscious juices from one each other's lips, sharing sweetness. When they fell asleep, however, they slept like brother and sister, hands clasped together.

Talitha wondered when things would change, but she felt shy. She took the plunge every day with her Shawnee sisters, and as she rubbed herself with sweet sage and other spicy herbs she received advice from some of the older sisters.

"Shawanese braves have never forced themselves on women as the whites do. You love White Buffalo, but he wants to make sure you are ready. Have you watched the men tame the wild horse? The horse must trust before it can be ridden." They turned away with naughty smiles.

While she wondered one day what more she could do to let White Buffalo know she trusted him, Dove Trees arrived, almost bursting.

"Talitha! I am with child! I know I am! Feel how hard." She placed Talitha's hand on her belly.

It felt no different than her own middle. "I don't feel anything. Are you sure?"

"I should have my moon blood, but it has not come. If you do not see me in the moon hut at the new moon, then you will know." Dove Trees flounced off.

The day of the hunt drew near, when she would leave with her husband, and she and Tepeke would be parted. One winter night before they left, Tepeke told the story of the People once more.

"Talitha, we soon part, but we will meet again. If we do not meet again before we travel the spirit road, you must remember this story for your children. You must tell them this:

'Washaa Moneto, the Great Spirit, made the world new again after a great flood. A giant sea turtle holds us on its back. He put the red people on this island, and he put our people, the Shawanoe, in the center, on the Shawanese River. The People are the first ones Moneto put here, a chosen band. Though all animals and men had a heart, this earth did not yet have its heart, and Moneto sent the People to Shawanese River, to be the heart of the Earth.'"

Tepeke voice was thin, like a reed blowing in the wind along the river's bank.

"Later he told them to go to the Mad River. Then he told them to go to the Mississippi. 'You will wait there,' said Moneto, 'and then you will find something coming to you that will make you very poor. Much misery. But Moneto makes you the heart of this land, and gives you a piece of his own heart, that you may endure.' "

The thin voice grew stronger. "Blue Jacket no longer speaks for us. Soon we leave to join others at Loramie's Store, where we will keep the old ways again."

She fell silent, and all they heard was the crackling of the fire. Talitha edged closer and clasped her mother to her.

Afterwards, she and White Buffalo, her own Shawanese Heart, made their way through the chilly night to their *wegiwa*. The sky above them was dark as soot, but sparkled with icy stars.

Their lodge was warm, and smelled of sweet smoke, the scent of Talitha's healing herbs mixed with the smoldering fire. When White Buffalo took her in his arms, his eyes burned, too.

Something had changed. He didn't talk, but pulled her down with him onto the bed of furs. He knelt before her and released her hair from its plaits. Then he twisted a lock of her hair round his hand and pulled her face to him, kissed her hard, then bit her softly on the lip.

He kissed her again and again, her mouth, her eyes, her throat. Then he groaned and pulled her up onto the pallet piled with furs and blankets, and laid her down. He pulled the buffalo robe back from her shoulders, kissing her all the while. He untied the laces on her shift, his fingers hot as they caressed her cool skin.

And then his fire entered her, and she could not tell where he started and she began, and soon they tumbled together and melted into one and the smoky world reeled round her head and stars seemed to sprinkle down through the window to the sky. White Buffalo shuddered, and she knew they were truly husband and wife.

Afterwards, he pulled his long hair back into a thong and gently kissed her lips, sore now, from so much pleasure.

His starlit eyes were wide and smiling. "We will make one for the People, my Talitha."

# CHAPTER 48

## Marie

**November 1794**

Sometimes it was good to be French. *Well, nearly half*, Marie thought as she pored over Aunt's copy of *Journal de la Mode et du Gout*, a magazine of the latest French fashions. But Aunt did not discriminate. She also had a copy of *The Ladies Magazine*, from Britain. Styles were changing: dresses had higher waists, some bodices ending right below the bosom. Stays were shorter and there were reports that some women did not wear them at all!

Marie and Aunt had been to the dressmaker several times in the few months of Marie's visit, and Marie had ordered some of the new styles, including short stays in a rare blue satin. Aunt Jo had raised her eyebrows at those, and Marie claimed they were for trade. She pretended many of the things she ordered were merchandise she would sell, and Aunt was none the wiser.

Marie's father, Aunt Jo's younger brother, had started out as a *coureur de bois*—free trader—and had since become a very wealthy merchant. He was among the first to travel to the camps and villages to trade. It was in a Delaware village that her father spied her mother and married her in the custom of the country—*a la facon du pays*, though later their union was blessed by a priest in Montreal. Like many others who had risen to wealth as he had, he was now a member of the famous Beaver Club of Montreal. Trading ran in Marie's blood, and Papa had agreed that she could have her own stores and dry goods to trade at the new Fort Wayne.

Her bed was covered with clothing to pack including a huge mound of cloaks, morning gowns—dishabille—shifts, a new riding skirt and coat, and a smaller pile of all the other things she would need, including handkerchiefs, gloves, stockings, bonnets, and shawls. She counted her six gowns: a variety of calico, sprigged cotton, broad striped, and silk. She laid the matching petticoats, beside them, and began to fold the muslin short gowns.

Ah, here was her favorite. She held it up to admire her handiwork, the pale embroidered forget-me knots, and fingered the delicate scraps of lace trim.

Aunt had sniffed. "Why do you go to such trouble? When no one will even *see* it!"

Such a question deserved no answer. She only smiled to herself.

Now she turned to the settee, loaded with clothing she had chosen for James. Aunt had not been invited on *these* shopping trips, she had only taken Sylvie, her aunt's maid, with her, and bought her silence by purchasing some sorely needed new items for the young girl.

Marie caressed the blue velvet waistcoat and jacket, to be worn with the tight fitting buckskin breeches. She'd had a blue broadcloth Great Coat made for him, single-breasted with cloth-covered buttons, turned-back cuffs, a high rollover collar and four shoulder capelets. There were four new hunting shirts. And, of course, after months on the march, James would need the new stockings and boots she had chosen some for him. She thought she well knew his size, but had enlisted the help of Polly Mann.

Polly had been delighted. "I know. I'll have him try on some of Adam's things while he's here, and then I will let you know how much larger or smaller to have them made for James." Polly was full of wonder and delight. "I'll let Uncle James think I'm sewing him a gift," she'd said.

Polly's sewing skills had definitely improved, but they were not up to the tailoring Marie had in mind.

Her favorite garment was the riding coat, similar to a frock coat, made of softest and creamiest elk hide, sun-bleached and exquisitely decorated and fringed. Woven quill-work covered the back seam and decorated the epaulets on the shoulders. Marie sighed as she pictured James wearing the beautiful coat, *reaching out for her*.

A loud clang disrupted her reverie, the doorbell announcing callers.

She listened to the footfalls of her aunt's maid, Sylvie, as she trudged to the door. There were some murmurs, and a slam as the door closed. Footsteps started up the stairs.

"I got you yer letter, ma'am."

*Sylvie could use some tips in maid deportment*, Marie thought, idly, as she opened the door, thanked her, then eagerly scanned the envelope.

Papa had written. Breathless, she ripped the letter open, and devoured the words she had longed for. The wagons and canoes had been hired, and the clerk was ready to accompany her to the place she would stay in Fort Detroit.

She pranced down the steps and entered the sitting room where aunt and beloved dog snored on a chaise before the fire.

"My letter's come!"

Startled, Aunt Josephine Therese spilled her spaniel, Bonnie Prince Charlie, onto the Turkey carpet. He yelped.

"*Quoi?*" Aunt Jo struggled to her feet. "Not word from your father already?"

"*Oui*, from him. He gives me permission to leave, and has all the arrangements settled."

"Oh dear oh dear!" Aunt Jo toddled about the room, fretting. The Bonnie Prince yipped again and snarled as she trod on his tail.

"*Ton père*, why does he come up with such the terrible plan for you?"

When Marie's mother died when she was quite small, Marie had intermittently been left in the care of Aunt Jo. And to Aunt Jo, Papa was always the irresponsible little brother.

"It is very safe now. I will read it to you."

"Oh *non*, oh *non*." Jo held her head in her hands and continued to totter about.

Marie sighed, rolled her eyes, and read. "My daughter Marie, has permission to come to Fort Wayne at once. I have planned her travel and escorts from Philadelphia to Fort Pitt. From there she will travel The Great Trail"—this was the Indian Waterway used by the *voyageurs*—"in *canot leger* with my most trusted clerk to Fort Detroit de Ponchartrain. Trade goods will be sent in the *canot du maitre*. In Detroit, she will stay at the home of my trusted friend, Madame LeBlanc, and from there be escorted to Fort Wayne." Marie stopped. She would not read aloud the most important part, the second part of the letter that contained the words of consent for Marie to marry James Halstead.

Aunt was too vain to wear spectacles, so there was no danger she would read it for herself. No, this would be Marie's most delicious secret, an elopement with the man she had loved these many years. Every item of clothing spread out upon her bed was chosen with the idea of pleasing James. Aunt did not need to know that either.

Aunt was aghast. "Send you to Fort Wayne?! To be *scalpé*! You will lose your beautiful hair. Or you will drown on the way." She collapsed in her chair, groaning, then sat up suddenly. "Your new gowns! I do not know how you will pack all of them. They will be ruined. They will go overboard. You will have to leave them *here*," she said with satisfaction, acting as if she had just played her trump card.

"I will *not* be leaving them here. As you know, Papa has made me the finest *cassettes* to store them in."

Aunt snorted. "And what will you do when you get there? Look at you, an old maiden, *célibataire*. All she has is her work and to be a shopkeeper. I do not know what will become of you." Aunt's English got worse when they argued.

A platter clattered onto the sideboard, where Sylvie should have been polishing silver but wasn't. Just listening, gawking, and gaping.

"Sylvie, why don't you bring in some wood for the fire? This room has suddenly grown quite chilly," said Marie.

Aunt Jo waved a bejeweled hand. "Why should she go? We have fuel. Let the child hear. She might learn something. What not to do."

"The wood, Sylvie," Marie repeated, and the young girl scuttled out. Sylvie was indentured for another year, but Marie doubted her aunt's employ would do anything to brighten her prospects.

Aunt Jo moaned. "Ah, you must always have your way, going off to the wilds. Ever since you were small you have left to desert me. So many times. And what am *I* to do without you?"

*Aye, there's the rub.* Scenes like this were among the many reasons Marie preferred life at the forts and outposts to life with Aunt Jo.

As for what Jo would do without her, Papa was most generous in his allowances to this older sister whenever Marie came to stay. Aunt Jo enjoyed the shopping excursions—compliments of Papa—as much as Marie, and had several new outfits to show for it

Aunt gave up her argument rather quickly. Josephine Terese lay back in the chaise with a hand on her forehead.

And Marie tried to keep from dancing as she made her way across the room to plant a kiss on her head. Why not be generous?

She was leaving to be with her beloved.

Marie gathered up a growling Prince Charlie and dumped him onto her aunt's lap. "You'll be fine, Aunt. You don't need me. You have The Bonny Prince."

Sylvie returned with the wood, disappointment scrawled across her face. The show was over.

And Marie *did* dance all the way up to her room.Marie felt only the tiniest twinge of guilt at keeping her marriage plans from Aunt. She simply could not bear to witness the horrified response, hear the warnings showered upon her if she should marry a soldier and frontiersman. She, who had gone to school in France! Yes, there would be dire predictions—of diseases he would no doubt have picked up at camp, prophecies about missing limbs, and Marie's future as a nursemaid to a broken man.

She would not have James spoken about like that. Her dream was at last within her reach. She had behaved herself for a very long time, while James was at war, while she traded alone at the forts, and fended off the attentions not only of clerks but chief factors.

Instead of attending balls in Philadelphia, Marie had gone to Mass, said her prayers, and James was delivered. After the victorious battle they called Fallen Timbers, he had written and asked her to be his wife.

She would. She could not—would not—wait any longer.

There was no need for Papa to attend her wedding. He had other children with Indian women, and now was kept busy with the antics and attractions of the famed Beaver Club of Montreal. *Don't worry daughter, after the passing of the calumet and the harangue, I always raise a glass to you!*

Yes, he had doted on her when she was small, but as the years went on, their dealings with one another had become that of business partners. Marie did not mind. Much. At least she would now have something—and someone—of her own.

The carriage to Pittsburgh waited below. Marie took a last glance at herself in the mirror She was twenty-five, no longer a *young* beauty. Her dear friend, Polly Mann—James's niece— had four children already, and probably another on the way. And Marie not even married. But there was no gray in her glossy black hair, no lines on her smooth, glowing face. Her dark eyes sparkled as she perched a new beaver hat— designed by herself— on her head. It was of coat fur, in the modified clerical style with a broadened heightened crown and ribboned hatband pinned with a small bunch of silk flowers.

Beneath her blue silk cloak, she wore one of her warmer blue gowns with a quilted petticoat, new stockings and boots. She winked at herself before she clicked down the stairs to bid *adieu* to Aunt Jo and Sylvie.

In a few short days, she would be with James.

They stood before the priest at St. Anne's Cathedral in Fort Detroit, an elderly cleaning woman as their witness. Marie thought her face would break from smiling. James wore the blue velvet jacket and waistcoat, the leather breeches, and over all, the gorgeous riding coat. He stood tall and strong, his white hair curled back, his blue eyes intense. She was almost frightened by how fiercely his eyes burned when he first saw her in her most delicious gown of silver tissue with low-cut bodice. He had looked at her just that way when she was a foolish girl in a fort.

The wedding was in French; she had coached James in the responses. There *was* the matter of the tiny lie she had told the priest— in French again—that James was Catholic. This had pricked her conscience just a little until she learned that even Anglicans occasionally married at St. Anne's. Who was to say he would *not* become Catholic? And certainly their children would be.

The service was short. The dour priest was only visiting, in rotation until a new one arrived, and he did not take much interest in them.

Outside, James stopped mid-stride, turned to her and enveloped her in his arms. The blue fire still burned in his eyes, setting her aflame.

"Truly, I cannot believe this day has come." His voice was husky.

She tilted her head up, pressed herself to him, and tasted the first sweet kiss. He lifted her and carried her as if she were light as a child into Madame LeBlanc's carriage. Once inside, they stared at one another, then burst into laughter.

Then he gathered her up, pulling her onto his lap. She sighed with happiness as he crushed her to him—a bruised bouquet. The sheer lace gown crinkled and puffed up around her like so many petals. She shivered as he pressed his face against the silken bodice, as she felt the warmth of his breath through the fabric and then on her bare skin. He pulled her face towards his, kissed her again and again, each kiss hotter and longer than the last.

There was not enough room for what she wanted him to do to her, what she wanted to do to him.

His mouth was sweet and spicy with a hint of cinnamon. Her heart beat faster as he gently tugged on the silken ribbon that closed her pelisse. It fell open, and he reached inside, to caress every inch of her. Her hat was knocked aside, and her pinned-up curls fell loose around her face.

The carriage rumbled to a stop.

James hastily wrapped her in the shawl crumpled on the seat beside her and tried to cover her disarray as she attempted to push her curls back under her hat.

"Just in time." He stepped down from the coach and held her tight as she tumbled out of the carriage into his arms.

After leading them to the meal they had spread out for them, the servants made themselves scarce.

James and Marie only picked at a few morsels, and then a maid reappeared to lead them to their chamber.

Warmth radiated from a small fire that whispering and crackling in the fireplace. Light danced off the walls; a golden glow spread from fragrant candles burning in crystal candelabras perched about the room. The swagged drapery covering the windows added to the warmth. The few sticks of furniture, including a small bedside table, were in the French *style étrusque* favored by Marie Antoinette.

The bed was lavishly covered, padded with rosy satin and silk pillows.

Disheveled and eager as she was, Marie's face burned and she turned shyly away.

James reached for her, gently unwrapped her shawl, and gazed at her as if she were a present he had just opened. A flush spread over her. He sat on the bed and took her hand.

"Come here, wife."

She liked the sound of *that*, grew even warmer with pleasure.

He pulled her onto his lap once more, and the delicious touching began again. He slowly moved one hand to the open bottle of French brandy on the bedside table.

"We must drink a toast. To this," he said. He touched her lips with his finger and kissed them softly. He reached around her for the glasses, and she helped, pouring the brandy into two small crystal goblets. They clinked them together, and after she took a sip, James took the glass from her, gently set it down and traced her cheek with his finger.

" 'Drink to me only with thine eyes, and I will pledge with mine,' " he murmured. *He* almost seemed a bit shy as he looked away from her a moment. "Or leave a kiss within the cup, and I'll not ask for wine.' That's from Shakespeare's friend, Ben Jonson. But it appears we *will* ask for brandy."

He held his glass to her lips, then leaned forward and pressed his warm lips against hers. He put a finger into the liquid and traced a brandy heart on the bare skin above her bodice. Then he leaned over and she gasped as he licked the spirits from her skin. Time froze as he pulled her down onto the luxurious quilts and covers. Her head spun in the sweetness of it all, and the world disconnected, and there was only Marie, only James, and then only one. She knew what it was to be possessed, and it was good.

She had not dared to dream it could be like this. Even though she was French.

*Well, nearly half.*

# CHAPTER 49

## Deliverance

*"…remaining prisoners among the Indians,*
*shall be delivered up in ninety days from the date hereof,*
*to the general or commanding officer at Greenville,*
*fort Wayne, or fort Defiance;*
*and ten chiefs of the said tribes*
*shall remain at Greenville as hostages,*
*until the delivery of the prisoners shall be effected."*
The Treaty of Greenville

**Polly**
**Indian Creek**
**Summer 1795**

"They weren't there." Exhausted, Polly flopped her dusty hat onto the porch rail and let out an exhausted sigh. She was with child again, and her latest baby, Henry, not yet a year old. All these folks depending on her and all she seemed to long for was her lost sister, Nancy, and her brother John.

Adam pressed her to him, put out his hand to greet James. "Bad luck," he said.

James, too, shook the dust from his hat. "We are not without hope. The Indian nations have a timeline. Ninety days from the start of August, and chiefs from the ten different tribes turn themselves in as hostages up at Greenville. They stay put until their people turn over what captives they have—bring them in either to Greenville or Fort Defiance. The treaty says Fort Wayne, too, but most of the captives are turning up at Greenville since that's where their chiefs are."

Polly felt a sting; the threat of tears pricked her eyes. To go all that way and come back with nothing—her heart felt likely to break.

"They still could turn up," James said gently.

"I suppose," Polly murmured, brushing her eyes with the back of her hand. She cleared her throat. "You know, Adam, there is a whole town there at Greenville, built specially for the treaty."

Adam raised his eyebrows in surprise.

"I saw my old commander, Hamtramck," James said. "He told me Indians are arriving at Greenville from more than four hundred miles away. Even from as far away as Fort Mackinac."

He grinned wryly as he continued. "The legion has artillery pointed right at the council houses, should the redskins change their minds and put up a fight. Wayne's going to set up a boundary line to let the redskins know where they can settle, have their own villages again."

Polly frowned. She had heard of treaties with the Indians. They never seemed to last. Why would this one be different?

"The northern tribes and Lake Indians have no captives to return and could care little about the new boundary lines—makes no never mind to them. But turns out they made this trip just so's they could see General Wayne, old Black Snake. They've given him another name, too— 'The Wind'—on account of how he tore up and drove out everything before him at that Battle of Fallen Timbers."

"Did *you* see the famous General?" asked Adam. Adam apparently wanted to add more to the heroic exploits of the General, whom both Adam and his brother, Jacob, knew from the late war with the British.

I only saw General Wayne from afar. That was close enough for me. Wouldn't want to have the General draft me into any of that building—the council houses and such—he had going on. But I did run into my old friend William Clark. He'd had a good long talk with the General."

"Turns out, Mad Anthony was not imagining things when it came to Wilkinson. There was a whole conspiracy against Wayne, all through the last campaign. Some rascals in the camp wanted to dismember the whole United States. The artificer who worked with us briefly, and then disappeared—name of Newman—turns out he *was* a spy the whole while. Had henchmen, too. A fellow named Cooper even left letters some of our plans lying in the road for the Indians to find. Wilkinson never had acted alone."

Adam gave a low whistle. "Well I'll be."

Polly thought on what a fragile thing a new country was when a whooping and a hollering interrupted. Chloe, Elsie, and Adam on their way up from the creek with little Sal stumbling after. Baby Henry could not yet walk, but Elsie carried him in her arms.

James pointed at Chloe, his eyes thoughtful. "That one there's proof, Polly."

Chloe ran to him, grabbed him around the waist. "Uncle James, I didn't know you snuck in. I'm a what?"

She was twelve now. Her younger sister nearly reached their Uncle's shoulders. Polly bit her tongue. Chloe *should* be acting more ladylike, but whenever Polly was away she managed to find herself a pair of castoff buckskins to wear. Polly reckoned she'd begged or stolen them from Adam's nephews. One might think she was a boy were it not for the long blonde curls, tangled right now with twigs and hay.

She liked to dress like a Shawnee. Mercifully, she was so young when returned that she did not remember any of her time with them.

*How would it be for the others, who had been gone so long? If they were ever found?*

James tipped Chloe off her feet and answered her. "You're proof that sometimes a pesky sister comes home to roost."

James laughed as Chloe screamed and kicked as he upended her and swung her around by arm and leg.

"Next time you may be too big for me, miss, but right now I can still lift you," he hollered.

"Me, me!" cried Little Adam. Elsie handed the baby to Polly, who cuddled and kissed him while Sally pulled at her skirts until her father reached down to take her into his arms.

James lowered shrieking Chloe and scooped up Adam. "Alright, little Mann, " he said, and began to swing him in a wide arc.

"Did anyone have any news at all?" Adam asked softly.

"Of Nancy, no," Polly answered. "But like James said, back before the battle, some folks reckoned they'd spied John. The stories never matched up. One would say they saw him on the Wabash, another up by Detroit. They never mentioned the same tribe twice." She let out a ragged breath. "There must be many boys who look like John. Though you wouldn't think so, his being lame and all."

"Hmmm. You said you heard not one word of Nancy?" he mused.

"No. But Adam—lots of them brought to Greenville to be returned didn't want to come back to their families." Her voice caught. "To their white kin. It was awful. Like to how I'd feel if I was pulled from you all, I suppose."

Again she blinked back tears while Adam gave her a reassuring squeeze.

She tried on a stern expression for James and the children. "Y'all are finished with your horseplay now?"

"Yes!"

"That's a 'yes *Ma'am!*'" James corrected the children, and they echoed him.

"Then I'll get to fixing supper." She started up the porch steps, then paused and sniffed. "Something already smells mighty good in here."

"Jacob's Mary was down while I worked with Jacob at the mill. She made supper and brought the *Kinder* to play with ours while she cooked. They will sleep well tonight." He ruffled little Adam's hair.

"Elsie and Cory laid the table. Let's have supper. Let's go wash up, *Kinder*."

"Yessir, time's awastin." Polly could not help winking at Adam as she patted James on the shoulder.

"We've got to hurry and get you back to your wife."

# CHAPTER 50

## Crow Moon

*One crow for sorrow*
*Two for mirth*
*Three for a wedding*
*Four for a birth*
*Five for laughing*
*Six for crying...*

**Talitha**
**Deer Creek**
**Winter 1796**

Tecumseh's face was wide with smiles. Small wonder, Talitha thought. The hunting and trapping had gone well, and tomorrow they would leave the winter camp and make their way to Loramie's Station, where they would share their bounty with the many widows and children who no longer had anyone to hunt for them.

Tepeke and Prairie Deer awaited them there, and Talitha had a secret. She was happy to have something to share besides game and furs.

First, though, the men would ride off for one last hunt. When they returned, they would leave an offering of tobacco, *tipwiwe*, to carry thanks to the Creator, and soon they would be on their way back to her *neega* at Loramie's Station.

"Little Sister." Tecumseh stopped beside her, and tugged on her braid, a habit he had carried with him since she was a child.

"You know I made exceptions—to take you with us these past two seasons. I broke my rule of no women on the hunt. For this one."

He waved at White Buffalo, who was readying his horse but stopped to flash them a grin.

"Yes, and now you see what good luck she brings," White Buffalo called in response. "So many deer, so many furs. More than ever. You should have brought her a long time ago."

Talitha looked up from her work bundling hides and smiled back at him in thanks.

It was true Tecumseh had set aside his rule for them, and it had been a most prosperous season, shattering Tecumseh's long held belief that a woman on the hunt would bring bad luck. All knew that Tecumseh was the best hunter, but some of the Kispoko who now were a permanent part of their band wanted a contest. Wagers had been placed.

"Each of us will kill as many deer in three days as you," they boasted.

But when the three days were up, not one had more than twelve deer. Tecumseh brought in more than thirty. Clearly, Moneto smiled on him and on their expedition.

Tecumseh headed towards his own mount, clipping White Buffalo on the shoulder as he went past. "We'll see," he said. "You get us more game today, little brother, and then we will see about our lucky Talitha."

The happy mood shimmered in the air even after they'd ridden away. Thankfully, Lalwethika did not stay behind with her but left with the others. A poor hunter, he was merely tolerated. Sometimes he lagged behind on pretense of fishing in the creek that ran through camp, but usually he headed back into his *wegiwa* and slept off the effects of whatever rum he managed to acquire from the French traders and trappers who passed their way. Tecumseh still had a soft spot for The Rattler, and not only tolerated—but perhaps even welcomed—his company. Talitha reckoned this was because Seewausekau was gone and Lalawethika was the only brother he had left.

The Rattler made her uneasy. Blind in one eye, due to a hunting accident long ago, his face was skewed, and he looked evil. Unlike the other men in their group, he had never had a vision quest. Instead he fed off Tecumseh's fine reputation. Yet Tecumseh loved him, and for that reason she tried to set aside her bad feelings and searched for good in him as well.

Sinnamatha—Big Fish— was the one she missed.

In the months after Fallen Timbers, he had disappeared for weeks at a time. And then they received news that he had reunited with his brother, Abram. In the months following the Treaty at Greenville, he and his brother together had crept into the gatherings with others who were being traded back to the whites. However, they had not rejoined the whites right away. First there was an angry meeting with Tecumseh, followed by tears from each when Big Fish left.

How could he choose to leave them?

Sadly, The Rattler, not lovable Big Fish, was their now constant companion.

The faces of others who had flitted between two worlds flashed before her. First came Johnny Logan, sometimes known as Spemica Lawba. His Bluebird had been exchanged, taken back from a white family, and now they were together, married, with a little one on the way.

The cawing of crows drew her thoughts away from another bird, the lovely Bluebird, Dove Trees' former rival for Johnny Logan. Talitha glanced up to see birds of another hue, at the black birds, clumped together on a bare branch, staring at her. It was *haatawi kiishthwa*, the Crow Moon. At this time of year, the cries of the crows let the People know that the end of *papoonwi*, winter, was near.

They continued to gaze at Talitha with bright eyes, and she thought back to an old rhyme a funny woman had taught her when she was a white child. The woman was like a soldier, with men's clothes and a loud voice. Only she said her rhyme was about magpies, not crows. How did it go?

*One for sorrow*
*Two for mirth*
*Three for a wedding*
*Four for a birth...*

Talitha could not bring the rest of it to mind. The past, her white family had faded into dim ghosts of memory. How could one choose the mist over this? This love. This life, as ragged as it could be.

She forced herself to hum a song as she packed the hides into bales. For some reason the cawing of the lucky crows did not sound lucky today. But Moneto *had* blessed them, and in more ways than this bounty of game. Her secret.

News. Good news, for once.

She was with child.

She had suspected this, but it was the second moon with no moonblood, and now she knew.

*Perhaps that was what the four crows meant. The coming birth of the child? Were there definitely four of them?* She counted them on their bare branches. Six.

No matter. With such good hunting, the crows, one of the twelve totems of the People, were sure to be a portent of good fortune. She folded a beaver pelt, tucking in a tobacco leaf to ward off fleas. The skin was so soft enough to make a nice blanket for the baby. She would tell White Buffalo their secret when he returned from the day's hunt. Then, together they would go to Loramie's and tell Tepeke and Prairie Deer.

She wished Dove Trees was at Loramie's with the others. The Greenville Treaty allowed peaceful Shawanese to return to the sites of some of the old villages of Kekionga. Dove Trees lived there with her

Seneca and their baby. White Doves, a small, happy one, was already trying to talk. Of course! She was like her mother.

Though many had resettled on the sites of the old villages, Talitha was reluctant to go back. It was better to start at Loramie's where she had never lived before. Surely there were plenty of ghosts near the old town of Silver Man, where she and White Buffalo had passed such happy times with Bright Wing, Henri, and the little ones. Many of the old friends were gone, some dead. The name had even changed. Now it was called Fort Wayne, after General Black Snake.

Tecumseh would not go with them to Loramie's. He planned to take his band up the Great Miami to a spot near Piqua, to plant corn. There was still the rumor of a wife in one of the villages, said to be joining him, but Talitha had yet to hear him speak of her. But he Kispoko, who especially loved teasing Tecumseh, always insisted the story was true.

How lucky they were to have a friend like him! Tecumseh's generous spirit was renowned, and would be even more so, after this hunt.

He followed his own warrior's path and had not signed any of the peace treaties. Unlike so many others, he refused to carry out the tortures against their enemies. Even so he had earned a place as one of the young war chiefs. Talitha's heart filled with pride—that her young husband took after such a good chief.

It was later in the day when she heard hoofbeats, the sound of the hunters returning.

*But it is too early for them to have finished.*

She stopped her work. Her breath hung in the cold air as she strained to hear voices that might explain why they had stopped. All she heard was muffled sounds.

She left the bales of furs she had been tying and ran towards the sound of the horses. Lalawethika, his dark face pale, and his one eye gleaming bleakly, led White Buffalo's horse. The saddle lay empty.

Then she saw Tecumseh. He rode slowly, and behind his horse trailed a litter, a *travois*, as the *voyageurs* called it. The litter was piled with a bundle of blankets. Talitha made out a hank of glossy black hair, hanging from a head that lolled limply as bed scraped its way over every lump in the ground.

Her husband.

She ran to him. The hunters stopped, dismounted, and Tecumseh came to where she knelt beside White Buffalo. His long eyelashes fluttered as she took his hand. The men unfastened the *travois* carried him to their *wegiwa*, and gently laid him on the floor. Then they left, all but Tecumseh.

White Buffalo's eyes flickered once more as she removed the blankets to see his wounds. Her stomach rose as she saw he was broken in too many places. A bone protruded from his upper leg, and blood soaked his leggings. One arm bent unnaturally. He could not move his head. There was nothing in her medicine bag that could fix this.

Tecumseh cleared his throat. He tried to make words but nothing came out. His mouth moved and a tear tracked down his face. He gulped, and then she heard his voice—low, breaking. His message came to her as if from miles away. "It was the pack horses. We were up on the bluffs, and White Buffalo led them, and then a bear came after us for the meat we packed. The horses panicked. He tried to save them, but got tangled up in the lines and they went over the bluff together."

She clutched White Buffalo's hand tightly. His eyes struggled to open again.

Tecumseh laid his hand on her head briefly and left.

"My love." She edged closer and held her husband's hand against the soft deerskin over her belly as she tried to keep the tears from her voice. "You will walk the Spirit Trail, but you have returned to me first so I can tell you I am with child."

*Could he hear her?*

His eyes rolled and she choked back a cry.

"We made one for The People. This one will live after you and be told of his father, the great man you are." She swallowed. "He will know—or she—all you have done."

He seemed to have heard, at last his eyes locked onto hers for just for a moment, and his mouth quivered, as if to favor her with one last smile.

Then his beautiful eyes widened for a moment at something beyond her shoulder. Just as quickly, the brightness of his eyes faded, and at the same time the light that spilled through the open door of the *wegiwa* grew dim. Talitha turned but saw nothing, just the flit of a crow's wing in flight.

When she turned back to White Buffalo, he was gone.

She closed his eyes, laid herself against the broken body, and sobbed.

Tecumseh reappeared and knelt beside her, mourning silently.

The crow moon was out, shrouded in a pale halo when the cousins returned, and they pried the body away from her, to wrap it as was their custom.

"We will take him to Loramie's Station tomorrow," Lalawethika said. There, she knew the cousins of the Turtle Clan would prepare his body for burial.

What would become of her then she did not know.

# CHAPTER 51

## Seven for Sickness

*One crow for sorrow*
*Two for mirth*
*Three for a wedding*
*Four for a birth*
*Five for laughing*
*Six for crying*
*Seven for sickness...*

**Nancy**
**The Old Villages of Kekionga**
**September 1796**

It was a lean summer. Tecumseh had moved to the Great Miami with his small band. It was rare that they saw him now, though whenever he came he always brought them meat for Tepeke, Prairie Deer, and herself.

After White Buffalo was laid to rest at Loramie's Station, Tepeke traveled with Talitha up to that area where the old villages of Kekionga once stood. There they planted meager gardens and a small cornfield, often fighting crows—*seven today*, Talitha thought idly—for the small crop. Since the death of White Buffalo she could not stop counting crows.

The People had little meat. There were not enough men to hunt for them. Dove Tree's Seneca seemed to begrudge the meat Dove Trees shared with them. And then, while he was on a hunting trip, Dove Tree's baby grew sick.

Talitha and her mother nursed her with all their remedies, but the babe was wasting.

"She needs milk." Dove's Trees eyes pleaded with her.

There was no milk cow in the cluster of *wegiwas* that formed their poor little village. "Talitha, you can go to the fort and bring us some. Please. You talk English so much better than we can. They will be kinder to you." Dove Trees clutched White Doves, now a small limp bundle, to her chest.

They gathered what coins they could, and Talitha made her way to the American fort named after General Black Snake. She arrived there, only to be told there would not be any milk until tomorrow.

"Is there any farm I can go to? There is a very sick child who needs milk," she begged.

The two men at the store spoke together for a moment. Then one gave her a brief hard stare—was it anger or sympathy? —and took a scrap of paper. He drew some lines to indicate the way.

"It's not too far. This farm's the one that'll be bringing milk in the morning, anyway. They might have some for you."

"Thank you," she whispered, and rushed off. She hoped to make it to the farm and and back to her people before night fell and White Doves grew worse.

# CHAPTER 52

**James**
**Farm Near Ft Wayne**
**September 1796**

Marie had married him, and it still hardly felt real. His strange new life suited him well. Husband and wife, and partners in a business, too—the land he'd received in payment for his service in the artificers enabled them to set up a farm together. The additional payment for his work on Fort Wayne got them off to a good start. They had dry goods on offer up at the fort and also traded their produce and milk.

He milked the cows, content in their soft lowing, the swish of milk in the pail, the cool shade of the shed that provided a dark, peaceful respite from the late summer heat. Marie was with the baby, out in their vast garden, gathering produce they would sell at tomorrow. They'd have some milk to trade, too.

He wiped his brow and paused. Thought he heard something. He turned to see if he could spy Marie—the sight of her still brought such pleasure to him—but all he saw was a pair of young calves as they frolicked in the twilight. He got back to milking when he definitely heard a noise and sat up once more.

A ragged squaw stood there in the doorway, belly swollen. With child and hungry, he reckoned. Some had returned to their old stomping grounds at Wayne's invitation, with the expectation they could behave peacefully, and live like white folks. Though living like white folks did not necessarily make anyone more peaceful, James knew.

The squaw fiddled with a pouch tied around her thickening waist, trying to fish out some coins. From the looks of her, he reckoned she didn't have much. Well, he and Marie could certainly afford to help her out.

He rose from his stool and noticed her eyes were a deep blue. A white Indian. This one had avoided being exchanged at Greenville, then. A tiny knife stabbed his heart.

"Milk. Please," she said in her soft Indian voice. Yet there was a hint of the familiar in it.

He gave her tattered clothing a second look. She was dressed in the Shawnee style, the shabby—though once fancy—leggings and decorated moccasins. She had a basket fastened to some sort of belt tied around her, and she pulled a piece of crockery out—a small British-made pitcher with a stopper—for him to pour the milk in. She held it out with her right hand, waiting.

James picked up his pail, and carefully filled her jug. He set down the pail as she put a stopper in the pitcher, which she then rested on the stool. She held out her left hand, while he reached out his own to receive what few coins she might have to drop into it. As the coins clinked down, he glimpsed a silvery scar on the back of her hand.

An outline, the faded map of Ireland.

He latched onto her hand. Coins scattered into the straw on the floor. The stool near his leg toppled; the bucket and pitcher crashed onto the ground and milk sloshed everywhere as the cow started bawling. He struggled with the woman, tried to hold her still.

"Marie!" Blue eyes wild, panicked, his captive acted as if the devil himself was after her.

Her. Nancy Flynn.

His niece.

In rushed Marie, face flushed, holding their babe in her arms.

He held up the scarred hand. "It's her," he managed to croak. "It's her. It's my niece, Nancy Flynn."

"*Mon Dieu.*" Marie crossed herself. She knelt on the ground, to set the baby aside and reached out to the stranger, who had squirmed into a kneeling position.

The woman had stopped fighting and now looked at them, not quite with terror, but an awful sort of fear, panting like a trapped animal.

Then a calm seemed to settle on her as James spoke.

"It's me. Your Uncle James. Nancy Flynn, you've come home."

# CHAPTER 53

## The Tree of Life

**Polly**
**Indian Creek**
**October 1796**

The children shouted and raced around in the cool autumn air. There was a new addition. Baby James, named after Polly's uncle, napped in the house, while Polly made kraut on the porch. She lifted her head for a moment to sniff the wood smoke of the mill, forge, and hearth.

She started at the gobble of a wild turkey in the distance. The sound, the smoke, the October sky—it took her back to that fateful October day so long ago.

"I'm an Injun, and I will scalp you." "Baby" Adam, now nine, leapt away from Auntie Cory, three years his elder, but still tomboy enough to race after him with a stick held aloft.

"Cory!" Polly shook a finger at her. "I'll not have that game." One might argue that all the young'uns around here played like that, but even pretend scalp-taking made Polly sick.

Sally and Henry looked up from the chickens they chased and watched as Cory tried to get in one more lick with her rod.

Polly raised her voice. " Put that switch down now!"

Cory stopped, panting and red-faced. "Yes ma'am," she sighed and lay down her weapon. Then she perked up, cocked that messy head of curls. "I hear company coming from over yonder, Polly."

At that moment, Elsie, who had been gathering more cabbage for kraut, skipped over from the garden. "I heard it, too. I think it might be Uncle James on Apollo. There's a lady with him. And an Indian."

Polly wiped her hands on her apron. She was right in the middle of chores. This was no time for company. "Elsie, I don't see why your uncle would be headed this way. Might be someone working on the road who needs some help."

They started off towards their visitors. Cory picked up her switch again and ran ahead while Young Adam and the little ones trailed behind her. Three horses rounded the bend. Polly's heart lifted. James and Marie. And Elsie was right. There was a third one, an Indian.

James hallooed out to them and Polly waved back.

"Brought you a surprise," James called out as they got closer.

"I can see that." She was not expecting James at all, and Adam would have told her if Fort Wayne was in need of supplies from the mill. Why had James brought Marie and the baby all this way? The road was still quite rough to be hauling around an infant.

Elsie picked up Henry, who straggled behind, and then grabbed Polly's hand as they trotted forward to meet their company. Cory, shy for once, hung back. James dismounted and then helped Marie, who had her baby in a sling across her chest, to dismount.

Her beautiful sister-in-law had a strange grin on her face. As Polly embraced her, she noticed Marie's eyes kept roaming back to the stranger—the Indian squaw still on horseback. James, too, smiled with a peculiar expression.

What was happening?

Polly's frowned. Her eyes lit on the Indian, traveled from the beaded moccasins up to the leggings, recently repaired, from the look of them. Shawnee, she thought. The buckskin dress stretched tight across the belly. She was expecting a child. Why had they brought her here?

She shielded her eyes from autumn's late afternoon sun and looked up into a tanned face framed by auburn hair. Red strands shone in the fading light. The pair of bright blue eyes was fixed upon her with—Was it fear? *Or recognition?*

Her stomach dropped.

"Nancy," she whispered.

James rushed up beside her and caught her just before her knees gave way. The children all looked on, some afraid, while some—like Cory—drew closer, eager.

"Polly, you mean this is our sister, Nancy, what got taken away with me?" Cory's face shone with wonder and delight.

Polly steadied herself, reached up, and grabbed the hand, which clutched a small, dusty, crumbling figure. Then she glimpsed a scrap of blue and realized it was the corn doll. Once more her head spun and her mouth wouldn't work.

James cleared his throat. "Yep. I knew her by that burn she had."

Still grasping that hand, Polly held it up to examine it. Through her tears, she saw the scar. She looked in her sister's eyes and saw Pa's blue ones—startling in the dark face. The doll fell and Cory knelt to pick it up—as the scarred hand reached out to touch Polly and then stopped.

"You are like our mother," Nancy said, her English strange but musical. The children gathered closer at her words.

And then she slid out of the saddle, down towards Polly, and Polly clung to her, sobbing like her heart would break. Nancy was stiff, hard as a stone. Then she softened. The lost sister's arms wrapped round Polly, embraced her, too.

# EPILOGUE: A FORTING LIFE

**John/Quetaske**
**Fort Wayne**
**November 1796**

He'd gotten tips from voyageurs he had come across. That one named Jean Baptiste—though many of them carried that name—told him that Black Snake's fort, where Kekionga used to be, was now called Fort Wayne. The Americans were trading again, with the tribes and the French, too. They needed folks who knew Indian ways and could speak the Indian tongues to help with the trading.

So he'd made his way up here on his own, then used the papers he still had from Colonel John Hardin, even spoke the peace words Hardin had taught him as an introduction. Still didn't really know what they all meant, but they all got a kick out of that. Those agents at the fort took a shine to him right away.

A warm bed, food, and work to do. And no one could trade *him* away again. Things were looking up.

*Counting Crows*
*One crow sorrow*
*Two for mirth*
*Three for a wedding*
*Four for a birth*
*Five for laughing*
*Six for crying*
*Seven for sickness*
*Eight for dying*
*Nine for silver*
*Ten for gold*
*Eleven for a secret that will never be told.*

# ACKNOWLEDGEMENTS, WORKS CONSULTED, AND EVERMORE THANKS

*A Sorrow in Our Heart: The Life of Tecumseh*, by Allan W. Eckert

The Fantastic Scholarly Works and Maps of Researcher and Historian Helen Hornbeck Tanner, including *Atlas of Great Lakes Indian History*

*Bayonets in The Wilderness*, by Alan D Gaff

*Boone, A Biography*, by Robert Morgan

*The Discovery, Settlement, and Present State of Kentucke, 1784*, by John Filson

*The Draper Manuscripts*, Lyman Draper

*Fallen Timbers 1794: The US Army's First Victory*, John F Winkler, Illustrated by Peter Dennis

*Follow the River*, by James Alexander Thom

*I Should Be Extremely Happy in Your Company: A Novel of Lewis and Clark*, By Brian Hall

*The Journals of Lewis and Clark*, introduction by John Bakeless

*King's Mountain*, Sharyn McCrumb

*Outpost on the Wabash , 1787-1791, Letters of Harmar and Hamtramck*, edited by Gayle Thornbrough

*The Shawnees and the War for America*, by Colin G Calloway

*Sources of the River: Tracking David Thomson Across North America*, by Jack Nisbet

*Tecumseh, A Life*, by John Sugden

*Tecumseh and the Quest for Indian Leadership*, by R. David Edmunds

*Undaunted Courage: Meriwether Lewis, Thomas Jefferson, and the Opening of the American West*, by Stephen E. Ambrose

*Wabash 1791: St Clair's Defeat*, John F Winkler, Illustrated by Peter Dennis

*Warrior Woman: The Exceptional Life Story of Nonhelema, Shawnee Indian Woman Chief*, by James Alexander Tom and Dark Rain Thom

*1776*, by David McCollough

Kinfolks: My grandparents, George and Grace Jarrell, kindled my earliest interest in Nancy Flynn. Annie Mae Jarrell, with her book on the John Chapman Jarrell family, fed the flames, as did her son, David Jarrell.

Cousins Joan and Wes, your interest in Nancy's story definitely helped it along, as did the interest of my sisters three, two of whom were the earliest captive listeners to my tales.

Nephew Joseph Jarrell and the Gales Creek Oregon Black Powder Brigade led me on our own "wild scampering foray" through the forests of Washington County where they shared their wondrous expertise on weaponry of the late 1700's.

Further afield, Wiley Alston Jarrell and Jarrell List-serv provided incredible resources. It was member "Honey Bee" who declared, "Yes, the John Chapman Jarrell line IS descended from Indians and you can read about it in The Draper Manuscripts." This story as it is told would not exist without the collection of Lyman Draper.

Other helpful researchers include Joan Horsley, meticulous genealogist, may you Rest in Peace, and Pam Lasher. (Yes, we will always be on the lookout for the lost portrait of Nancy's baby…) And to Long Lost Cousin WMD Miller: Your excitement upon finding the early Flynn/Miller connections was contagious.

Others who guided me with their reading, editing, kind support, and so much more include:

Judy Voth, head cheerleader. From driving me across the rainy Kentucky fields, hills, and hollers in search of Cabin Creek, to spending hours with the manuscript—your friendship and enthusiasm are priceless. Debbie Kimery—you are an editing treasure! Not to mention super fun musical compañera. Muchas Gracias! And Angie Cathey, your humor and comments, (not to mention sense of style) as always are most treasured. Last but not least, warm thanks to Laurie Mosher-Paulin for a sharp eye and a sharp wit, and Door County Wine.

Deepest gratitude also must go to Mirella Patzer and my partners in her Historical Fiction Group, especially Rosemary Morris and Corinne Van Housen. What a joy to work and learn from you all. Thanks also, to Portland author Roseanne Parry, for words of wisdom after having a look at a snippet.

To my many music and dance friends—well, you helped me hear the ancient echoes of the tunes that form a backdrop to this tale.

Thanks, Irisa, for the picture!

Thanks and love also to some of my earliest writing partners: Cathy, Bev, and Marty. Pouring out one's heart when one is fifteen is great practice. I still miss waiting for the mail on hot summer days. XO.

Finally, to my husband, Mark Roberts: eternal gratitude for being a good sport and sharing in my joy when we not only finally found Indian Creek as we wandered Monroe County, West Virginia, but also found the very spot where Mann's Station once thrived. Huzzah! And thanks to Colin, for being Colin.

NOTES: Discrepencies about when Anne Bailey's ride took place: some say 1789, some say '90 or '91. I am going with '89 since most men in '91 were involved in fighting the Western Confederacy, and fewer fort attacks were happening in '91 than in '89. The Ballad memorializing her ride (and stating it was in 1791) was written nearly 100 years later, during the Civil War.